The Canadian Writer's Market

Eleventh Revised Edition

THE CANADIAN WRITER'S MARKET

Eleventh Revised Edition

Adrian Waller

and

Jem Bates

M&S

CANADIAN CATALOGUING IN PUBLICATION DATA

The National Library of Canada has catalogued this publication
as follows:

Main entry under title:

The Canadian writer's market

ISSN 1193-3305

ISBN 0-7710-8795-0 (11th rev. ed.)

1. Authorship – Handbooks, manuals, etc. 2. Publishers and
publishing – Canada – Directories. 3. Canadian periodicals –
Directories. 4. Advertising agencies – Canada – Directories.
5. Journalism – Study and teaching – Canada – Directories.

PN4908.C3   070.5'2'02571   C92-032255-7

The support of the Government of Ontario through the
Ministry of Culture and Communications is acknowledged.
Typesetting by M&S, Toronto
Printed and bound in Canada by Webcom Ltd. on acid-free paper

McClelland & Stewart Inc.
The Canadian Publishers
481 University Avenue
Toronto, Ontario
M5G 2E9

1 2 3 4 5   98 97 96 95 94

A NOTE ON CHANGES
IN THE ELEVENTH EDITION

The eleventh edition of *The Canadian Writer's Market* is both larger and more focused than previous editions in a number of specific ways. In several chapters, the information provided has been expanded substantially. Each of these changes has enhanced the book's usefulness as a reference guide for Canadian writers and a resource for people in publishing.

In Chapters 1 and 2, Consumer Magazines and Literary & Scholarly, pay rates have been introduced wherever these could be established. Sometimes fees for freelancers are standardized; more often they will depend on the complexity and level of research needed and the writer's experience, among other factors. Publishers were asked to indicate some typical rates where they couldn't be definitive. They were then invited to elaborate their specific editorial needs, and many responded by providing useful insights. Current circulation figures are also included, where provided by the publisher.

Entries in Chapter 5, Book Publishers, have been considerably expanded in many cases, too. Again, we encouraged publishers to be specific on the kinds of submissions that interest them. We also invited each publisher to nominate a "notable title" from their 1993 list. It must be stressed that the chosen title does not necessarily represent the publisher's best or most important book of the year, nor does it claim to be representative of a house's often wide-ranging list. It simply offers an intriguing taste of the particular after a summary that necessarily errs towards the general.

Chapter 6, Literary Agents, provides an overview of each agency's subject interests, client base, and operating framework. The response did not permit standardization (for reasons touched on in the chapter's introduction) but provided some interesting insights anyway! A new section in Chapter 7, Awards, Competitions, & Grants, outlines provincial and federal support programs for which individual writers may apply. The name change of Chapter 8, Professional Development, itself suggests this section's broadened parameters. As well as backgrounding the top creative writing and journalism programs offered by Canada's colleges and universities, a new section now introduces the pick of the country's writing schools, workshops, and retreats.

Finally, a word on consistency. So far as possible, we have tried to provide information that is complete and consistent. Of course, life's not like that. A few key magazine publishers, whose editorial needs are more than fully provided for, chose not to be listed this time. We could have researched various data not provided directly by publishers, but we decided that this would be inappropriate. If phone or fax numbers are not listed, it is often because the publisher or editor prefers not to be contacted by these means. Some magazines are sensitive about their pay rates or their circulation figures; a few book publishers prefer not to reveal the number of books they publish each year or to isolate one notable title from their list. In each case, where they have not provided information, we have not sought it out.

ACKNOWLEDGEMENTS

Many editors and other publishing staff and course co-ordinators took time out from their busy schedules to respond to our questionnaires and answer our specific or general questions. Their co-operation is gratefully acknowledged. Also, thanks once again to Vicky Ridout, of the Writers' Union of Canada, and Catherine Keachie, of the Canadian Magazine Publishers Association, for their insights and support.

J.B.

Contents

INTRODUCTION

Back in the 1970s, when *The Canadian Writer's Market* was first published, the country sported a mere 100 consumer magazines, about 150 trade journals, two dozen or so farm publications that appeared somewhat sporadically, and 147 book publishers. As time went on, however, the industry was caught in an upswing and, five or six years later, there were 225 consumer magazines in Canada, most sold by subscription or delivered to selected households free of charge, and almost as many trade publications distributed in various corners of the workplace and business world. As well, there were 50-odd farm publications and 160 book publishers.

According to *Canadian Advertising Rates & Data* (*CARD*), published monthly by Maclean Hunter Ltd., as the 1990s dawned there were over 400 consumer magazines, and trade journals were keeping pace. By Statistics Canada figures, in 1990-1 (the most recent year for which reliable data are available) there were 1,500 periodicals in Canada. The number of national book publishers had almost doubled!

Publishing, however, has always been an extremely transient business. In today's Canada, magazines come and go faster than they ever did. Thus, keeping *The Canadian Writer's Market* up-to-date over the years has required much research and revision.

A number of publications are distributed free as corporate public relations vehicles. However, a large number of magazines are still sold by subscription, while many are kept in business almost entirely by either government grants or funds from specific organizations.

Whatever their method of funding or distribution, most Canadian magazines that buy freelancers' work have been included in the eleventh edition of *The Canadian Writer's Market*, making it a useful tool for all who seek to sell their words.

As we all know only too well, the recession of the past few years has put great pressure on the publishing industry. Since the last edition of this book, a significant number of publications have folded because of this pressure, and a number of publishers have been forced to reduce their operations, or cut back on their lists. Many good writer's markets have disappeared as a result.

This edition again focuses on English-language publishers and publications. In earlier editions we carried many francophone magazines and trade publications. By 1991, however, we had become uncomfortably aware that to do full justice to Quebec's large and dynamic publishing industry we would need virtually to double the size of this book. Yet any halfway point seemed to us an unacceptable compromise. So, as with the last edition, this is a guide to the English-language publishing world, though we have again retained many bilingual publishers. We would refer readers looking to work in Québécois to the *CARD* directory for French-language magazines, and to *Quill & Quire*'s biannual guide, *Canadian Publishers Directory*, for a full listing of French-language book publishers.

Again we have chosen in general not to list the specialist educational and professional publishing houses, which offer few opportunities for the unspecialized writer, while retaining those publishers that also have a trade operation, and not to carry the many very small publishers who produce on an occasional basis, perhaps no more than one or two volumes a year.

For some writers, particularly those just starting out who need to build a portfolio of published works to show editors on larger magazines later, money can be secondary. Publication in a respected literary journal with little or no remuneration can only benefit a serious writer in the long term, particularly one who seeks to turn one day to books.

Few could have imagined, when *The Canadian Writer's Market* first appeared, the technical aids from computerized libraries, word processors, and memory typewriters to telephone answering machines, facsimile machines, and electronic mail communications that would become available to writers. Now it is possible to transmit story ideas – even clearly typed manuscripts – through the telephone lines from one side of the world to the other. More and more editors, in fact, solicit faxed story proposals and manuscripts to save time. This edition again includes the fax numbers of book publishers and magazines, and other contacts where these are available.

Except where editors have asked us not to, we have also included regular telephone numbers with each listing. Writers are always advised, however, to try to sell their work by letter or fax. While it is often perfectly acceptable to phone a publication to ask for its contributor's guidelines (which usually say how much it pays for those articles needed for its various editorial departments), business with editors is nearly always more effectively accomplished with a carefully compiled story proposal. And this may be faxed, too.

We have again opted to arrange the magazines into logically appropriate groups. The three main classes remain Consumer Magazines; Literary & Scholarly; and Trade, Business, Farm, & Professional Publications. And to better facilitate a quick and easy reference for writers seeking a suitable market for a good idea, or for those wanting to recycle an article to other buyers, we have narrowed down these groups even further, according to subject. Inevitably, however, these classifications are somewhat arbitrary at times and have a tendency to overlap. Even the distinction between consumer and trade publications is sometimes difficult to delineate. Some "trade" periodicals – the book industry's *Quill & Quire*, for instance – have such a general popularity that they are equated to consumer magazines. In this edition, we have introduced a section of notable business journals in Chapter 1 in order to describe the market they offer in greater detail. Most comparable business publications retain a simplified listing in Chapter 3. Women's magazines have been reinstated as a sub-group in Chapter 1. These popular, high-circulation magazines are among the most successful areas in Canadian publishing and can offer freelancers some of the best markets.

Consumer magazines, therefore, appear in thirteen sub-groups: the arts; business; city & entertainment; the environment; feminist; general interest; home & hobby; lifestyle; news, opinions, & issues; special interest; sports & outdoors; women's; and youth & children's. Trade publications are divided into twenty sub-sections according to the professions or trades they serve. These groups range from advertising, business, and data processing to electronics, transportation, and travel.

To sharpen this reference book as a marketing tool, we provide thumbnail sketches for each consumer magazine to explain in the limited space available what kinds of articles it carries. This is useful because so many magazines have names that give little indication of what they really are, who reads them, and, consequently, the kinds of articles or stories they buy. No one would ever guess, for instance, that a monthly Vancouver magazine called *Kinesis* is a forum for feminists. Nor that, far from being a farm publication, as one might first suspect, *Grain* is a spunky little literary publication that has been produced quarterly in Regina since 1973.

We use the term publication often throughout this book because, strictly speaking, many of its listings are not really magazines as we have come to know them. Some may be tabloid newspapers, some simple, one-colour, staple-bound periodicals that feed the needs, sometimes sporadically, of a smallish group of loyal readers. Others, however, are magazines in the truest sense: glossy, highly professional consumer or trade journals that boast respectable circulations. The word publication, then, seems to safely cover all listings, both large and small.

Much more important to the writer is that all these publications provide opportunities both for estabished freelancers wanting to break fresh ground and for neophyte writers seeking to have their work published. Each magazine listed accepts outside contributions with varying frequency and for equally varying fees.

Some publications, particularly among the scholarly journals and the literary and arts magazines, do not pay their writers at all. Others pay fees that are among the highest in North America, and expect high standards of writing and reporting in return.

Marketing

Too few novice writers understand that marketing is as vital an element of their craft as style and subject matter. Without a successful marketing strategy, their words and ideas may never see print.

The professional way to sell your writing is with a coherently written proposal. This eliminates the risks inherent in producing work on speculation. When an idea is accepted, the writer and the editor discuss fee, deadline – an *obsession* in the business, by the way – and the preferred writing style for the finished article.

Writers should always study the magazines for which they would like to write so they can immediately address the question, What does this particular editor want? Ultimately, though, they are aiming to satisfy not the editor but the editor's readers, and the only way to find out what *they* like is by reading the kind of material they have been purchasing in the past.

Another sure-fire way of becoming acquainted with a specific group of readers, and getting a feel for what they want, is to take careful note of the type and quality of the advertising within the magazine. In other words, you can only really know what to suggest to an editor after diligently studying his or her issues – and lots of them –as regularly as you can, in libraries, on the newsstands, or in doctors' offices.

Unquestionably, the hardest writing to sell is the novel. No matter how timely or ingenious a story may be, the effect a piece of fiction ultimately has on readers will depend almost entirely on how well it is constructed and written. Some of this, of course, also applies to non-fiction writing, particularly first-person experience pieces so much a part of the writer, and essays that must intelligently set out opinions and arguments. But, whereas the worthiness of most suggestions for magazine articles can be demonstrated aptly in a proposal, the power of a novel really cannot.

Some publishers are able to judge the merits of a piece of fiction from two or three sample chapters accompanied by a synopsis of the entire work. Ideally, this should explain the plot and show the very thing that holds fiction together – the theme. On the basis of this initial work, some publishers will give an experienced writer a contract and an advance against royalties to complete the book. Usually, though, they commit themselves to novels submitted by an unknown author only after seeing the completed text.

To help sell their work, fiction writers often seek out literary agents like those we have listed in Chapter 6. But don't expect agents to possess magic wands that they can wave to find a market for everything that crosses their desks. On the contrary, they must work extremely hard to sell whatever they can, and their best acquisitions, usually from experienced writers, are nearly always the first to find a buyer. So, to make their lives easier, reputable agents only ever handle a work they think will sell so well that it will be financially beneficial for both themselves and their clients.

In some large cities in the United States, agents also place magazine articles and essays, but only those written by frequently published authors who are exceptionally well-known. In Canada, however, this is seldom the case. Virtually all articles are sold directly to magazines and publishing houses by authors themselves – with well-crafted proposals.

Not surprisingly, then, the query letter to an editor and the full, detailed proposal or outline that follows it, may well be the most significant piece of work the beginning writer ever undertakes. It not only sells a suggestion, after all, but the writer with it. It should serve to demonstrate to an editor that, beyond any shadow of doubt, the person who conceived the idea and refined it really *is* the one best able to turn it into a strong, informative piece of writing for a lot of readers to enjoy.

Copyright

Whatever you sell, and by whatever means you choose to do it, one of the most crucial legal elements of the writing craft is copyright. This is usually discussed the moment an editor responds favourably to a writer's suggestion.

Copyright is an *extremely* complex area of law, and writers are advised to read up on it all they can before negotiating the sales terms of their work, thus putting themselves in a stronger bargaining position. A helpful booklet, *Copyright Questions and Answers*, is available from the Department of Consumer and Corporate Affairs, Copyright and Industrial Design Branch, 5th Floor, 50 Victoria Street, Place du Portage, Tower 1, Hull, Que. K1A 0C9.

Put simply, copyright means the sole right to reproduce – or allow others to reproduce – a literary or artistic work. It begins upon creation rather than on publication, and exists until fifty years after the creator's death.

The *assignment* or *licensing* of copyright is what is negotiated in any deal between a publisher and a writer. Depending on the nature of the contract, the author can sell rights in many different ways.

Some publishers, often book publishers, will ask an author to assign copyright. This means that the publisher has control of all aspects of the copyright, including subsidiary rights such as translation rights, reprint rights, or even film rights, for the period of the agreement. The work is then published with copyright in the publisher's name. Such a contract will generally stipulate that once the publisher has allowed the book to go out of print, the rights revert to the author. The writer will likely find that it is preferable to *grant a licence* to a publisher, specifying the rights of the publisher with respect to territory and time. In this way, the publisher is given the right to use the work in different markets or at a later date, and will be able to negotiate separately for subsidiary rights.

Terms of a copyright agreement may vary greatly in nature or content – a contract, after all, can include whatever conditions one party feels pertinent – but not in principle. Canadian magazines with large circulations most often buy North American rights – the right to publish an article to be read by an audience scattered across the entire continent. Some large Canadian magazines are content simply to buy Canadian rights – the right to publish a work that will be read only within the country. Some acquire serial rights – the right to publish a work in a sister publication without having to pay extra for it.

Some smaller publications, however, simply buy one-time rights. Under this type of agreement, copyright ownership automatically reverts to the writer, either immediately upon publication or shortly afterwards, depending on the agreement. This leaves the writer legally free to sell the same article in the same words to what is called a secondary market. If that new market also buys only one-time rights, the same article may then be re-sold to a third magazine without the need for any alteration, then a fourth, and so on down the line.

Another variation of one-time rights, which is preferred by many of the larger magazines, is for *first-time* rights, giving the publisher the right to be the first to publish an article. In other words, they may indeed want one-time rights, but these must be first-time.

This usually leaves writers with two main options. They can

either sell a story several times over to those magazines willing to buy one-time rights, not caring if these are first, second, or even third, or they can take what most experienced freelancers have come to regard as the more lucrative road. That is, they can write a piece for a top fee from a large magazine first, then try selling the same idea to smaller magazines later.

Be careful here, though. While ideas can't be copyrighted, the words used to express or explain them can, and are. This is why our copyright laws came into being: to prevent people from taking and using something – in this case, words, phrases, expressions, literary structures – that does not belong to them. So if you have sold North American, Canadian, or even world rights to a magazine, remember that before being offered elsewhere, your piece must be totally rewritten and restructured. As it passes from the original buyer to others wanting first-time rights, each text must avoid any of the original word combinations, structures or echoes. If, on the other hand, you have sold one-time rights and the copyright has reverted to you, you may send off your article in its original, unaltered form as many times as you wish.

Some magazines – *Reader's Digest*, for example – buy what are known as reprint rights, yet another corner of the maze of copyright. Under this agreement, editors may pick up and re-publish articles that have appeared elsewhere so long as they pay the original publishers, and/or the writers, fees for their one-time use. This practice is always restricted to publishers and must *never* be confused with recycling. It is merely an arrangement made between two magazines, with the copyright laws in mind, which gives the writer a little extra money as a bonus for his or her initial efforts.

Here are some of the most frequently posed questions about copyright, with general answers:

Is every piece of written work copyrighted?

No. In Canada, copyright on a work lasts for the life of the author plus fifty years. After that, the work falls into the public domain and may be legally copied at will.

How can I tell who the rightful owner of a copyright is?

In the first few pages of a book or magazine there is a copyright notice. Typically, it will read: Copyright Josephine Blow, 1994; or Joseph P. Blow & Sons, Publishers, 1994. Beneath this will usually appear the publisher's address. Even if the copyright is held in the author's name, it is generally the publisher who has the right by contract to authorize reprints of excerpts. If, however, the author has retained these rights exclusively, which may sometimes be the case, he or she can be contacted through the publisher.

How does copyright infringement occur?

Usually through carelessness or ignorance. Few writers, after all, deliberately set out to steal something that doesn't belong to them. They either quote too much of someone else's work without first seeking permission to do so, or use previously written words without making a sufficiently concerted effort to rework them.

What is too much of someone else's work?

The answer to this isn't easy. It depends on several factors, principally the quantity and quality of the portion taken and whether its use will detract from the impact and/or the marketability of the original. No one loses sleep if a writer uses a line or two from a book and attributes its source; to reproduce three or four key paragraphs without permission, however – even *with* attribution – could lead to problems. The writer is always advised to contact the copyright holder, quoting the extract(s) he or she wants to use in full, giving a true indication of context, details of format (magazine article, script, or book), and size of audience, and ask for permission to reproduce it. A neophyte writer wanting to use a hundred words for publication in a small magazine probably will not be charged what a name writer would be expected to pay for a similar-sized extract in an article for one of the big players. Many copyright holders, however, do not charge for so few words.

How can I copyright my work?

The moment you have written something it is automatically copyrighted. If, however, you feel there is a chance someone may one day say your manuscript is theirs, you may register it for a fee with the Federal Department of Communications' Copyright and Industrial Design Branch. If your work is registered in this way, should a dispute over copyright arise, you would be in a much stronger position if the case ever went to court. It would be up to the other party to prove that you are not the creator of your work. You can also mail a copy of your manuscript to yourself in a registered package. This would provide you with a dated receipt, which you would be able to produce when opening the package before a judge, should the manuscript's rightful ownership ever become a legal issue.

If I work for a newspaper, who owns the copyright on my work?

Usually, if you are employed by a company, it automatically owns the copyright of everything that is published by it in the course of your work. This cannot be reproduced or re-sold in any form without permission first being obtained. Often, newspapers generously allow articles, or portions of them, to be reprinted without charge.

Can a magazine editor steal the idea contained in my story proposal and assign it to someone else to write?

Yes, but the good ones won't. For this reason, it is not necessary to write copyright on your proposal. You would be wasting words anyway. Ideas like titles are in the public domain and cannot be protected by copyright laws unless they are part of an invention. And that is yet another branch of copyright law. If you intend to sell movie scripts in Hollywood (in which case you will definitely need an agent to negotiate rights on your behalf), have faith in the people you deal with. Good magazines and publishing houses stay in business because their editors are ethical.

Should I copyright the book I have been contracted to write before sending it to the publisher?

No. All publishers will copyright your work for you, under either their name or yours, depending on the terms of the contract you should already have signed. They will also register it for you, at the National Library in Ottawa, as an original Canadian work.

Libel

Jonathan Swift, in *A Tale of a Tub*, complained loudly and logically that writers were no longer able to lash out at particular people for particular vices and had to content themselves with general satire on mankind. More than two hundred years later, we still must take heed. We must do our best not to make any direct, unfair, or inaccurate allusion to the living that might compromise their reputations.

Libel suits are notoriously complex – and the traps are wide. Many writers hold the mistaken belief that the use of fictitious names, or a statement saying that any resemblance between the characters in the book and living persons is purely coincidental, will automatically protect them from the possibility of a libel suit. This assumption is wrong. If the average reader associates a character described in a manuscript with an actual person, and the description reflects unfavourably on that person's reputation or integrity, there is always the danger of libel.

Fiction writers must always strive to assure that the resemblance really *is* coincidence, and must certainly avoid the intention. Apparent *intention* to libel an actual person, even in fiction, could be interpreted by legal minds as a personal attack, and could possibly lead to an action.

All writers need to understand enough about Canadian libel laws to protect both themselves and their publishers against court action. This is absolutely necessary since nearly all publishers' contracts provide for indemnification by the author in cases where a person maligned in a manuscript resorts to a suit.

Libel in Canada is mostly covered by civil law and comes under provincial jurisdiction. Its principles are based on English common law for all provinces, except in Quebec, where the law stems directly from the French Civil Code. But the principles remain: libel is a printed statement or picture that exposes a person to hatred, ridicule, or contempt, and imputes to that person immorality, crime, or disorderly conduct, or tends to injure that person in the pursuit of a profession, office, or trade. In short, anything that might discredit a person may be construed as libellous. Under some circumstances, this can also apply to corporations or their individual members.

If such a statement or picture is printed, the publisher must be prepared to defend his publication on three fronts: truth of the statement; privilege; and fair comment on a matter of public interest. If the author's statements are accurate and true, there may be no basis for a civil action for libel, but any false or defamatory statement that tends to harm a person's reputation may constitute libel.

Privileged reports fall into two classifications: absolute privilege and qualified privilege. If published at the same time as they took place, a fair and accurate report without editorial comment on proceedings heard before a court of justice is absolutely privileged. Qualified or conditional privilege is enjoyed by reporters while covering proceedings in any government body, whether legislative or administrative, any commission of inquiry or organization whose members represent any public authority in Canada, or municipal council, school board, or board of health meetings.

The defence of qualified privilege extends to the findings or decisions of those Canadian organizations formed to promote the interests of any art, science, religion, or learning; any trade, business, industry, or profession; any game, sport, or pastime to which members of the public are invited as spectators or participants.

Fair and honest comment on matters of public interest, as long as it is true, is privileged. An author who comments on current affairs or writes a biography is permitted to express honest opinions or fair criticism of someone's works or accomplishments because this is usually in the public interest and serves to promote a useful purpose. Fair comment extends to criticism of books, magazines, articles, plays, and films.

Another defence often resorted to by newspapers and magazines is mitigation of damages based on a retraction of a statement that was made in error. While this action does not absolve the publication from libel, it nevertheless tends to show that any injury was purely accidental, and this may lessen the amount of the damages levied by the court.

Simultaneous submissions

There is absolutely nothing wrong with writers sending the same article, proposal, or book manuscript to more than one potential market at the same time. It is their work, after all, so they can do whatever they please with it. But unless they are sending off material simultaneously to those magazines that are happy to buy second, third, or fourth rights, they could run into problems.

The practice can sometimes be unethical. Busy magazines need about a month to assess an idea or a manuscript properly, sometimes more. During this time, several people may be assigned to the job of writing an informed critique explaining to both the writer and the senior editor how the manuscript or article is effective, how it isn't, and what revisions may be necessary.

In publishing houses, this work takes considerably longer and is correspondingly more expensive. Judging a promising book proposal or an intriguing manuscript of several thousand words usually means that an editor must set aside present work. If the editor is rushing to complete a book for the upcoming spring list, an outside reader might have to be hired to do this job instead. Readers are also hired for their specialized expertise, to judge whether a writer has covered a topic, fact or fiction, properly and accurately. If an idea or manuscript appears tempting, the publisher may recruit market researchers to assess its sales potential. By sending the same material to several houses, the writer may automatically involve them all in the expense of assessing something only one of them would eventually be able to acquire.

Indeed, to established writers, the idea of simultaneous submissions is distasteful. Knowing how busy editors can be, they give them reasonable time to respond – about six weeks on a magazine and as long as three months in a publishing house. If after that they have heard nothing, they fire off a reminder, then turn immediately to other productive work. The publishing business is notorious for its slowness and, unfortunately, this is something all writers have to learn to accept.

Photocopies

Simultaneous submission often means sending out photocopies of manuscripts, rather than the original. Editors on good magazines will sometimes refuse to read photocopies – they immediately suspect that they have been sent a copy because other copies are in the process of being offered elsewhere. And why should editors bother investing time in something they are not quite sure they will even have the chance to buy? But there is also a strong argument for keeping originals safe to preclude their getting lost in the mail. It is usually wise to explain to an editor that you are sending a photocopy for precisely this purpose, and that the original *is* available if required. If you are using a computer, however, none of this needs to be considered, since you will always have a back-up on your disk. You can simply print out and send off "originals" as the need arises.

Word processing

Thanks to modern technology, more and more writers are crafting their poems, articles, and books on personal computers using a word processing program. (A word processor is a machine that is dedicated to one particular word processing system. They have been largely replaced by the microcomputer, which can use a variety of different word processing software packages, depending on the manufacturer, and can also run a variety of programs.) Most publishers prefer authors to use computers, not because it saves them money, but because typesetting from disk speeds up the production process and helps prevent errors from creeping into the manuscript at a later stage.

The word processor enables the writer to compose words and keep them in files – one file per story or article, perhaps, or one per chapter – then recall them. As long as a file has been properly stored, it can be retrieved any time. Word processing enables writers to edit, cut, and paste limitlessly, without resorting to such traditional and perfectly respectable writers' tools as scissors, stapler, or glue. Thus they are spared the drudgery of seemingly endless retyping while striving to make their prose sparkle or their narrative flow in a smoother, clearer line. At the end of the day, with the final text saved on a disk, a clean copy can be printed out in a matter of minutes.

Many word processing programs contain a spell-check and a thesaurus. The spell-check, of course, helps eliminate poor spelling and typographical errors, and the thesaurus gives the writer instant access to a wide choice of synonyms and antonyms. With just another keystroke, any word can be selected from the thesaurus to replace one that is no longer wanted in the text.

In recent years, as personal computers have flooded the market, the consumer has become increasingly confused about what product to buy. Strange as it may seem, the least important part of word processing is the computer itself. This – the hardware – is really nothing more than an electronic box with switches, coils, and microchips. It is only as good as whatever program – the software – is inserted into a drive to make it perform in a specific way. Thus, software capabilities must always be foremost in the writer's mind, and he or she is far better off seeking out the most suitable word processing program first, then buying the right computer to accommodate it.

Your choice of program will ultimately determine the type of hardware you buy to run it. Powerful software packages need equally powerful computers to absorb them, make them run, and still have enough working memory, or RAM. A small, inexpensive computer with between 64 and 256 kilobytes of memory might be fine for a student's essays, or a smallish piece a reporter may want to write for a newspaper, but it will not have sufficient capacity to accommodate a top-notch word processing program. The serious writer would quickly outgrow it.

To be able to store a healthy bank of 2,000-word magazine pieces and have quick and easy access to them, the writer will need a computer with a minimum of 512K RAM. Many busy freelancers have found, however, that it is wiser to spend an extra two hundred dollars or so on a computer with 640K memory. This not only has sufficient power for virtually any word processing program available, but would guarantee more than enough working memory should the computer one day be used for writing books.

For books, by the way, a powerful computer and decent software is essential. When buying a computer you should consider getting a built-in hard-disk drive. This allows you plenty of storage memory in which to keep your programs and your files, and means an end to relying on floppy disks for all your operations. Some writers do manage to write books on small home computers, but all too often their software restricts them and the computer's capacity is such that they can only get one or two chapters on a single disk. If you find yourself with half of a chapter on one disk, and the other half on another, you can bank on awkward technical problems when the time comes for you to print out your work.

Power, memory, and software capability are one thing. Another aspect of word processing worthy of almost equal consideration is your working speed, which lies largely in using a good keyboard, one with which you feel comfortable.

It is also important to remember that just how quickly a manuscript can be produced does not necessarily depend on how good or expensive your printer is, but how suitable. Your printer should provide a clear, draft-quality text in an easy-to-read typeface. Script typefaces resembling italics or Old English should be avoided because they are harder to read. This rule applies to both a computer and a typewriter, electric or otherwise.

Another component of the home computer, and one more integral to comfort than any other, is the piece of equipment you must stare at for hours on end – the screen. Many efficient home computers are sold with colour screens. These are fine for games and, for some graphics, imperative. But for simple word processing, they are not only superfluous, but expensive. Conversely, other computers come with much cheaper screens that show bulky, disjointed lettering that is difficult and uninviting to read.

Ideally, the writer should aim somewhere between these two extremes. Best is what is called a high-resolution screen. This not only costs significantly less than a colour screen, but helps to reduce eyestrain. Suffice it to say that endlessly watching your work spring to life on a screen you are not comfortable with will make word processing a chore, and certainly not a pleasure.

Before buying a word processor, shop around, and talk to other writers to ascertain what computers and software packages *they* bought, and why. Judge your needs by theirs. And make certain that your sales clerk understands the amount of revising and polishing you will be doing, so that you obtain the type of software best suited to the writer's needs.

Manuscripts

It goes without saying that manuscripts that have been poorly typed and are littered with spelling errors look amateurish. Editors don't necessarily expect word processed texts, but they should be well-prepared and double-spaced on white bond letter-size paper, with a covering page bearing a title. If your article is accepted, it is doubtful that the title you gave it will survive. It is likely to undergo several changes as editors put their heads together to dream up something that suits it better, according to the style of their magazine. When first submitting a piece, then, its title is of little consequence. Your job is merely to call your work *something* so it can be recorded as such when the editorial department receives it.

A greater priority is the other information you must put on the title page – your name, complete address, and telephone number.

Of course, editors are most interested in such ingredients as uniqueness or importance of subject, and whether it has been properly covered and deftly illustrated with anecdotes. They look, too, for good writing – this does not translate to clever or fancy as much as it does to clear and coherent. Editors do find, however, that a neat manuscript is infinitely more inviting to read than an untidy one.

When submitting a book manuscript, each new chapter should be denoted as such by starting partway down the page. All pages must be numbered, double-spaced, and have margins about an inch wide. The text will require a title page, too, and others devoted to a full, accurate listing of any permissions the author needed to acquire to be legally entitled to quote from copyrighted works. Do not bind or staple your manuscript.

While editors used to like to see an entire manuscript, this is usually no longer the case. Many publishing houses will not accept unsolicited manuscripts, and if you do manage to convince a busy editor to take a look at your work, a sample two chapters plus synopsis will be sufficient. You can always courier the balance of the manuscript if required.

When using a computer it is always wise to co-ordinate your efforts with those of the publisher so that your disks will not be useless. Many instructions are specific to the type of software used, but some are general: 1) each article or chapter should have its own file; 2) never fill your disks – always leave room, at least 40K "working space" on each, for the typesetter's format instructions; 3) always make back-up disks; 4) never centre or justify the text, which makes it difficult for the publisher to obtain an accurate word count and creates problems for the typesetter during formatting; 5) set your margins so that there are no more than sixty characters per line; 6) never hyphenate a word at the end of a line unless that word has a hyphen already; 7) make very clear your codes for accents, currency symbols, fractions, and footnote or endnote numbers, and don't overuse bold and italic typefaces.

Style

By style, most book and magazine editors mean the conventions of spelling, punctuation, and capitalization. There is, of course, no universally accepted manual for style because it varies from periodical to periodical, publishing house to publishing house, not to mention from fiction to non-fiction, from genre to genre, and from discipline to discipline. Writers should remember, however, that style is an integral part of their craft and, by showing a blatant disregard for it, they can quite inadvertently prejudice an editor against their work.

Writers are expected to observe at least *some* of the basic house rules, and these should be obvious in what has already been published by those magazines and book publishing houses for which they aspire to write. If they are not, the writer is always wise to find out as much as possible about what these rules are, and what stylistic traits – as idiosyncratic as many may appear to be – are preferred.

Canadian newspapers generally follow *The Canadian Press Stylebook* (which also contains some good tips on reporting, by the way), and magazines tend to develop their own standards and preferences from one authoritative source, or a compilation of several. Book publishers, however, usually adhere to well-known manuals. A selection of the best style and resource books is provided at the end of this book.

Very often, a publishing house has compiled its *own* guide to house style, and the aspiring writer should never be afraid to ask for a copy of this.

The word count

The number of words a manuscript contains is another consideration for editors. A large part of their job is to ensure that stories will fit into an allotted space. When they order 2,000 words, the manuscript should not be appreciably longer, and preferably 100 words or so less.

For books, the word count is more crucial, because cutting, even merely trimming to a publishable size, is a lot more work than many writers realize. Doing it properly almost always means having to judiciously remove material – a sentence here or a couple of paragraphs there – throughout an entire text and not just from one part of it. The time involved explains why authors lament that they have had potentially good works either rejected out of hand, or returned swiftly to them for drastic shortening.

Always remember that the real skill in writing is being able to tell a story, fact or fiction, in the shortest number of necessary words. To achieve this, good writers develop keen powers of self-criticism. They are constantly scrutinizing their work for wordiness, clutter, unnecessarily long quotes, or characters that do nothing to enhance the subject of their story, or move the action along. The moment they come upon any of them, they ruthlessly pare away the superfluous material so as to make their text tighter.

They also check regularly to see how many words they are writing. A simple way to count them is to set the left-hand margin of the typewriter or word processor at twenty and the right at seventy-five so that each line of type will then contain an average of ten words. Twenty-five double-spaced lines on a standard-size page, therefore, will equal roughly two hundred and fifty words.

Postage

These days all publishers are under pressure to reduce costs wherever possible. Postage rates have soared in recent years and so, for any business that relies heavily on our mail system, they represent a bigger expense than ever. It should now be taken for granted that if you want your manuscript returned you must include a self-addressed, stamped envelope, so that it can be returned without cost. Increasingly, publishers will assume that you do not want your material back if an SASE is not included, and will simply throw it away. During the research for this edition, magazine and book editors stressed this point again and again, and writers ignore it at their peril. If submitting to U.S. publishers, keep a supply of American stamps. You can stock up on a visit, arrange for a friend visiting the States to bring some back for you, or buy them through a Canadian dealer (*Canadian Author* magazine often carries advertisements for these).

Income tax

In Canada, the Income Tax Act is good to writers, allowing them to deduct legitimate work expenses from their taxable incomes. In return, writers are trusted to show all their earnings, particularly fees that are unsupported by T4, T4A, or T5 slips from magazines and publishing houses that have printed their work.

Basically, writers come under three classifications:

- Salaried employees who supplement incomes by earning a little extra money as occasional freelance writers.
- Part-time writers whose major income comes from another job that will almost certainly be cast aside the moment writing becomes more profitable.
- Totally self-employed, full-time writers not on any payroll, who are expected to file honest returns mindful that no income taxes have been deducted at source.

Writers with other jobs need only attach to their income tax returns a statement summarizing writing income and expenses, and to show whether this extra work resulted in a profit or a loss. Any profit must be added to that taxable income earned from the other job. Losses, however, may be used to reduce it.

Writers living entirely from their craft must keep many more details – a list of all income and its sources, and receipts and vouchers to support expenses. Maintaining proper financial records not only serves as a reminder of cash that has flowed both in and out, but also helps to reduce problems that might be encountered should a tax return be audited.

All writers may reasonably deduct the cost of all stationery, including letterhead, envelopes, typewriter ribbons, computer paper and ink cartridges, pencils, pens, and paper clips. Telephone costs, particularly long-distance calls, are also deductible, as are postage, membership dues in writers' organizations, union dues, accountants' fees, secretarial help, research assistance, subscriptions to newspapers and magazines, reference books, copyright costs, and photocopying charges.

Many writers find that their biggest annual deduction is for their work space. Those who work in an outside office may claim its rent as an expense. If, however, they work at home, they may write off a reasonable portion of their living space. A writer using one room as an office in a six-room apartment, for example, may claim one-sixth of the rent plus one-sixth of such other expenses as municipal taxes, heating, lighting, minor repairs, and ordinary maintenance. However, work space related costs can only be deducted from your *net income from writing* after you have deducted all your other costs.

An area of tax deduction often overlooked is the depreciation of office furniture and equipment. Both may be written off according to a fixed percentage determined by the income tax regulations. A typewriter or word processor can be depreciated by 20 per cent of the total cost each year for five years. The same tax saving may be applied to printers, cameras, tape recorders, filing cabinets, desks, chairs, and telephone answering machines.

Travel is also an allowable expense, whether it is to visit a publisher or gather research for an article. Here the non-fiction writer is at a distinct advantage, because in most cases, interviewing people in a different town is absolutely necessary. This could conceivably mean a bus trip from downtown Vancouver to nearby Burnaby, on the one hand, or a flight from Halifax to Istanbul, on the other.

The simple rule is that to be tax deductible, travel *must* relate to work. For the novelist who cannot secure an advance commitment from a publisher, a legitimate business trip may be extremely hard to prove. All is not lost, however. If a visit to Turkey is necessary to gather material that cannot be found elsewhere, it can either be claimed as an expense when the work is published, or written off against royalties.

Car travel, hotels, meals, and entertainment – the drinks you may want to buy a useful contact, the dinner you host for a person who is figuring prominently in your story, or the editor on your latest book – are also legitimate writers' expenses. Remember, though, that you cannot claim on your income tax form any expenses that a magazine or publishing house may already have refunded to you. Apart from being illegal, it is dishonest.

American markets

The English-speaking Canadian who has begun to sell with some consistency enjoys a unique geographical advantage over colleague writers overseas. Canada has a southerly neighbour with a population of some 260 million people, most of whom speak English and are thus potential readers of English writing.

The most recent edition of *Writer's Market* (see Chapter 10, Resources) lists more than 4,000 paying markets in the United States for novels, short stories, fillers, plays, gags, verses, even photographs the freelancer may take during travels. This book also gives the names and addresses of editors, and sets out their requirements –

what they expect from a manuscript in content and length, and how long it takes them to report back to a writer with a decision on whether or not to publish.

Two U.S. monthly magazines are also indispensable to Canadian writers seeking new markets south of the border – *Writer's Digest* itself, the publisher of the annual *Writer's Market*, produced in Cincinnati for practical-minded freelancers, and *The Writer*, published in Boston for those with more literary tastes. These journals not only keep readers informed about markets and trends, but provide both a stimulus and a constant flow of fresh ideas. Writer's Digest Books, by the way, publishes an astonishing range of practical books for writers – from guides to writing genre fiction to manuals on magazine article writing.

The much-repeated rule about studying markets, as you must when writing for Canadian magazines, applies more than ever in the U.S., because the array of American publications is awesome. And those that may at first appear similar most certainly are not on closer examination. Nearly all magazines have their own special character and narrow, specific needs to go with it.

The enormous selection of American magazines, however, in no way diffuses the difficulty in breaking into the huge market they have come to constitute, particularly with a Canadian story. The first point to ask yourself here is, "Why would an American magazine be interested in Canada?" A quick answer to the question is that most really aren't unless they can be *made* to be interested in Canada, or unless the story has a broad appeal to both nations.

Some Canadian stories, of course, will have an obvious and natural tie-in with American events. A perceptive article on NAFTA from a Canadian perspective might attract the interest of a U.S. business magazine. As a Canadian writer you will have to work hard to penetrate the American market, especially with ideas for the consumer magazines.

Most Canadians who have consistently sold their writing in the United States can thank those opportunities provided by the vast collection of American trade publications. If Canada is related to the United States at all, it is through sharing common trade channels, and having similar concerns about world politics and business. The moment American equipment and/or expertise is brought to bear on a Canadian building site, for example, there could legitimately be the makings of a story for an American trade or professional magazine. Sometimes, there may also be a story in how Canada sees, or deals with, problems specific to both countries.

But there is yet another hurdle to cross. Many American trade magazines are staff-written. This means that a staff writer will travel to Canada to cover an American story rooted here, so a manuscript from a Canadian freelancer must be exceptionally strong to win a place.

The odds can be beaten, though. After accepting a few manuscripts from a Canadian contributor, the editor of an American trade magazine might be willing to publish a monthly feature written by a Canadian on the Canadian viewpoint: what his or her country thinks about mutual problems and issues, and what solutions it can offer.

It is well worth trying to secure a foothold in the American market, for purely economic reasons. It is still difficult, after all, for Canadians to make a satisfactory living by writing exclusively for magazines and publishing houses in their own country, which helps explain why most combine crafting poetry, novels, magazine articles, and non-fiction with other work. The situation may change though. Writing opportunities for Canada's writers have certainly increased since this book first appeared; with more settled economic times they are almost certain to continue to do so. And when they do, *The Canadian Writer's Market* will be there with a richer list than ever.

Adrian Waller

1

CONSUMER MAGAZINES

"Magazines constitute the only national press we possess in Canada. . . Magazines, in a different way from any other medium, can help foster in Canadians a sense of themselves." – *Report of the Special Senate Committee on Mass Media*, 1970

At the time of this report, 70 per cent of all magazines sold in Canada originated in the United States. Since then, protective federal legislation has helped to foster the growth of a vigorous local industry: twenty years on, Canadian magazines had captured 40 per cent of the local market, and had done so despite the fact that a mere 6 per cent of Canadian magazines ever reached our American-dominated newsstands. Today, this remarkable success story faces threats from all sides. The first strike was to the postal subsidy.

Canada's enlightened federal postal subsidy program was established almost a century ago to help compensate for the isolation of many Canadian communities. The guiding principle was that all Canadians, wherever they lived, should have equal access to their nation's magazines. Over the years, the preferential postal rates have played a vital role in fostering the growth of the local industry by subsidizing distribution costs for magazines heavily reliant on subscription sales. The Canadian Magazine Publishers Association and other industry advocates had long warned that removing or reducing the subsidy would threaten many fragile publishing operations. Nevertheless, in December 1989, a cash-strapped government announced the incremental phasing out of the program. Controlled-circulation trade publications were hit hard by the subsidy's removal. As yet, most paid-circulation consumer magazines have been exempted, though their postal costs *have* risen, and the future looks grim.

Magazines struggling with extra postal costs face strong consumer resistance to price hikes in the wake of the 7 per cent increase imposed by GST. Coinciding with the recession, the introduction of the GST in 1991 was a body blow to the industry. According to a new report by the CMPA, the first year of GST brought a devastating 62.5 per cent decrease in magazine profits. On top of the direct impact on subscription and advertising sales, Canadian magazines now face an extra 7 per cent competitive disadvantage in relation to their U.S. competitors, as more than 50 million copies of U.S. magazines enter Canada each year without being taxed.

The stealthy introduction of split runs from across the border is the latest threat to the industry. Split runs are special editions of magazines imported into Canada with U.S. editorial content but discounted Canadian advertising. They siphon off advertising that would otherwise go to Canadian magazines, eroding their market share. Consumer magazines simply cannot survive without a reliable level of advertising, their main source of revenue.

In the past three years, as a result of these combined assaults, Canadian magazines have suffered heavy losses in revenue. The CMPA estimates that the number of full- and part-time magazine employees has decreased by over 30 per cent, while the number of unpaid voluntary staff has increased by some 60 per cent. At least 129 magazines ceased publishing during 1991–92, according to the industry magazine *Masthead*.

To underscore just how fragile the magazine publishing industry is, 47 per cent of the periodicals surveyed by Statistics Canada in 1984 ran at a loss, while only 41 per cent reported after-tax profits. In 1990–91, according to StatsCan, average pre-tax profit was 2 per cent, but a breakdown of this figure reveals how unequally this "profit" was spread: while the market leaders averaged a 4 per cent profit, a larger number of magazines – those with modest annual revenues below $100,000 – were averaging pre-tax losses of 22 per cent. The big players will sometimes use the profits from their successful, high-circulation publications to support a smaller one not making a profit – an option not available to solo magazines.

It is perhaps a cause for wonder that the industry survives at all, let alone as the dynamic profusion of voices that it is. It is also a tribute to those who make it happen – to loyal Canadian readers, who continue to support their national press through their subscriptions; to the freelance writers who are its creative backbone; and to the publishers, editors, designers, and production staff who dream up and sustain the magazines. So when you're feeling especially frustrated about how poorly paid you were for that last article, spare a thought for your "tight-fisted" employer. During the research for this book, it was striking how many publishing ventures (smaller arts magazines stood out especially) are kept alive – indeed, in creative terms, are flourishing – through the enthusiasm, hard work, and sheer willpower of a few committed, stubborn, often unpaid individuals.

Most consumer magazines continue to rely heavily on freelancers, and in spite of these bleak economic times the range of opportunity for the skilled and imaginative writer remains broad. Large-circulation consumer magazines that are heavily supported by advertising can usually afford to pay most for a writer's work – fifty cents to a dollar a word at the top of the scale. The standouts here are high-calibre general interest magazines like *Equinox*, *Canadian Geographic*, and *Saturday Night*, glossy inflight magazines like *Canadian* and *enRoute*, top women's magazines like *Chatelaine*, and leading business journals like *Profit* and the *Globe*'s *Report on Business*.

Many other magazines pay fees that can amount to between $1,000 and $1,500 for a professionally written feature article. Magazines with smaller circulations, which include most of those listed in the following pages, for obvious reasons tend to pay less – anything from $100 to $800 for an article of up to 3,000 words – though there is often some room for negotiation over the fee, depending on the writer's experience and the amount of research needed.

A last class comprises those magazines and journals that either generate much of their own editorial copy, or rely almost entirely on the voluntary contributions of professional colleagues or qualified readers. They may pay only occasionally for freelance contributions, sometimes in the form of free magazines. The committed freelance writer should consider contributing to these too, recognizing the long-term benefits in terms of experience and professional development. It is a reflection of the times that more entries than ever before fall into this class in the present edition of *The Canadian Writer's Market*. More positively, however, it also reflects the large number of exciting and stimulating small magazines that are determinedly holding their own despite hostile market conditions. They should be supported.

Today, more than ever, writing for publication is an intensely competitive business, and to succeed requires the right approach, good research, and plenty of hard work. The first, golden rule is to familiarize yourself thoroughly with the magazine's agenda and style before you approach the editor with a proposal. Find out whether they have an editorial calendar or run special or theme issues (the *CARD* directory sometimes lists these – see Chapter 10, Resources). You will often have time to prepare your submission ahead of schedule. Seasonal stories may need to be submitted up to six months in advance.

Note the magazines that interest you in the following pages and send for sample copies, or search them out in a good bookstore or your public library. Generally, it is not a good idea to send unsolicited work without an initial written inquiry. Always request contributors' guidelines where these are available. They may be a few short, practical remarks or several pages of background and advice, but close attention to these guidelines will often make the difference between your submission being taken seriously or not. Be sure to check what form your submission should take. Many magazine editors now prefer to receive them on disk. Ensure that you provide it in the appropriate program, or in a readily convertible, text-only form. Provide hard copy back-up, too, in case the disk presents problems or the editor chooses to do an initial edit on paper.

Nothing will endear you less to a hard-pressed editor than to present him or her with an unintelligible disk or a poorly presented article. A submission full of spelling and punctuation errors, and betraying a manifest ignorance of basic grammar, will not impress. On the other hand, clean copy, delivered on time, may win you an important friend. Your first submission to a periodical should always include a story outline along with a brief summary of your professional experience and cuttings of previously published stories (tearsheets). Mention any experience that qualifies you to write on the topic. For most editors, evidence of previous experience is initially the single most attractive feature in a submission. Always be businesslike in your dealings with editors – respond immediately to letters or phone calls, and be friendly and co-operative. Include an SASE with *every* inquiry or submission that requires a response.

The successful freelancer keeps abreast of the changes and developments in the industry. One excellent conduit for this information is the Periodical Writers Association of Canada. PWAC membership entitles you to a subscription to their informative bimonthly newsletter, *PWAContact*; a comprehensive listing in their annual directory, sent to editors and publishers nationwide; a free subscription to *Sources*, a biannual directory of contacts for journalists and other writers; and, not least, the opportunity to exchange market information and make important contacts with other writers. The monthly *Canadian Autho*r magazine carries a useful section on new magazine markets for writers, and you'll also learn about new magazine launches in the pages of *Masthead*.

The most financially secure freelancers are those who are most versatile. They may feed feature articles steadily to a handful of consumer magazines, develop a working relationship with the editors of a couple of specialist trade publications, and write a regular column for a weekly newspaper. Or perhaps they have approached the director of communications of a government department or corporation and now have irregular (but often startlingly lucrative) commissions to write reports, newsletters, or information packages. As professionals, they are ready to practise their craft in unexpected – even initially unappealing – contexts as well as in their chosen areas of interest.

Target your articles, but remember that other publications might also be interested in the fruits of your research. Always look for research follow-on ideas. Research for a feature on city gardens for a general interest consumer magazine might also turn up useful background material for an article on the gardening centre phenomenon for a business journal or a more technical piece for a trade publication.

In this edition we have dropped information on specific rights bought by each periodical. As discussed in the introduction, rights are a complex, thorny issue. In general, however, it is in the writer's interest to limit the transfer of rights. Be wary of selling all rights to your work, since you may be giving up several opportunities for milking further payment from your efforts. Most magazines seek first Canadian serial rights – that is, first-time publication in a Canadian periodical. Once your piece has appeared in print you are free to recycle it elsewhere if you can. With bilingual publications, restrict your agreement to English-language rights so that you are paid again if your piece is translated for the French edition. Maclean Hunter, for instance, will pay you up to 40 per cent of your original fee for articles translated for their French-language sister publications. Before signing a contract, check out PWAC's Standard Agreement. You'll also want to know what "kill fee" is offered – that is, what percentage of the agreed fee you will be paid if the magazine for some reason doesn't publish your assigned piece. Again, PWAC can offer advice in this area.

The Arts

Applied Arts Magazine
885 Don Mills Road, Suite 324, Don Mills, Ont. M3C 1V9
Phone: (416) 510-0909   Fax: (416) 510-0913
Contact: Peter Giffen, editor
Circulation: 11,000
Published 5 times a year
   Targeting the communication arts market, *AAQ* spotlights the work of graphic design, advertising, photography, and illustration professionals, featuring outstanding examples of their work. Carries profiles and interviews. Pays 60¢/word on acceptance for articles of 500 to 2,000 words.

Artfocus Magazine
P.O. Box 1063, Station F, Toronto, Ont. M4Y 2J7
Phone: (416) 925-5564   Fax: (416) 925-5564
Contact: Pat Fleisher, publisher/editor
Circulation: 6,000
Published quarterly
   Features art gallery reviews, museum previews, profiles of contemporary artists, dealers, and collectors, and articles on media and technique by prominent artists. Also comments on controversial

issues in the arts. Carries short articles of 500 to 600 words, features of 1,500 to 2,000 words. Fees average $200 to $250, paid after publication. Query first with samples of written work.

Art Impressions Magazine

P.O. Box 96, 22 Keele Street S., King City, Ont. LOG IKO
Phone: (905) 833-2737 · Fax: (905) 833-3763
Contact: Michael J. Knell, editor
Circulation: 18,000
Published quarterly

For collectors of Canadian art, especially realistic, impressionist, and wildlife. Carries articles on Canadian art, art history, artists, and art-related issues. Preferred length 2,500 to 3,500 words. Pays on publication at negotiated rates. Written proposals always welcome.

ArtsAtlantic

145 Richmond Street, Charlottetown, P.E.I. CIA IJI
Phone: (902) 628-6138   Fax: (902) 566-4648
Contact: Joseph Sherman, editor
Circulation: 3,500
Published 3 times a year

Award-winning arts review carrying features, reviews, and reports on Atlantic Canada's fine arts, cinema, video, artisanship, performance, and literature. Reviews are 600 to 800 words, feature articles 1,200 to 3,000 words. Pays a flat rate of $65 per review, 15¢/word for features – up to a maximum of $250 – on publication. Welcomes approaches by mail, phone, or fax.

Arts Bridge

10405 Jasper Avenue, 7th Floor, Standard Life Centre, Edmonton, Alta. T5J 3N4
Phone: (403) 427-2968   Fax: (403) 427-0263
Contact: Dave Ponech, co-ordinator
Circulation: 28,000
Published quarterly

An informative package produced by the provincial government for Alberta's artists and arts-related organizations, institutions, and related business. Pays 30¢/word for articles of 500 to 2,000 words.

"Articles are assigned. Send me a résumé and samples of published work, preferably dealing with the arts, along with short ideas for proposed articles."

Azure

2 Silver Avenue, Toronto, Ont. M6R 3A2
Phone: (416) 588-2588   Fax: (416) 588-2357
Contact: Nelda Rodger, editor
Circulation: 12,000
Published bimonthly

A design review, covering developments in graphic, interior, and industrial design and art in Canada and abroad, directed towards designers, architects, and the visually aware. Pays on publication. Guidelines available.

Border Crossings

393 Portage Avenue, Suite Y300, Winnipeg, Man. R3B 3H6
Phone: (204) 942-5778   Fax: (204) 949-0793
Contact: Meeka Walsh, co-editor
Circulation: 3,300
Published quarterly

An interdisciplinary arts review featuring articles, book reviews, artists' profiles, and interviews covering the full range of the contemporary arts in Manitoba and the West. Subjects include architecture, dance, fiction, film, painting, photography, poetry, politics, and theatre. Pays a negotiated fee on publication. Writers should use the magazine as their guide when formulating submissions.

C Magazine

P.O. Box 5, Station B, Toronto, Ont. M5T 2T2
Phone: (416) 539-9495   Fax: (416) 531-7610
Contact: Joyce Mason, editor/publisher
Circulation: 3,000
Published quarterly

A leading Canadian review of contemporary Canadian and international visual art and criticism. Features should be 1,500 to 3,000 words, reviews 650 to 750 words. Feature rates vary; $125 paid per review. Pays on publication. Guidelines available.

Camera Canada

1140 South Dyke Road, New Westminster, B.C. v3m 5a2
Phone: (604) 524-5332
Contact: Marilyn McEwen, editor
Circulation: 3,000
Published quarterly

Showcases the work of up-and-coming photographers through their portfolios, method, philosophy, and biographical information. Contributors are unpaid, but inquiries welcome.

Canadian Art

6 Church Street, 2nd Floor, Toronto, Ont. m5e 1m1
Phone: (416) 368-8854   Fax: (416) 594-3375
Contact: Sarah Milroy, editor/publisher
Circulation: 27,000
Published quarterly

Covers visual arts in Canada in a lively and opinionated way. Includes articles on painting, sculpture, film, photography, architecture, design, video, and television, with critical profiles of new artists and assessments of established art-world figures. Articles 150 to 2,000 words. Pays $100 for 150 words, up to $1,000 for 3,000 words, on publication. Inquire first. No unsolicited submissions.

Canadian Musician

23 Hannover Drive, Unit 7, St. Catharines, Ont. l2w 1a3
Phone: (905) 641-3471   Fax: (905) 533-8303
Contact: Shauna Kennedy, editor
Published bimonthly

A magazine for professional and amateur musicians, as well as serious music enthusiasts and industry personnel. Accepts articles of 2,000 to 3,000 words. Most articles are assigned and fees are negotiable. Pays on acceptance. All writers are required to be technically and musically literate. Guidelines available.

Canadian Theatre Review

Department of Drama, Queen's University, Kingston,
   Ont. k7l 3n6
Phone: (519) 824-4120, ext. 3147 (A.F.), (613) 545-2104 (N.R.)
Contact: Alan Filewod or Natalie Rewa, editors

Circulation: 1,200
Published quarterly

Publishes playscripts, essays of interest to theatre professionals, and interviews with playwrights, actors, directors, and designers. Issues are thematic, with guidance from guest editor. Preferred article length 1,500 to 3,000 words. Pay scale and guidelines available on request.

Canadian Writer's Journal

P.O. Box 6618, Depot 1, Victoria, B.C. v8p 5n7
Phone: (604) 477-8807
Contact: Gordon M. Smart, editor/publisher
Circulation: 250
Published quarterly

Not a significant market for the writer, but freelancers are finding it a useful source of ideas on professional, motivational, and marketing aspects of the profession. Length 400 to 1,200 words. "Queries or complete mss. welcome. Writers should present specifics rather than generalities, and avoid overworked subjects such as overcoming writer's block, handling rejection, etc." Runs annual contests for poetry and short fiction. Guidelines available.

CineACTION!

40 Alexander Street, Apartment 705, Toronto, Ont. m4y 1b5
Phone: (416) 964-3534
Contact: editorial collective
Circulation: 2,000
Published 3 times a year

A film magazine that explores neglected and unconventional cinema, both mainstream and independent productions, from a feminist and socialist perspective. Submission inquiries welcome. It is the magazine's policy to pay for contributions, but limited funds mean payment is sometimes delayed.

Classical Music Magazine

121 Lakeshore Road E., Suite 207, Mississauga, Ont. l5g 1e5
Phone: (905) 271-0339   Fax: (905) 271-9748
Contact: Derek Copperthwaite, associate editor
Circulation: 7,000

Published 5 times a year

Featuring classical music in all its aspects, including news stories, photo features, historical articles, personality profiles, and interviews. Pays on publication for articles of 2,500 to 3,000 words. Appropriate short news items (100 to 200 words) earn $50; longer articles up to $300. Send $5 for writer's guidelines.

Coda Magazine

P.O. Box 1002, Station O, Toronto, Ont. M4A 2N4
Phone: (416) 593-7230   Fax: (416) 593-7230
Contact: Bill Smith, editor
Circulation: 3,000
Published bimonthly

The Canadian jazz and improvised music magazine with an international reputation, published since 1958, with articles, essays, personality profiles, and reviews. "*Coda* is a specialized periodical and only publishes work by experts in this field, so all is negotiable."

Dance Connection

815 – 1st Street S.W., Suite 603, Calgary, Alta. T2P 1N3
Phone: (403) 263-3232   Fax: (403) 237-7327
Contact: Heather Elton, editor
Circulation: 2,500
Published 5 times a year

Reflects a commitment to a broad view of dance. Through feature articles, critical essays, profiles, and literature, it examines contemporary issues relating to dance. Pays 10¢/word on publication for articles of 800 to 2,500 words. Guidelines available.

Dance International

Roedde House, 1415 Barclay Street, Vancouver, B.C. V6G 1J6
Phone: (604) 681-1525   Fax: (604) 681-7732
Contact: Maureen Riches, editor
Circulation: 2,000
Published quarterly

Formerly *Vandance International.* Provides a forum for lively and critical commentary on the best in national and international dance, including features, reviews, reports, and commentaries. Preferred length 1,000 to 2,000 words. Pays on publication $100 to $150 for features, $65 to $80 for commentaries, $40 to $60 for reviews, $60 to $75 for notebook. Full guidelines available.

errata
5996, rue St. Urbain, Montreal, Que. H2T 2X5
Phone: (514) 278-3555
Contact: Stephen Evans, publishing editor
Circulation: 1,000
Published quarterly

Features many aspects of writing and art. Preferred length 3,000 to 5,000 words. "*errata* welcomes submissions from all aspiring writers/artists. At least half our content is from unpublished writers. Our mission is to promote the work of new writers and artists." Contributors are unpaid. Guidelines available.

FUSE Magazine
183 Bathurst Street, 1st Floor, Toronto, Ont. M5T 2R7
Phone: (416) 367-0159   Fax: (416) 360-0781
Contact: Kathleen Pirrie-Adams, editorial co-ordinator
Circulation: 5,000
Published 5 times a year

Addresses all aspects of contemporary culture. Special emphasis on issues relating to different cultural communities, including feminist issues, gay and lesbian culture and politics, minority and labour struggles, and economic and policy analysis. Also reviews visual arts, from independent production to mass media, including video, film, television, music, performance art, theatre, and books. Articles from 700 to 5,000 words. Pays 10¢/word on publication for reviews, and a flat rate of $700 for full-length features. "Please request guidelines before submitting unsolicited copy."

Inuit Art Quarterly
2081 Merivale Road, Nepean, Ont. K2G 1G9
Phone: (613) 224-8189   Fax: (613) 224-2907
Contact: Marybelle Mitchell, editor
Circulation: 4,000

Devoted exclusively to Inuit art, and directed towards art specialists, artists, historians, teachers, and all interested readers with the purpose of giving Inuit artists a voice. Carries feature articles, profiles, interviews, news and reviews, and reader commentary. Pays 50¢/word, or $500 for a feature article of 1,000 to 1,500 words, on publication. Query editor first.

MUSICWORKS: The Journal of Sound Exploration

179 Richmond Street W., Toronto, Ont. M5V 1V3
Phone: (416) 977-3546   Fax: (416) 208-1084
Contact: Gayle Young, editor
Circulation: 2,500
Published 3 times a year

Distributed with audio component – cassettes or CDs – to illustrate articles and interviews covering a broad range of contemporary classical and experimental music. Also ethnic music and sound related to dance and visual art. Features are 1,000 to 3,500 words. Fees depend on length, complexity, and other factors. Pays on publication. Welcomes inquiries. Guidelines available.

The Mystery Review

P.O. Box 233, Colborne, Ont. KOK 1S0
Phone: (613) 475-4440   Fax: (613) 475-3400
Contact: Barbara Davey, editor
Circulation: 2,500
Published quarterly

For readers of mystery and suspense. Carries information on new mystery titles, interviews with authors, real-life unsolved mysteries, puzzles, and word games relating to the genre. Pays honorarium depending on type of submission. Contact editor for guidelines.

Opera Canada

366 Adelaide Street E., Suite 434, Toronto, Ont. M5A 3X9
Phone: (416) 363-0395   Fax: (416) 363-0396
Contact: Jocelyn Laurence, editor
Circulation: 4,000
Published quarterly

Devoted for more than 30 years to Canadian opera. Reviews international performances, interviews Canada's best singers, and addresses opera-related cultural issues. Reviews up to 300 words; features 1,000 to 1,500 words. Accepts submissions and submission inquiries. Pays on publication. Fees negotiable.

Parachute
4060 St. Laurent Boulevard, Suite 501, Montreal, Que. H2W 1Y9
Phone: (514) 842-9805
Contact: Chantal Pontbriand, editor
Circulation: 3,000
Published quarterly

A bilingual review offering readers in-depth articles on the theory and practice of art today – interviews with artists, and articles on music, cinema, photography, theatre, dance, and video. Pays about $100 for reviews and issues column (to a maximum of 1,000 words), up to $500 for articles and interviews (3,000 to 5,000 words), on publication. Guidelines available.

Parallélogram
183 Bathurst Street, 1st Floor, Toronto, Ont. M5T 2R7
Phone: (416) 869-3854   Fax: (416) 360-0781
Contact: Lynne Fernie, editor
Circulation: 5,000
Published quarterly

A national bilingual magazine that traces developments in contemporary art, including painting, sculpture, installations, video, new music, dance, and performance. Articles 2,000 to 2,500 words. Contact editor for guidelines and pay rates.

Performing Arts & Entertainment in Canada
1100 Caledonia Road, Toronto, Ont. M6A 2W5
Phone: (416) 785-4300   Fax: (416) 785-4329
Contact: Karen Bell, editor
Circulation: 30,000, with issue over-runs up to 100,000
Published quarterly

Explores the issues and trends affecting performing arts in Canada – primarily theatre, dance, opera, ballet, and film. Also carries profiles on individual performers, companies, and troupes. Prefers articles of 1,200 to 1,800 words. Fees $150 to $300, paid on publication. Query first.

Proscenium
189 Laurier Avenue E., Ottawa, Ont. KIN 6PI
Phone: (613) 238-3561   Fax: (613) 238-4849

Contact: Jocelyne Dubois, editor
Circulation: 2,500
Published bimonthly

A bilingual arts and culture news magazine presenting innovative cultural ideas. Follows political, cultural, and educational developments, at national and provincial level, of concern to artists and arts administrators. Preferred length 750 to 1,000 words. Pays $200 for columns, $350 (maximum) for features.

The Reader

1701 West 3rd Avenue, Vancouver, B.C. v6J 1K7
Phone: (604) 732-7631   Fax: (604) 732-3765
Contact: Celia Duthie, publisher
Circulation: 11,000
Published quarterly

A free-circulation book review selection of new titles of interest to the general reader. Preferred length 200 to 800 words. Pays on publication with a $100 gift certificate for major reviews, a $50 gift certificate for brief reviews. Welcomes unsolicited reviews, but acceptance not guaranteed. "Submissions should be succinct, interesting, and positive." Guidelines available.

Shift Magazine

10 King Street E., Toronto, Ont. M5C 1C3
Phone: (416) 868-6565   Fax: (416) 360-5694
Contact: Andrew Heintzman, editor
Circulation: 2,500
Published quarterly

A broad cultural magazine with a vigorous and youthful editorial agenda. Preferred article length 800 to 2,000 words. Cannot pay but welcomes submissions, which should include author bio.

Studio Magazine

124 Galaxy Boulevard, Toronto, Ont. M9W 4Y6
Phone: (416) 675-1999   Fax: (416) 675-6093
Contact: Barbara Murray, executive editor
Circulation: 14,000
Published 7 times a year

A large-format, full-colour design magazine. Buys factual articles with appeal to professional designers, illustrators, and photographers. Pays on publication. Mail inquiries only, enclosing published samples and references. Length and fee discussed case by case.

Theatre Research in Canada
Graduate Centre for the Study of Drama, 214 College Street,
    Toronto, Ont. M5T 2Z9
Phone: (416) 978-7984   Fax: (416) 971-1378
Contact: the editors
Circulation: 500
Published twice a year
    Addresses all aspects of research into both English- and French-language theatre in Canada. Also publishes book reviews and articles (up to 4,000 words), in English and French, on companies and people who have contributed to theatre and criticism. Pays on publication. Submission guidelines outlined in journal.

Theatrum
P.O. Box 688, Station C, Toronto, Ont. M6J 3S1
Phone: (416) 493-5740   Fax: (416) 493-5740
Contact: Sarah Hood, editor
Circulation: 3,000
Published quarterly
    Directed towards both patrons and practitioners of the theatre, as a forum for the working professional to discuss his/her craft. Provides a place for discussion and exposure, in "an art form that is becoming increasingly exciting and complex." Includes feature articles, artist profiles, production and book reviews, and festival reports. Welcomes unsolicited manuscripts. Pays an honorarium of from $50 (reviews) to $300 (articles) two weeks after publication.

West Coast Line
2027 East Academic Annex, Simon Fraser University, Burnaby,
    B.C. V5A 1S6
Phone: (604) 291-4287   Fax: (604) 291-5737
Contact: Miriam Nichols, managing editor
Circulation: 600
Published 3 times a year
    A creative arts magazine focusing mostly on West Coasters and

featuring contemporary poetry, short fiction, drama, and photography. Devoted to "contemporary writers who are experimenting with, or expanding the boundaries of, conventional forms of poetry, fiction, and criticism." Pays $4/page for prose, $5/page for poetry, after publication. Query first. Guidelines available.

Writer's Lifeline
P.O. Box 1641, Cornwall, Ont. K6H 5V6
Phone: (613) 932-2135   Fax: (613) 932-7735
Contact: Stephen Gill, editor
Circulation: 2,000
Published 3 times a year
Publishes articles, news, book reviews, poems, author interviews – anything concerning the world of books that could prove useful to writers. Preferred length 500 to 3,000 words. "Please read our publication before submitting." Pays in copies. Guidelines available.

Business

Atlantic Business Report/Brunswick Business Journal
140 Baig Boulevard, Moncton, N.B. E1E 1C8
Phone: (506) 857-9696   Fax: (506) 859-7395
Contact: Lynda J. MacGibbon, managing editor
Circulation: *ABR* – 14,000; *BBJ* – 7,000
Published monthly
Two regional business magazines that aim to foster economic development in Atlantic Canada by publishing stories about economic trends and issues and featuring successful businesses. Preferred length 800 to 1,200 words. Pay around 15¢/word on publication. Guidelines available.

Atlantic Lifestyle Business Magazine
197 Water Street, St John's, P.O. Box 2356, Nfld. A1C 6E7
Phone: (709) 726-9300   Fax: (709) 726-3013
Contact: Adrian Smith, editor
Circulation: 25,000
Published bimonthly
Examines culture, lifestyle, and business in Atlantic Canada.

Pays 15¢/word on publication for articles of 2,000 to 2,500 words. Guidelines available.

BC Business
4180 Lougheed Highway, Suite 401, Burnaby, B.C. V5C 6A7
Phone: (604) 299-7311   Fax: (604) 299-9188
Contact: Bonnie Irving, editor
Circulation: 26,000
Published monthly

Directed towards managers, entrepreneurs, and professionals, it aims to inform readers of the trends, people, and companies shaping the business environment in British Columbia. Pays 35¢/word on acceptance for articles of 1,000 to 2,500 words. "Tell us something we don't know." Guidelines available.

Canadian Business
70 The Esplanade, 2nd Floor, Toronto, Ont. M5E 1R2
Phone: (416) 364-4266   Fax: (416) 364-2783
Contact: Randall Litchfield, editor
Circulation: 90,000
Published monthly

Canada's premier national business journal, carrying incisive and thoughtful commentary and advice on business issues and profiles of successful business people. Articles 800 to 4,000 words. Pays $500 to $3,000 on acceptance, depending on assignment and experience. Prefers initial inquiries by mail.

Canadian Business Life
1 St. John's Road, Suite 501, Toronto, Ont. M6P 4C7
Phone: (416) 766-5744   Fax: (416) 766-1970
Contact: Darryl Simmons, vice-president
Circulation: 50,000
Published quarterly

Focuses on the concerns of small business. Preferred length 1,000 to 2,000 words. Pays on publication. Welcomes inquiries.

Edmonton Business Report
3228 – 105th Street N.W., Edmonton, Alta. T6J 3A2
Phone: (403) 499-7849   Fax: (403) 988-5932

Circulation: 25,000
Published monthly

A new regional business magazine that aims to become indispensable to small and medium-sized business operators in and around Edmonton. Carries news stories, columns containing how-to information, and features, mostly originating with freelancers, offering analysis of issues of interest to the business community. *EBR* is actively seeking freelance queries and submissions. Rates vary, but are at the high end for a regional publication. Pays on publication.

The Financial Post Magazine

333 King Street E., 3rd Floor, Toronto, Ont. M5A 4N2
Phone: (416) 350-6172   Fax: (416) 350-6171
Contact: Maryanne McNellis, editor
Circulation: 200,000
Published 11 times a year plus *FP 500* annual

An executive lifestyle magazine featuring political, business, and general interest articles and personal finance columns, mostly written by experts or seasoned journalists. Articles 1,500 to 3,000 words. Pays top rates on acceptance.

The Home Business Report

2949 Ash Street, Abbotsford, B.C. V2S 4G5
Phone: (604) 857-1788   Fax: (604) 854-3087
Contact: Barbara Mowat, publisher
Circulation: 100,000
Published quarterly

A magazine to link home-based businesses across the country, providing a network for sharing experiences, including advice for launching new businesses and support for those that are struggling. Articles 600 to 1,200 words. Pay rates depend on assignment – from 10¢/word to $250 to $400 for a 1,200-word feature – paid on publication. Very interested in successful rural and small-town home-based businesses offering an unusual product or service. Guidelines available.

Lethbridge Business Magazine

239 – 12th Street A. N., Lethbridge, Alta. T1J 4A4
Phone: (403) 327-3200   Fax: (403) 320-6049

Contact: Suzanne Zintel, editor
Circulation: 6,000
Published bimonthly

Informs Lethbridge business people about current business issues. Preferred length 700 to 1,500 words. Pays around 12¢/word on publication. Guidelines available.

PROFIT: The Magazine for Canadian Entrepreneurs

70 The Esplanade, 2nd Floor, Toronto, Ont. M5E 1R2
Phone: (416) 364-4760   Fax: (416) 362-4505
Contact: Rick Spence, editor
Circulation: 100,000
Published quarterly

Features regular columns and departments along with articles on management topics and issues of interest to owner/managers of small to medium-sized businesses. Offers insights and practical advice in the areas of marketing, technology, finance, innovators and trends, and personnel management. Pays up to 75¢/word on acceptance for features of 1,000 to 2,500 words and shorter items. "You must know something about business and be prepared to rewrite."

Report on Business Magazine

444 Front Street W., Toronto, Ont. M5V 2S9
Phone: (416) 585-5499   Fax: (416) 585-5705
Contact: David Olive, editor
Circulation: 300,000
Published monthly

A news magazine covering the national business scene and international developments affecting Canada. Carries profiles of prominent business and political personalities, book reviews, and regular columns on personal finance and national opinion. Pays around $1/word. Full-length feature fee varies from $1,500 to $4,000, depending on length, complexity of topic, and writer's style and experience. Pays on acceptance.

Small Business Week Magazine

108 – 93 Lombard Avenue, Winnipeg, Man. R3B 3B1
Phone: (204) 942-2214   Fax: (204) 943-8991
Contact: Stuart Slayen, editor

Circulation: 35,000
Published twice a year

Provides a range of helpful material for Manitoba-based small business owners, managers, and staff. Article length 700 to 2,000 words. Pays about 17¢/word, or $200 for 1,500 words, on publication. "Rates are negotiable, depending on the story. Writers are encouraged to phone the editor to discuss story ideas before submitting." Guidelines available.

Trade and Commerce

P.O. Box 6900, 1700 Church Avenue, Winnipeg, Man. R3C 3B1
Phone: (204) 632-2606   Fax: (204) 694-3040
Contact: Laura Jean Stewart, editor
Circulation: 10,000
Published 5 times a year

Profiles companies and communities with an emphasis on their contribution to the economy or economic development activity. Pays 20¢ to 30¢/word on publication for 1,500 to 2,500 words. Works with freelance writers all over Canada and the United States. Guidelines available.

Victoria's Business Report

1609 Blanshard Street, Victoria, B.C. v8w 2J5
Phone: (604) 382-7777   Fax: (604) 381-2662
Contact: Gery Lemon, editor
Circulation: 14,000
Published monthly

Focuses on the concerns of south Vancouver Island business. Articles 500 to 1,000 preferred. Rates range from $50 to $400, paid on publication.

City & Entertainment

Cityscope

1133 Kensington Road N.W., Calgary, Alta. T2N 3P4
Phone: (403) 270-9590   Fax: (403) 283-2223
Contact: Valerie Berenyi, editor
Circulation: 62,500

Published bimonthly

A city magazine focusing on arts and entertainment, sports and recreation, business, and politics in and around Calgary, and promoting local talent. Articles 250 to 3,500 words. Pays 30¢/word on publication plus some expenses. Guidelines available.

Georgia Straight

1235 West Pender Street, 2nd Floor, Vancouver, B.C. v6e 2v6
Phone: (604) 681-7000   Fax: (604) 681-0272
Contact: Charles Campbell, managing editor
Circulation: 93,000
Published weekly

Event-oriented yet thoughtful articles on the arts, music, movies, style, food, sports, and outdoor recreation, anchored by a general interest news feature. Articles 200 to 4,000 words. First send an inquiry with writing samples. Pays 15¢ to 30¢/word on publication. Guidelines available.

Hamilton This Month

361 King Street W., Hamilton, Ont. L8P 1B4
Phone: (416) 522-6117   Fax: (416) 529-2242
Contact: Wayne Narciso, editor/publisher
Circulation: 40,000
Published 8 times a year

A news and general interest magazine for Hamilton and its suburbs, focusing on public issues, events, and concerns – and the personalities behind them. Also covers fashion, interior decorating, electronics, cars, and restaurants. Feature length 3,000 to 5,000 words. Phone with ideas. Fees negotiable.

Home Movies

2400 Midland Avenue, Unit 112, Scarborough, Ont. M1S 1P8
Phone: (416) 412-4429   Fax: (416) 299-9750
Contact: Michael Ryan, editor
Circulation: 2,500
Published bimonthly

For people who collect movies on laserdisc and have a general interest in home theatre. Article length 100 to 1,500 words. Pays on acceptance $20 to $80, depending on length and quality. "We're looking for writers to review laserdiscs but will consider any article that relates to home theatre. We welcome unpublished writers and will work with those who show promise." Guidelines available.

Key to Kingston

P.O. Box 1352, Kingston, Ont. K7L 5C6
Phone: (613) 549-8442   Fax: (613) 549-1608
Contact: Kim Wright, publisher/editor
Circulation: 17,000
Published 8 times a year

News of events and attractions for visitors. Also includes restaurant reviews, shopping guides, local history, and suggestions for area tours. Cover stories highlight things to do and see. Articles/stories 1,000 to 1,500 words. Cannot pay but welcomes inquiries.

London Magazine

231 Dundas Street, Suite 203, London, Ont. N6A 1H1
Phone: (519) 679-4901   Fax: (519) 434-7842
Contact: Jackie Skender, editor
Circulation: 40,000
Published 9 times a year

Covers lifestyles, fashion, city issues, art, food, history, business, sports, and entertainment for Londoners and residents of southwestern Ontario. Features regular columns by local writers. Articles 200 to 2,000 words. Fees negotiable, paid on acceptance. Guidelines available.

Marquee Magazine

77 Mowat Avenue, Suite 621, Toronto, Ont. M6K 3E3
Phone: (416) 538-1000   Fax: (416) 538-0201
Contact: Ron Base, editor; Alexandra Lenhoff, managing editor
Circulation: 700,000
Published 9 times a year

Now distributed in newspapers across Canada, *Marquee* continues to carry short feature stories, previews, and profiles of upcoming movies and personalities while expanding its coverage of video, music, and fashion. Given the magazine's advanced deadline, writers need access to on-set and on-location interview opportunities. Articles 300 to 1,500 words. Pays on publication. Fees vary.

Montreal Mirror

400 McGill Street, 2nd Floor, Montreal, Que. H2Y 2G1
Phone: (514) 393-1010   Fax: (514) 393-3173
Contact: Peter Scowen, managing editor
Circulation: 80,000
Published weekly

An alternative tabloid featuring articles on major issues written from a local perspective. Also reviews restaurants, films, art shows, books, and new music. Pays on publication.

Network

287 MacPherson Avenue, Toronto, Ont. M4V 1A4
Phone: (416) 928-2909   Fax: (416) 928-1357
Contact: Maureen Littlejohn, editor
Circulation: 150,000
Published bimonthly

A national entertainment magazine featuring predominantly pop/rock music interviews and reviews, with some movie and video coverage. Pays on publication $40 to $300 for short pieces between 150 and 700 words. Three-month lead time. Query letter advisable.

The Newfoundland Herald

P.O. Box 2015, Logy Bay Road, St John's, Nfld. A1C 5R7
Phone: (709) 726-7060   Fax: (709) 726-8227
Contact: Greg Stirling, editor-in-chief and general manager
Circulation: 11,000
Published weekly

An entertainment and local interest magazine focusing on people. Preferred length 1,000 to 1,800 words. Pays 8¢/word on publication. "Read at least three recent issues before deciding on story angles, then contact the editor by phone or mail with ideas."

NOW

150 Danforth Avenue, Toronto, Ont. M4K 1N1
Phone: (416) 461-0871   Fax: (416) 461-2886
Contact: Michael Hollett, editor/publisher
Circulation: 95,000
Published weekly

A news, entertainment, and listings magazine for Toronto's

young adults. Covers film, music, theatre, art galleries, books, fashion, personalities, and current events. Most work assigned. Uses very few out-of-town writers. No freelance entertainment submissions. Toronto region news submissions with alternative perspective have best chance. All fees negotiable. Inquiries welcome.

Ottawa Magazine

192 Bank Street, 2nd Floor, Ottawa, Ont. K2P 1W8
Phone: (613) 234-7751   Fax: (613) 234-9226
Contact: Rosa Harris-Adler, editor
Circulation: 45,000
Published 7 times a year

A city magazine exploring the news, social issues, cultural and consumer interests, and personalities of the capital. Pays 30¢ to 50¢/word on acceptance for articles between 1,000 and 2,500 words. Inquire by mail or fax. Guidelines available.

Sound & Vision

99 Atlantic Avenue, Suite 302, Toronto, Ont. M6K 3J8
Phone: (416) 535-7611   Fax: (416) 535-6325
Contact: Alan Lofft, editor
Circulation: 30,000
Published bimonthly

An entertaining, informative, and technically literate magazine that explores new audio and video technology, tests new products, and looks at trends in home entertainment. Pays $500 to $900 on acceptance for features of 2,000 to 4,000 words. "Writers must combine technical knowledge with a lively, entertaining prose style."

Starweek Magazine

1 Yonge Street, Toronto, Ont. M5E 1E6
Phone: (416) 869-4901   Fax: (416) 865-3635
Contact: Bob Hallam, editor
Circulation: 806,000
Published weekly

Carries profiles of top entertainers plus articles on sports, music, videos, and cooking, to complement Toronto-area weekly television listings. Pays on publication for articles of 800 to 1,100 words. Mail or fax queries. Fees negotiated for new freelancers.

TV Guide
50 Holly Street, Toronto, Ont. M4S 3B3
Phone: (416) 482-8600   Fax: (416) 482-6054
Contact: Richard Charteris, editor
Circulation: 820,000
Published weekly
   Carries television listings and articles on the entertainment industry, children's programming, sports, food, and showbiz personalities. Pays 50¢/word on acceptance for articles of 750 to 1,000 words.

Uptown
2314 – 11th Avenue, Suite 206, Regina, Sask. S4P 0K1
Phone: (306) 359-0199   Fax: (306) 359-9060
Contact: Pat Rediger, editor
Circulation: 27,000
Published monthly
   Distributed directly to downtown employees. Focuses on the people, events, and issues affecting the city of Regina, with a special emphasis on the downtown core, and including entertainment and the arts. Articles 750 to 2,000 words. Pays 20¢/word on publication. Guidelines available.

Vancouver Magazine
555 West 12th Avenue, Suite 300, S.E. Tower, Vancouver,
   B.C. V5Z 4L4
Phone: (604) 877-7732   Fax: (604) 877-4849
Contact: Judith Hogan, assistant editor
Circulation: 80,000
Published monthly
   A glossy city magazine focusing on current affairs and entertainment. Most issues cover municipal politics, business, media, music, and high society. Also covers upcoming events, wine, and fine dining. Articles must be Vancouver specific. Pays on acceptance. Guidelines available.

What's Happening
P.O. Box 171, Foxboro, Ont. K0K 2B0
Phone: (613) 969-8896   Fax: (613) 969-1836
Contact: Jo Anne Lewis, editor

Circulation: 21,000

Published bimonthly

An events magazine serving the Belleville community, covering what's new in business and local events. Pays $75 to $100 on publication for articles. Guidelines available.

Where Calgary

1 Palliser Square, 125 – 9th Avenue S.E., Suite 250, Calgary, Alta. T2G 0P6

Phone: (403) 266-5085   Fax: (403) 290-0573

Contact: Jennifer MacLeod, editor

Circulation: 25,000

Published monthly

News of events and attractions for visitors. Also includes restaurant and entertainment reviews, and shopping guides. Cover stories highlight things to do and see. Buys non-fiction of 500 to 1,000 words, and pays a $275 standard rate on publication.

Where Halifax/Dartmouth

5475 Spring Garden Road, P.O. Box 14, Suite 302, Halifax, N.S. B3J 3T2

Phone: (902) 420-9943   Fax: (902) 429-9058

Contact: Karen Matheson, editor

Circulation: 25,000

Published 10 times a year

What to do and where to go in the Halifax/Dartmouth area. Shopping, sightseeing, events – anything of interest to visitors. Welcomes written inquiries with story ideas. Fees average $150 for 800 words, paid on publication.

Where Vancouver

2208 Spruce Street, Vancouver, B.C. V6H 2P3

Phone: (604) 736-5586   Fax: (604) 736-3465

Contact: Louise Whitney, editor

Circulation: 40,000

Published monthly

A visitors' guide incorporating entertainment listings, its aim to provide an intelligent city guide for the upscale traveller. Monthly events sections are popular features. Cover stories usually feature West Coast life. Articles 1,200 to 1,500 words. Pays 15¢ to 20¢/word on acceptance. Writers should first contact editor as all assignments are commissioned.

Where Victoria

1001 Wharf Street, 3rd Floor, Victoria, B.C. v8v 3T7
Phone: (604) 388-4324   Fax: (604) 388-6166
Contact: Anna Feindel, managing editor; Janice Strong, editorial
   director
Circulation: 27,000
Published monthly

A guide for visitors and residents featuring dining, shopping, entertainment, galleries, and attractions. Articles 500 to 1,000 words. Pays 25¢/word on publication. "We also welcome student submissions for no pay but carrying byline." Guidelines available.

The Environment

Borealis

P.O. Box 1359, Edmonton, Alta. T5J 2N2
Phone: (403) 439-8922   Fax: (403) 433-9646
Contact: David Dodge, editor
Circulation: 15,000
Published quarterly

Covers wilderness, nature, and environmental issues in Canada, with a strong emphasis on photography. Seeks to inspire and inform through a wide range of feature-length essays, news items, and book reviews. Pays honoraria on publication for submissions of 100 to 3,000 words. Include published samples. Guidelines available.

Common Ground

P.O. Box 34090, Station D, Vancouver, B.C. v6J 4M1
Phone: (604) 733-2215   Fax: (604) 733-4415
Contact: Joseph Roberts, editor/publisher
Circulation: 360,000
Published bimonthly

Aims to inform and inspire readers in the areas of personal growth, ecology, and healthy living. Pays 10¢/word on publication for articles from 500 to 1,800 words. "Make your first sentence and first paragraph great, or the article won't even get read."

Earthkeeper

P.O. Box 1649, Guelph, Ont. N1H 6R7
Contact: Scott Black, editor
Circulation: 11,000
Published bimonthly

A national environmental magazine, carrying well-researched feature articles and news reports, that seeks to provide a constructive context for change. Pays $50 to $300 on publication for articles between 750 and 3,500 words. Guidelines available.

Everwild Environmental Newspaper

4041 Hastings Street, Burnaby, B.C. V5L 2J1
Phone: (604) 298-0766   Fax: (604) 298-0765
Contact: Lauren Mulholland, editor
Circulation: 30,000
Published bimonthly

Provides an open forum for varied opinion and information on environmental issues, including features of 600 to 1,200 words on business, health, and Native issues. Pays $75 for features, $25 to $50 for other submissions, on publication. "We are looking for positive and informative articles. We try to resist 'blaming' others for the predicament we find ourselves in." Guidelines available.

Green Teacher

95 Robert Street, Toronto, Ont. M5S 2K5
Phone: (416) 960-1244   Fax: (416) 925-3474
Contact: Tim Grant, general editor
Circulation: 4,000
Published 5 times a year

A magazine by and for educators that aims to provide ideas, inspiration, and classroom-ready materials to help all educators (including parents) promote environmental and global awareness amongst young people, pre-school to college, in school and in the community. Articles 550 to 2,000 words. All writers are volunteers. Submissions welcome.

Harrowsmith

7 Queen Victoria Road, Camden East, Ont. KOK 1J0
Phone: (613) 378-6661   Fax: (613) 378-6123
Contact: Arlene Stacey, editor
Circulation: 160,000
Published bimonthly

A magazine for a thoughtful, critical audience interested in self-reliance and country living. Subject areas most frequently covered include country life, food gardening, solar and wind energy, folk arts, ecology, and owner-builder architecture. Pays around 60¢/word on acceptance for 1,200 to 2,500 words; rate varies according to the writer's experience and the complexity of the article. Guidelines available.

Natural Life

195 Markville Road, Unionville, Ont. L3R 4V8
Phone: (905) 470-7930
Contact: Wendy Priesnitz, editor
Circulation: 5,000
Published bimonthly

An environmental magazine focusing on ways to live a self-reliant, environmentally friendly, and sustainable lifestyle. Pays 10¢/word ($100 maximum) on publication for articles of 800 to 1,000 words. Query first. Guidelines available.

Nature Canada

1 Nicholas Street, Suite 520, Ottawa, Ont. KIN 7B7
Phone: (613) 562-3447   Fax: (613) 562-3371
Contact: Barbara Stevenson, editor
Circulation: 15,000
Published quarterly

Published by the Canadian Nature Federation. Began in 1939 as *Canadian Nature*. Focuses on all aspects of Canadian wildlife, from butterflies to beluga whales and wildflowers to Halley's Comet. Also carries how-to stories on outdoor recreation and tales of life in the field. Designed to enhance readers' understanding, enjoyment, and awareness of nature. Features vary from 1,000 to 4,000 words. Pays 20¢/word on acceptance. Guidelines available.

Seasons

355 Lesmill Road, Don Mills, Ont. M3B 2W8
Phone: (416) 652-6556   Fax: (416) 444-9866
Contact: Gail Muir, editor
Circulation: 16,000
Published quarterly

A nature and outdoors magazine published by the Federation of Ontario Naturalists and designed to enhance knowledge about natural history and the environment in Ontario. Features Ontario wildlife, wilderness, parks, and conservation issues. Preferred length 2,000 to 3,000 words. Pays up to $700 on publication. Query first, but study the magazine before you do. Guidelines available.

Watershed Sentinel

P.O. Box 25, Whaletown, B.C. V0P 1Z0
Phone: (604) 935-6992   Fax: (604) 935-6992
Contact: Delores Broten, editor
Circulation: 1,500
Published bimonthly

Environmental news for Georgia Strait with a provincial, national, and international perspective. Articles are 450 to 1,500 words. Pays in copies. Guidelines available.

Wildflower

90 Wolfrey Avenue, Toronto, Ont. M4K 1K8
Phone: (416) 466-6428
Contact: James Hodgins, editor
Circulation: 3,000
Published quarterly

Devoted to the conservation, cultivation, and study of North American wildflowers and other flora. Contains essays, book reviews, notices of coming events, and plant sources. Articles 1,500 to 5,000 words. Published by the Canadian Wildflower Society, for gardeners, naturalists, field botanists, and teachers. Cannot pay but welcomes submissions. Guidelines available.

Feminist

Fireweed: A Feminist Quarterly
P.O. Box 279, Station B, Toronto, Ont. M5T 2W2
Phone: (416) 323-9512   Fax: (416) 516-8869
Contact: Nalini Singh, office co-ordinator
Circulation: 2,000

A feminist journal of politics and the creative arts, combining analytical articles, fiction, poetry, photos, and drawings. Fiction runs to 3,500 words, articles to 5,000 words. Pays on publication. Guidelines and pay schedule available.

Healthsharing
14 Skey Lane, Toronto, Ont. M6J 3S4
Phone: (416) 532-0812   Fax: (416) 588-6638
Contact: Hazelle Palmer, managing editor
Circulation: 5,000
Published quarterly

Examines issues relating to women's health (mental, physical, and social) from a feminist perspective to provide insight, advice, and alternatives for women. Articles 2,500 to 3,000 words. Pays on special theme issues only (pending funding). Guidelines available.

Herizons
P.O. Box 128, Winnipeg, Man. R3C 2G1
Phone: (204) 774-6225
Contact: Penni Mitchell, editorial co-ordinator
Circulation: 5,000
Published quarterly

A feminist periodical focusing on women's issues and the women's movement. Articles 500 to 3,000 words. Pays 10¢/word. Send query and sample of previous published work written from a feminist perspective. Guidelines available.

Kinesis
1720 Grant Street, Suite 301, Vancouver, B.C. V5L 2Y6
Phone: (604) 255-5499   Fax: (604) 255-5511
Contact: Fatima Jaffer, editor

Circulation: 3,000

Published 10 times a year

A nationwide feminist newspaper for all women. Articles of 800 to 1,600 words cover the struggles of women activists in Canada and abroad. Issues of interest include health politics, poverty, violence against women, and aboriginal women's news. Also discusses music, dance, literature, film, and the visual arts from a feminist perspective. Contributors are unpaid. Guidelines available.

Quota Magazine

648A Yonge Street, Suite 9, Toronto, Ont. M4Y 2A6

Phone: (416) 929-2820   Fax: (416) 929-2889

Contact: Elaine J. Doy, editor

Circulation: 160,000

Published monthly

A lesbian/feminist magazine committed to giving women a voice. Article length 1,000 to 1,500 words. Pays 5¢ to 10¢/word (negotiable) one month after publication.

The Womanist

41 York Street, 3rd Floor, Ottawa, Ont. KIN 5S7

Phone: (613) 562-4081   Fax: (613) 562-4033

Contact: Joan Riggs, editor

Circulation: 20,000

Published quarterly

A national newspaper featuring feminist commentary and in-depth analysis on a range of subjects, from legislation on Parliament Hill to women's movement issues. Articles are from 750 to 2,000 words. Cannot pay but welcomes inquiries.

Women and Environments

736 Bathurst Street, Toronto, Ont. M5S 2R4

Phone: (416) 516-2379   Fax: (416) 531-6214

Contact: Kim Pearson, assistant editor

Circulation: 1,200

Published quarterly

A feminist periodical exploring women's relationships to their various environments and focusing on women's needs in housing, the workplace, urban centres, neighbourhoods, and other natural and built environments. Contributors are unpaid, but submission inquiries welcome. Guidelines available.

Women's Education des femmes
47 Main Street, Toronto, Ont. M4E 2V6
Phone: (416) 699-1909   Fax: (416) 699-2145
Contact: Christina Starr, editor
Published quarterly

A bilingual journal directed towards adult educators, teachers, students, education administrators, literacy workers, and women. A feminist connection to the world of learning and education. Feature articles cover such diverse issues as antiracist education, violence as a barrier to education, women-positive learning and literacy, and feminist pedagogy. Articles 1,500 to 2,500 words. All contributions voluntary. Submission inquiries welcome. Guidelines available.

General Interest

Above and Beyond
P.O. Box 2348, Yellowknife, N.W.T. X1A 2P7
Phone: (403) 873-2299   Fax: (403) 873-2295
Contact: Jake Ootes, editor
Circulation: 30,000
Published quarterly

Glossy, full-colour inflight magazine for First Air and Air Inuit carrying articles pertaining to Arctic areas (mainly Northwest Territories, Arctic Quebec, and Greenland), its people, communities, lifestyles, tourist attractions, and commercial activities. Prefers articles 1,000 to 1,500 words. Pays $300 per article on publication. "Assignments are not given to new freelancers. Commitment to publish provided only upon receipt of article with colour photos / slides." Guidelines available.

Arctic Circle
16 Concourse Gate, Suite 200, Nepean, Ont. K2E 7S8
Phone: (613) 727-5466   Fax: (613) 727-6910

Also P.O. Box 8, Iqaluit, N.W.T. XOA OHO
Phone: (819) 979-6468   Fax: (819) 979-4763
Contact: Jim Bell, editor-in-chief
Circulation: 15,000
Published bimonthly

Strives to present the real Arctic, mainly in Canada but also around the circumpolar world, to a Northern and national audience. Targeting an educated readership, its subjects include society, the environment, wildlife, business and economics, politics, health, education, Native North Americans, history, and literature. Controversial and ironic, presenting the inside stories in a provocative and entertaining way. Pays 25¢/word for features, departments, and columns ranging in length from 1,200 to about 4,000 words. Usually pays on publication. Inquire first with proposal.

The Beaver
450 Portage Avenue, Winnipeg, Man. R3C OE7
Phone: (204) 786-7048   Fax: (204) 774-8624
Contact: Christopher Dafoe, editor
Circulation: 44,000
Published bimonthly

A market since 1920 for lively, well-researched, informative articles on Canadian social history, with a special emphasis on the frontier region of the country and its life and culture. References to the publisher, the Hudson's Bay Company, and its history not mandatory. Articles based on unpublished journals or letters are of particular interest. Prefers articles of 3,000 to 4,000 words. Pays honoraria of $300 to $500 on acceptance. Guidelines available.

Bluenose
1459 Hollis Street, Halifax, N.S. B3J IVI
Phone: (902) 492-7006   Fax: (902) 429-1171
Contact: Edward Sutcliffe, editor/publisher
Circulation: 10,000
Published bimonthly

A general interest magazine for and about Nova Scotia and "the Nova Scotia family," modelled on New England's *Yankee*. Articles of 500 to 5,000 words. Fees negotiable, with rates varying from 10¢ to 30¢/word, paid on publication.

Canadian

199 Avenue Road, 3rd Floor, Toronto, Ont. M5R 2J3
Phone: (416) 962-9184   Fax: (416) 962-2380
Contact: Kathleen Hurd, managing editor
Published monthly

An inflight magazine for several airlines, including Canadian Airlines International. Welcomes high-quality contributions from writers and illustrators. Especially interested in profiles of successful entrepreneurs, adventure travel, and people with unusual hobbies. Articles 300 to 1,200 words. Pays $1/word on publication. Mail rather than phone inquiries, please. Guidelines available.

Canadian Geographic

39 McArthur Avenue, Ottawa, Ont. K1L 8L7
Phone: (613) 745-4629   Fax: (613) 744-0947
Contact: Ian Darragh, editor
Circulation: 250,000
Published bimonthly

Published by the Royal Canadian Geographical Society. Describes and illuminates, with fine colour photography, all aspects of Canada. Concerned with geography in its broadest sense, from archaeology and climatology to geology and wildlife. Pays $1/word on acceptance for articles of 2,000 to 3,500 words. A large paid circulation helps make it one of the most lucrative freelance opportunities. Written queries preferred. Guidelines available.

Canadian West

P.O. Box 3399, Langley, B.C. V3A 4R7
Phone: (604) 534-9378
Contact: Garnet Basque, editor/publisher
Circulation: 9,000
Published quarterly

A full-colour adventure and history magazine focusing on the early life and times of British Columbia, Alberta, and the Yukon. Topics include exploration and explorers, the pioneers, and their adventures in early Western Canada. Buys well-researched articles of around 3,000 words. Pays 5¢ to 8¢/word – more with photos – on publication. Guidelines available.

enRoute

150 John Street, Suite 900, Toronto, Ont. M5V 3E3
Phone: (416) 591-1551   Fax: (416) 591-3511
Contact: Matthew Evan Church, editor
Circulation: 125,000 printed, 350,000 readership
Published monthly

Air Canada's inflight magazine. Publishes strong Canadian pieces on business and technical trends, travel, successful personalities, fashion, and fine dining, aimed at the business flier. Pays a competitive, negotiable rate on acceptance. Uses published writers only. Inquire first with ideas, enclosing tearsheets. Guidelines available.

Equinox

7 Queen Victoria Road, Camden East, Ont. K0K 1J0
Phone: (613) 378-6661 or 1-800-267-0965   Fax: (613) 378-6123
Contact: Alan Morantz, managing editor
Circulation: 170,000
Published bimonthly

A world-class magazine of science and geography, serving Canadians who seek to discover more about their country and the world around them. Addresses geography in its broadest sense, encompassing biology, astronomy, the earth sciences, the arts, architecture, industry, travel, and adventure. Features of 1,500 to 5,000 words earn $1,500 to $3,500 on acceptance – more paid for photos. Guidelines available.

Imperial Oil Review

111 St. Clair Avenue W., Toronto, Ont. M5W 1K3
Phone: (416) 968-4268   Fax: (416) 968-4272
Contact: Sarah Lawley, editor
Circulation: 60,000
Published quarterly

This high-quality current affairs magazine, published by Imperial Oil since 1917, carries articles on important facets of Canadian living, profiles on our celebrated institutions, people, places, and culture, nostalgia, and in-depth pieces on travel and oil exploration. Pay rates vary, but you can expect about $2,500 for 2,500 to 3,000 words. Pays on acceptance.

The Kootenay Review
S.19, C.15, R.R. 1, Nelson, B.C. VIL 5P4
Phone: (604) 825-4663   Fax: (604) 352-3013
Contact: Lorna Lynch, managing editor
Circulation: 2,500
Published monthly
A respected regional magazine with nationwide subscribers. Contains broad, often humorous commentaries, a monthly short story, and book and video reviews. Preferred length of articles 500 to 1,000 words. Assigned articles paid $35 per 500 words on publication; short stories unpaid. Recommends freelancers first submit short stories. Guidelines available.

Leisure World
1253 Ouellette Avenue, Windsor, Ont. N8X 1J3
Phone: (519) 971-3208   Fax: (519) 977-1197
Contact: Doug O'Neil, editor
Circulation: 318,000
Published bimonthly
Circulated to CAA members, this lifestyle magazine features travel, leisure, and automotive stories and articles. Seeks dramatic narratives of real-life experiences involving compelling characters. Articles 800 to 1,600 words. Pays $100 to $150 for travel and destination features, $75 to $125 for short pieces, on publication. Guidelines and editorial calendar available.

LeisureWays
2 Carlton Street, Suite 1707, Toronto, Ont. M5B 1J3
Phone: (416) 595-5007   Fax: (416) 924-6308
Contact: Deborah Milton, editor
Circulation: 580,000
Published bimonthly
A Southern Ontario travel and leisure magazine financed by the CAA and circulated among Ontario members. Carries articles on personalities, interesting places, recipes, culture, current events, and ingenious entrepreneurs. Articles (800 to 1,500 words) should be accompanied by suitable colour slides. Pays 50¢/word on acceptance. Guidelines available.

Maclean's

777 Bay Street, Toronto, Ont. M5W 1A7
Phone: (416) 596-5386   Fax: (416) 596-7730
Contact: Robert Lewis, editor
Circulation: 579,000
Published weekly

Canada's most widely read news magazine, with about 2.6 million readers. Examines news events, trends, and issues from a Canadian perspective. Has a broad network of bureaus, with correspondents in 5 Canadian cities and 35 other countries. Staff writers and freelancers contribute to weekly sections on politics, business, entertainment, sports, leisure, science, medicine, and technology. Pays a variable but competitive fee on acceptance.

Newfoundland Lifestyle

197 Water Street, St John's, P.O. Box 2356, Nfld. A1C 6E7
Phone: (709) 726-9300   Fax: (709) 726-3013
Contact: Edwina Hutton, managing editor
Circulation: 15,000
Published quarterly

Designed to reflect a positive image of Newfoundland and Labrador through articles about the people and unique way of life. Feature articles 2,000 to 3,000 words. Pays 10¢/word on publication for 1,500 to 2,500 words. Guidelines available.

Passage

1609 Blanshard Street, Victoria, B.C. V8W 2J5
Phone: (604) 382-6188   Fax: (684) 381-2662
Contact: Gery Lemon, managing editor
Circulation: 150,000
Published 7 times a year

B.C. Ferries Corp's official on-board magazine. Carries coastal stories, profiles, and features of interest to tourists and locals. Pays a variable rate on publication for 600 to 1,000 words.

Reader's Digest

215 Redfern Avenue, Westmount, Que. H3Z 2V9
Phone: (514) 934-0751
Contact: editorial department

Circulation: 1,266,000
Published monthly
   This mass-interest magazine is among the freelancer's most lucrative potential markets. Carries articles on everything from nature, science, and politics to drama, self-improvement, and people, prominent or otherwise. All pieces contain advice, an experience, or a philosophical message of value to the magazine's more than 2 million readers. No fiction or poetry. Commissions original articles and adaptations of Canadian subjects of between 3,500 and 5,000 words, which earn $2,700. Also buys material previously published in books, magazines, or newspapers. Buys all rights and pays on acceptance for original articles, one-time rights for previously published "pickups." No unsolicited manuscripts. Send letter of inquiry with a two-page outline. Guidelines available.

Saturday Night
184 Front Street E., Suite 400, Toronto, Ont. M5A 4N3
Phone: (416) 368-7237   Fax: (416) 368-5112
Contact: John Fraser, editor
Circulation: 420,000
Published 10 times a year
   A sophisticated, award-winning magazine first published in 1887. Features profiles of the men, women, and institutions that shape and run Canadian society. Its insightful reporting goes far beyond explanations of events and focuses on why things happen, who makes them happen, and how they may affect our future. Also publishes high-quality fiction and poetry. Boasts a list of contributing editors that reads like a *Who's Who* of Canadian literature. Pays about $1/word: $500 for one-page stories, $2,500 for short columns, and $5,000 for full-length features.

STITCHES
14845 Yonge Street, Suite 300, Aurora, Ont. L4G 6H8
Phone: (905) 841-5607   Fax: (905) 841-5688
Contact: Simon Hally, editor
Circulation: 40,000
Published 10 times a year
   Formerly *Punch Digest for Canadian Doctors,* a magazine of humour for practising physicians. Pays 30¢ to 35¢/word on pub-

lication for 20 to 2,000 words. "Aspiring contributors are encouraged to request a free sample copy of the magazine. We are eager to hear from genuinely funny writers."

This Country Canada
P.O. Box 39, Pakenham, Ont. KOA 2XO
Phone: (613) 624-5000   Fax: (613) 624-5952
Contact: Barbara Sibbald, editor
Circulation: 50,000
Published quarterly

A glossy, large-format magazine celebrating the people of Canada, carrying a mix of modern and historical features. Preferred length 1,500 to 2,000 words. Pays on publication. First send a one-page outline. Guidelines available.

Toronto Life
59 Front Street E., 3rd Floor, Toronto, Ont. M5E 1B3
Phone: (416) 364-3333   Fax: (416) 861-1169
Contact: John Macfarlane, editor
Circulation: 96,000
Published monthly

A classy city magazine that tells readers how Toronto works, lives, and plays. Examines city politics, society, business, entertainment, sports, food and restaurants, and shopping in a unique mix of hard-nosed reporting and rigorous service journalism. Also publishes supplements. Draws on a stable of experienced writers and rarely accepts outside submissions. Pays on acceptance between $1,000 and $4,500, depending on assignment. Guidelines available.

Travel à la carte
136 Walton Street, Port Hope, Ont. L1A 1N5
Phone: (905) 885-7948   Fax: (905) 885-7202
Contact: Donna Carter, editor
Circulation: 145,000
Published bimonthly

Destination travel articles both international and Canadian. Focuses on attractions, customs, and historical background where appropriate. Stories of 1,500 to 2,500 words concentrate on well-frequented destinations rather than the remote. Submissions must include colour slides. An initial query letter along with a sample of published writing advised. Fee negotiable. Pays within 60 days of publication. Guidelines available.

Up Here: Life in Canada's North

P.O. Box 1350, Yellowknife, N.W.T. X1A 2N9
Phone: (403) 920-4652   Fax: (403) 873-2844
Contact: Ken Schmaltz, assistant editor
Circulation: 40,000
Published bimonthly

A lively, informative magazine about Northern travel, wildlife, arts, culture, lifestyles, and especially the people who travel the region and cope with the harsh winters there. Articles 750 to 3,000 words. Pays 20¢ to 25¢/word on publication for articles and features, with a standard fee for columns and photos. Complete manuscripts with photos welcome. "We're looking for solid reporting and research, and top-notch photos. Always tell your story through the people involved." Written queries only, please. Guidelines available.

Western Living

555 West 12th Avenue, Suite 300, East Tower, Vancouver,
    B.C. V5Z 4L4
Phone: (604) 877-7732   Fax: (604) 877-4849
Contact: Paula Brook, editor
Circulation: 265,000
Published 10 times a year

A general interest and lifestyle magazine with a special emphasis on the home. The largest regional magazine in Canada. Regular features address social issues, trends, personalities, travel, fashion, recreation, and cuisine. All stories should have Western Canadian focus. Articles 1,500 to 3,000 words. Pays 50¢/word on acceptance for pieces from 200 to 3,000 words. Guidelines available.

Western People

P.O. Box 2500, Saskatoon, Sask. S7K 2C4
Phone: (306) 665-3611   Fax: (306) 653-1255
Contact: Karen Morrison or Wendy Roy, features editors
Circulation: 100,000
Published weekly

A general interest, rural-oriented magazine featuring histories, memories, poetry, fiction, and contemporary profiles of Western Canadians. Especially interested in well-researched Western history. Preferred length 800 to 2,500 words. Pays $100 to $300 on acceptance for articles, depending on length – less for poetry. "Eastern and U.S. writers have a hard time catching the flavour of this magazine. People profiles are seldom of big names, almost never politicians. We require photos for most articles." Guidelines available.

Westworld Magazine

4180 Lougheed Highway, Suite 401, Burnaby, B.C. V5C 6A7
Phone: (604) 299-7311   Fax: (604) 299-9188
Contact: Robin Roberts, editor
Circulation: 500,000
Published quarterly

Distributed to members of the BCAA. Features local and international travel and automotive-related articles. Pays 50¢/word on publication for articles of 800 to 1,200 words. "Query with a one-page outline of proposed article, and include published samples." Guidelines available.

Home & Hobby

BC Home Digest

4180 Lougheed Highway, Suite 401, Burnaby, B.C. V5C 6A7
Phone: (604) 299-7311   Fax: (604) 299-9188
Contact: Nancy Ryder, editor
Circulation: 210,000
Published 5 times a year

A home improvement guide to help homeowners maintain and renovate their homes. Includes ideas on renovation, design, gardening, and money management. Articles 1,000 to 2,000 words. Pays 30¢/word on publication. Submission inquiries welcome. "We generally hire B.C. writers exclusively."

Canadian Coin News

202 – 103 Lakeshore Road, St. Catharines, Ont. L2N 2T6
Phone: (416) 646-7744   Fax: (416) 646-0995

Contact: Bret Evans, editor
Circulation: 14,000
Published semi-monthly

A tabloid magazine for Canadian collectors of coins and paper money. Pays a month after publication. Fees negotiable. Prefers phone or fax queries.

Canadian Gardening

130 Spy Court, Markham, Ont. L3R 5H6
Phone: (905) 475-8440   Fax: (905) 475-9246
Contact: Liz Primeau, editor
Circulation: 115,000
Published bimonthly

A magazine geared towards the home gardener. Carries people-oriented feature articles on home gardens, garden design, and tips and techniques on gardening in the Canadian climate. Pays on acceptance for pieces between 300 and 3,000 words – $100 to $200 for short, "upfront" pieces, $300 to $700 for features, depending on length and research required. "Our readers are real gardeners who want complete, relevant information. We're strong on the 'how-to', but expect thoughtful, stylish writing as well." Guidelines available.

Canadian House & Home

511 King Street W., Suite 120, Toronto, Ont. M5V 2Z4
Phone: (416) 593-0204   Fax: (416) 591-1630
Contact: Cobi Ladner, editor
Circulation: 105,000
Published 8 times a year

Focuses on creative home decoration and design. Inspires and teaches through pictorial essays and how-to articles, featuring Canadian artisans, designers, and architects. Articles between 300 and 1,000 words. Always include colour photos with written submissions as visual confirmation of descriptions. Pays on publication. Fees range from $250 to $1,200. Guidelines available.

Canadian Stamp News

202 – 103 Lakeshore Road, St. Catharines, Ont. L2N 2T6
Phone: (416) 646-7744   Fax: (416) 646-0995
Contact: Ellen Rodger, editor

Circulation: 9,500
Published semi-monthly

A tabloid magazine serving Canadian philatelists and enthusiasts around the world who collect Canadian stamps. Pays a month after publication. Fees negotiable. Query first.

Canadian Workshop

130 Spy Court, Markham, Ont. L3R 5H6
Phone: (905) 475-8440   Fax: (905) 475-9560
Contact: Bob Pennycook, editor-in-chief
Circulation: 120,000
Published monthly

Elucidates a variety of home projects for the avid do-it-yourselfer and woodworker – from laying floors and cleaning furnaces to renovating basements and making kitchen cabinets. Articles should be between 1,000 and 2,000 words. Rates negotiable. Pays on acceptance. Guidelines available.

Century Home

12 Mill Street South, Port Hope, Ont. L1A 2S5
Phone: (905) 885-2449   Fax: (905) 885-5355
Contact: Joan Rumgay, publisher
Circulation: 40,000
Published 7 times a year

A magazine for lovers of vintage homes. Carries articles (1,000 to 1,500 words) about decorating, furnishings, art, crafts, architecture, restoration, renovation, gardens, and country fare. Fees vary according to project.

City and Country Home

777 Bay Street, 8th Floor, Toronto, Ont. M5W 1A7
Phone: (416) 596-5936   Fax: (416) 593-3197
Contact: Anita Draycott, editor
Circulation: 100,000
Published bimonthly

An upscale lifestyle magazine concentrating on fine interior design in Canadian homes and residences. Publishes articles on collecting, art and antiques, heritage buildings, gardens, shopping, travel, cuisine, and fashion. Also profiles up-and-coming designers. Pays $500 to $1,000 on acceptance for 700 to 2,000 words.

Collectibles Canada

103 Lakeshore Road, Suite 202, St. Catharines, Ont. L2N 2T6
Phone: (416) 646-7744   Fax: (416) 646-0995
Contact: Bret Evans, editor
Circulation: 19,000
Published 7 times a year

A magazine about art collecting, containing information on collector plates, figurines, limited edition lithographs, new products, and interviews with Canadian artists. Also publishes *Canadian Collectibles Retailer*. Pays a month after publication for articles of 750 to 1,500 words. Fees negotiable. Phone or fax inquiries preferred.

Cottage Life

111 Queen Street E., Suite 408, Toronto, Ont. M5C 1S2
Phone: (416) 360-6880   Fax: (416) 360-6814
Contact: Ann Vanderhoof, editor
Published bimonthly

An award-winning magazine directed towards those who own and spend time at cottages on Ontario's lakes. Examines and celebrates the history, personalities, and issues of cottaging. Also provides lots of practical advice to help readers keep their cottages, docks, and boats in working order. Pays on acceptance for articles of 150 to 3,000 words. Query all ideas before submission. Guidelines available.

Country Estate

178 Main Street, Unionville, Ont. L3R 2G9
Phone: (905) 479-4663   Fax: (905) 479-4482
Contact: Rise Levy, editor
Circulation: 70,000
Published quarterly

Established in 1971. A luxury lifestyle magazine on home-related topics, covering social functions, charitable activities, and society gatherings around Southern Ontario. Prints regular articles on travel, food, cultural events, country sports, social trendsetters, cars, real estate, home decor, interior design, home improvement, home entertainment, and new products. Pays $300 on publication for features of about 1,000 words.

Crafts Plus Magazine
130 Spy Court, Markham, Ont. L3R 5H6
Phone: (905) 475-8440   Fax: (905) 475-9560
Contact: Bob Pennycook, editor
Circulation: 90,000
Published 8 times a year

A practical magazine featuring instructional, project-based articles on sewing, knitting, floral arranging, folk art, and a range of other handicrafts. Pays on acceptance for articles between 450 and 2,000 words. Fees negotiable. Guidelines available.

Hi-Rise Magazine
95 Leeward Glenway, Unit 121, Don Mills, Ont. M3C 2Z6
Phone: (416) 424-1393   Fax: (416) 467-8262
Contact: Valerie Dunn, editor
Circulation: 38,000
Published 11 times a year

A magazine mirroring the concerns of high-rise dwellers. Carries self-help articles about tenants' rights and legal issues, issues of interest to condominium owners, plus regular features on food, travel, sports, hobbies, and business. Pays $25 for short pieces of 300 to 600 words. Guidelines available.

Homes & Cottages
6557 Mississauga Road, Suite D, Mississauga, Ont. L5N 1A6
Phone: (905) 567-1440   Fax: (905) 567-1442
Contact: Janice Naisby, editor
Circulation: 45,000
Published 8 times a year

For consumers building or renovating homes as well as builders, lumber retailers, and architects. Articles 1,500 to 2,000 words. Fees vary according to complexity. Pays on acceptance.

Ontario Craft
Chalmers Building, 35 McCaul Street, Toronto, Ont. M5T 1V7

Phone: (416) 977-3551   Fax: (416) 977-3552
Contact: Anne McPherson, editor
Circulation: 4,500
Published quarterly
   Represents the contemporary craft movement. Profiles interesting craftspeople and reviews their work. Articles 750 to 2,000 words. Pays on publication. Fees vary. "Familiarize yourself with *Ontario Craft* by looking through back issues."

Professional Renovation
178 Main Street, Unionville, Ont. L3R 2G9
Phone: (905) 479-4663   Fax: (905) 479-4482
Contact: Rise Levy, editor
Published quarterly
   Serving the Greater Toronto area, features home renovation projects performed by professionals. Subjects include advice on hiring professionals and profiles of completed projects. Most freelance projects assigned. Articles 500 to 1,500 words. Pays on publication.

RE-NEW: Canada's Magazine of Renovation and Restoration
12 Mill Street S., Port Hope, Ont. L1A 2S5
Phone: (905) 885-2449   Fax: (905) 885-5355
Contact: J. Rumgay, publisher
Circulation: 25,000
Published 5 times a year
   A home improvement magazine delivered to paid circulation consumers and the building trades, architects, etc. Preferred length 1,000 to 1,500 words. Fees negotiable, paid on publication. "We prefer visual elements – pictures, catalogue shots – to accompany text."

Lifestyle

Alive Journal of Health and Nutrition
7436 Fraser Park Drive, Burnaby, B.C. V5J 5B9
Phone: (604) 435-1919   Fax: (604) 435-4888
Contact: Rhody Lake, editor
Published 11 times a year

A national magazine for health-conscious Canadians featuring articles of 600 to 800 words by health professionals and personalities. Also carries short book reviews. Pays 15¢/word on publication.

Body & Soul
444 Front Street W., Toronto, Ont. M5V 2S9
Phone: (416) 585-5000   Fax: (416) 585-5705
Contact: Cathrin Bradbury or David Olive, co-editors
Circulation: 150,000
Published twice a year

A glossy supplement focusing on current health and lifestyle trends, circulated twice a year to *Globe and Mail* subscribers. Articles 500 to 3,000 words. Pays on acceptance around $1/word, depending on complexity of assignment. Written queries, which should be accompanied by tearsheets of published work, preferred to unsolicited phone calls.

Campus Canada
287 MacPherson Avenue, Toronto, Ont. M4V 1A4
Phone: (416) 928-2909   Fax: (416) 928-1357
Contact: Sarah Moore, managing editor
Circulation: 125,000
Published 4 times during school year

A student lifestyle magazine featuring sports, entertainment, issues on campus, travel, and other topics of interest to university and college students. Short articles of between 500 and 1,200 words preferred. Pays an average of $100 for 800 words on acceptance. Query first, by mail or fax, with story idea.

Canadian Money Saver
P.O. Box 370, Bath, Ont. K0H 1G0
Phone: (613) 352-7448
Contact: Dale Ennis, publisher/president
Published 11 times a year

A national consumer finance magazine offering articles (750 to 1,500 words) on such current topics as personal finance, investment techniques, retirement planning, consumer purchases, small business practice, and discount service. Cannot pay but welcomes submission inquiries. Guidelines available.

The Cottage Magazine
4611 William Head Road, Victoria, B.C. V9B 5T7
Phone: (604) 478-9209   Fax: (604) 478-1184
Contact: Peter Chettleburgh, editor/publisher
Circulation: 10,000
Published quarterly
    For cottage owners in Westen Canada (B.C. and Alberta). Feature articles of 1,000 to 2,500 words include entertaining profiles on individuals and companies and analysis of political issues that affect cottage owners. Regular columns and departments on small boats, solar power, and other practical topics. Pays on publication $200 to $500 for features, $150 to $200 for columns; news items up to 400 words are paid at 20¢/word. Query the editor by phone or with a brief written proposal. Guidelines available.

The Country Connection
P.O. Box 100, Boulter, Ont. KOL 1GO
Phone: (613) 332-3651   Fax: (613) 332-5183
Contact: John Keith, editor, ph. (613) 332-0287
Circulation: 15,000
Published quarterly
    A country magazine publishing informative, how-to, and historical pieces with rural themes and/or relating to central and eastern Ontario. Also humorous or light short fiction. Prefers articles and stories around 1,000 to 2,000 words. Where appropriate, link submission ideas to the season. Submit article *ideas* and short fiction. Pays 10¢/word on disk, 7¢/word typewritten, on publication. Guidelines available.

Destinations
444 Front Street W., Toronto, Ont. M5V 2S9
Phone: (416) 585-5348   Fax: (416) 585-5705
Contact: Cathrin Bradbury, editor
Circulation: 300,000
Published 8 times a year
    A travel and leisure magazine published with the *Globe and Mail*. Carries articles on travel, hiking, scuba diving, sailing, golf, mountain climbing, and holidays that cater to such specific hobbies as wine and art collecting, and wildlife photography. Articles from 150

to 3,500 words. Pays on acceptance, with fees negotiable. "Read recent issues. Then, if you have ideas you think might be appropriate, send us a written *proposal* with recent samples of your work. We're especially open to ideas for the Departures section."

Expecting

37 Hanna Avenue, Unit 1, Toronto, Ont. M6K 1X1
Phone: (416) 537-2604   Fax: (416) 538-1794
Contact: Bettie Bradley, editor
Circulation: 145,000
Published twice a year

A magazine for expectant parents, written mostly by healthcare professionals. Pays on publication.

Good Times

5148 St. Laurent Boulevard, Montreal, Que. H2T 1R8
Phone: (514) 273-9773   Fax: (514) 273-9034
Contact: Denise Crawford, editor-in-chief
Published 10 times a year

Addresses the concerns of retired Canadians and those planning retirement. Topics include financial planning, health and fitness, personal rights, interpersonal relationships, profiles of celebrities, and leisure activities. Articles are assigned. Welcomes inquiries, noting areas of expertise and suggestions, with writing samples. Pays 40¢/word on publication. "No phone or fax queries; material must be supplied on IBM-compatible disk."

Great Expectations

269 Richmond Street W., Toronto, Ont. M5V 1X1
Phone: (416) 596-8680   Fax: (416) 596-1991
Contact: Fran Fearnley, editor
Circulation: 135,000
Published quarterly

Articles directed towards expectant and new parents, promoting healthy pregnancy and an active role in the birth and early care of the child. Encourages informed consumer choice, breastfeeding, and gentle parenting. Fees around $550 for departments, $450 to $1,000 for features, depending on level of research and medical complexity as well as length, which should fall between 900 and 2,500 words.

Pays 30 days after acceptance. "Most editorial is provided by our regular freelancers. We are especially interested in writers with some background in childbirth issues." Guidelines available.

Okanagan Life Magazine

P.O. Box 1479, Station A, Kelowna, B.C. VIY 7V8
Phone: (604) 861-5399   Fax: (604) 868-3040
Contact: Holly McNeil, editor
Circulation: 18,000
Published bimonthly

A lifestyle and personality-oriented magazine directed towards middle and high income families. Strictly local issues and people. Preferred length 1,000 to 1,500 words. Pays 15¢/word for articles, 10¢/word for fiction, on publication. Guidelines available.

The Rural Voice

P.O. Box 429, Blyth, Ont. NOM IHO
Phone: (519) 523-4311   Fax: (519) 523-9140
Contact: Keith Roulston, editor/publisher
Circulation: 15,000
Published monthly

A regional periodical featuring agricultural news, profiles, and politics, with regular sections on marketing, the law, finances, and home life. Pays 12¢/word on publication for articles of 1,000 to 2,000 words. Guidelines available.

The Senior Times

4950 Queen Mary Road, Penthouse, Montreal, Que. H3W IX3
Phone: (514) 735-0722   Fax: (514) 735-1492
Contact: Barbara Newborn, publisher
Circulation: 30,000
Published biweekly

An informative news source targeting the English-speaking, 50-plus community of Montreal and surrounding areas. Pays a variable amount on publication for pieces of 400 to 600 words.

Today's Parent

269 Richmond Street W., Toronto, Ont. M5V IXI
Phone: (416) 596-8680   Fax: (416) 596-1991

Contact: Fran Fearnley, editor-in-chief
Circulation: 135,000
Published 9 times a year

A parenting magazine for parents of children up to the age of 8. Carries articles about child development, education, health, and family life. Preferred length 1,200 to 2,500 words. Pays $700 to $1,500 for features, $650 for departments, 30 days after acceptance. "Always query first and include samples of published work. Do not send manuscripts." Guidelines available.

Wedding Bells

120 Front Street E., Suite 200, Toronto, Ont. M5A 4L9
Phone: (416) 862-8479   Fax: (416) 862-2184
Contact: Crys Stewart, editor
Circulation: 102,000
Published twice a year

A fat, glossy magazine with editions in Atlantic Canada, Saskatchewan, Calgary, Edmonton, Hamilton, London, Ottawa, Montreal, Toronto, Vancouver, and Winnipeg, and a national edition. Directed towards brides and grooms and their families, offering information about every aspect of wedding planning. Pays on acceptance for articles of 1,000 to 2,000 words. Inquire by mail, but first read a couple of issues. Fees negotiable.

Westcoast Reflections

2604 Quadra Street, Victoria, B.C. V8T 4E4
Phone: (604) 383-1149   Fax: (604) 388-4479
Contact: Joy Bretz, editor
Circulation: 20,000
Published monthly

A magazine for people 50 and older, carrying pieces on things to do, places to go; personalized travel stories; and positive, well-researched stories on health, hobbies, and activities with interviews. Pays 10¢/word on publication for articles of 400 to 800 words.

Your Baby

269 Richmond Street W., Toronto, Ont. M5V 1X1
Phone: (416) 596-8680   Fax: (416) 596-1991

Contact: Holly Bennett, editor
Circulation: 150,000
Published 3 times a year
  For parents of babies up to 24 months. Focuses on baby care, health, fun and games, practical tips, and the experience of parenting. Emphasis on developmental issues. Distributed with *Chatelaine* magazine. Also published in French as *Mon Enfant*. Pays $400 for departments (700 to 800 words), $500 to $1,000 for features up to 2,000 words, about a month after acceptance. Inquire in advance with writing samples. Guidelines available.

News, Opinions, & Issues

Adbusters Quarterly
1243 West 7th Avenue, Vancouver, B.C. v6H 1B7
Phone: (604) 736-9401   Fax: (604) 737-6021
Contact: Kalle Lasn, publisher
Circulation: 20,000
  A combative, uncompromising commentator on the politics of media control and environmental strategy. Produced by the Media Foundation. Pays on publication for pieces from 100 to 1,500 words. Guidelines available.

Alternatives: Perspectives on Society, Technology & Environment
Faculty of Environmental Studies, University of Waterloo, Waterloo, Ont. N2L 3G1
Phone: (519) 885-1211, ext. 6783   Fax: (519) 746-0292
Contact: Robert Gibson, editor
Circulation: 3,300
Published quarterly
  Critical analysis, informed comment, and dedicated advocacy on contemporary problems facing our natural and social environments. Welcomes feature articles (4,000 to 5,000 words), short news reports (500 to 1,000 words), humour, book reviews (750 to 1,000 words), and essays (2,500 to 3,000 words). "Feature articles are peer refereed. Reports are written in news style. Our podium offers an

opportunity to stand on the soapbox and share your opinion." Contributors are unpaid. Guidelines available.

Anglican Journal

600 Jarvis Street, Room 224, Toronto, Ont. M4Y 2J6
Phone: (416) 924-9192, ext. 305   Fax: (416) 921-4452
Contact: Sam Carriere, news editor
Circulation: 270,000
Published 10 times a year

National publication of the Anglican Church of Canada, established in 1875. Contains news and features from across Canada and abroad. Subjects include news of all denominations and faiths, and articles on a range of social and ethical issues. Stories should be of interest to a national audience. Length 600 to 1,000 words maximum. Major articles earn $200 to $500; lesser features and news stories, $75 to $200; book reviews, $35 (plus the book). Initial inquiry recommended. Guidelines available.

Annals of Sainte Anne de Beaupré

Basilica of Sainte Anne, Ste.-Anne-de-Beaupré, Que. G0A 3C0
Phone: (418) 827-4538   Fax: (418) 827-4530
Contact: Roch Achard, editor
Circulation: 50,000
Published monthly

A general interest religious magazine, established in 1878. Buys fiction and articles with a Catholic dimension. Pays 3¢ to 4¢/word on acceptance for "educational, inspirational, objective, and uplifting" articles up to 1,200 words. Seeks analysis rather than reportage. Guidelines available.

bout de papier

45 Rideau Street, Suite 600, Ottawa, Ont. KIN 5W8
Phone: (613) 241-1391   Fax: (613) 241-5911
Contact: Debra Hulley, managing editor
Circulation: 2,500
Published quarterly

A bilingual journal of diplomacy and foreign service. Discusses international politics and global economic and security matters. Each issue includes guest columns, interviews, book reviews, media coverage, and reports on major issues. Contributors are not paid. Welcomes submission inquiries from qualified writers.

Briarpatch
2138 McIntyre Street, Regina, Sask. S4P 2R7
Phone: (306) 525-2949   Fax: (306) 565-3430
Contact: George Martin Manz, managing editor
Circulation: 2,000
Published 10 times a year
An award-winning regional magazine providing alternative views on issues concerning Saskatchewan and Canada. Carries short critical articles of 650 to 1,200 words on the environment, agriculture, aboriginal and women's rights, and labour. Specializes in investigative, activist journalism. No poetry. Contributors are not paid.

Canadian Dimension
228 Notre Dame Avenue, Suite 707, Winnipeg, Man. R3B 1N7
Phone: (204) 957-1519   Fax: (204) 943-4617
Contact: Yvonne Block, office manager
Circulation: 3,000
Published bimonthly
Fact and analysis that bring Canada and the world into focus. Carries alternative information on issues concerning women, the labour movement, peace politics, Native peoples, the environment, economics, and popular culture. Preferred length 600 to 2,000 words. "We will occasionally pay those whose sole income comes from writing." Guidelines available.

The Canadian Forum
804 – 251 Laurier Avenue W., Ottawa, Ont. KIP 5J6
Phone: (613) 230-3078   Fax: (613) 233-1458
Contact: Duncan Cameron, editor
Published 10 times a year
Tackles a wide range of subjects, including politics, national and international affairs, the arts in Canada, economics, travel, civil liberties, the environment, film, and literature. Carries some high-quality fiction. Publishing for more than 70 years. Articles 2,500 to 3,000 words. Pays an honorarium of $100 per article and $50 per review on publication.

Canadian Lawyer

240 Edward Street, Aurora, Ont. L4G 3S9
Phone: (905) 841-6480   Fax: (905) 841-5078
Contact: Catherine Kentridge, executive editor
Circulation: 28,000
Published 9 times a year

Written for and about Canada's legal world, focusing on the people, the issues, and the practice. International and entertaining items, too. Articles 1,000 to 2,500 words. Pays on acceptance, $800 to $1,200 for a cover story. "Make sure you have read several issues of the magazine before submitting queries. We look for lively, well-informed contributions and contributors."

Canadian Public Policy/Analyse de politiques

Department of Economics, Simon Fraser University, Burnaby,
    B.C. V5A 1S6
Phone: (604) 291-3442   Fax: (604) 291-5944
Contact: John Chant, acting editor
Circulation: 1,500
Published quarterly

A bilingual, refereed journal providing a forum for information about economic and social policy developments affecting all Canadians. Reviews books, articles, and government reports. Accepts submissions up to 5,000 words. Submission inquiries welcome, but no payment is made. A per page printing fee is charged.

Chinatown News

459 East Hastings Street, Vancouver, B.C. V6A 1P5
Phone: (604) 254-2533   Fax: (604) 254-3033
Contact: Roy Mah, editor
Circulation: 48,000
Published twice a month

Reports important developments locally, provincially, and nationally on issues affecting Canada's Chinese communities. Mostly news, but carries profiles of influential figures behind it. Submission inquiries welcome. Fees negotiable.

City Magazine

1464 Wellington Crescent, Winnipeg, Man. R3N 0B3
Phone: (204) 489-8145 or 489-2452   Fax: (204) 783-8564
Contact: Marcia Nozick, publisher/managing editor
Circulation: 3,000
Published quarterly

Covers urban politics, city planning, public art, architecture, and urban culture. Canada's only national urban magazine. Carries articles on urban ecology, community development, suburbia, housing, and such social issues as prostitution and slum clearance. Through critical analysis of current structures, it explores new models for urban living. Features 2,000 to 3,000 words. Interested in articles, comment, stories, and poetry. Contributors are not paid.

Compass: A Jesuit Journal

10 St Mary Street, Suite 300, Toronto, Ont. M4Y 1P9
Phone: (416) 921-0653   Fax: (416) 921-1864
Contact: Robert Chodos, editor
Circulation: 18,000
Published bimonthly

A review for Catholic and informed general readers, publishing articles on contemporary social and religious issues with an ethical and ecumenical perspective. Judged best Catholic magazine in North America by the Catholic Press Association. Articles 750 to 2,000 words. Pays $150 for 750 words, $250 for 1,000 to 1,500 words, $500 for 2,000 words, on publication. Guidelines available.

Connexions

P.O. Box 158, Station D, Toronto, Ont. M6T 3J8
Phone: (416) 537-3949
Contact: Ulli Diemer, editor
Circulation: 2,000
Published quarterly

A digest containing reprints from other sources as well as original pieces addressing social and environmental issues from a grassroots perspective. Carries analytical articles on social change and justice, projects, and organizations, and reviews of books, films, and new resources and teaching materials. Pays honoraria when possible. Phone or mail inquiries with ideas welcome.

Edges: New Planetary Patterns

577 Kingston Road, Suite 1, Toronto, Ont. M4E 1R3
Phone: (416) 691-2316   Fax: (416) 691-2491
Contact: Brian Stanfield, editor
Circulation: 25,000
Published quarterly

Exclusive articles by innovative writers and activists from around the world on art, ecology, economics, feminism, and spirituality, for the intelligent but non-academic reader. Focus is on changing cultural patterns in education and learning. Articles 1,000 to 2,500 words. Contributors earn a subscription. Submission inquiries welcome. Guidelines available.

Education Forum

60 Mobile Drive, Toronto, Ont. M4A 2P3
Phone: (416) 751-8300   Fax: (416) 751-3394
Contact: Neil Walker, editor
Circulation: 43,000
Published 3 times a year

A magazine of news, views, adventure, and personal experience. Published by the Ontario Secondary School Teachers' Federation and distributed to Ontario education workers. Buys articles of 2,000 to 3,000 words. Fees vary. Inquiries welcome. Guidelines available.

International Journal

15 King's College Circle, Toronto, Ont. M5S 2V9
Phone: (416) 979-1851   Fax: (416) 979-8575
Contact: Marion Magee, associate editor
Circulation: 1,800
Published quarterly

Published by the Canadian Institute of International Affairs and written by contributors worldwide. Reviews books on international affairs and foreign policy. Articles 7,000 to 8,000 words. Welcomes submission inquiries. Contributors are unpaid.

Legion
359 Kent Street, Suite 504, Ottawa, K2P OR6
Phone: (613) 235-8741   Fax: (613) 233-7159
Contact: Marla Fletcher, managing editor
Circulation: 502,000
Published 10 times a year

A general interest magazine for Canada's war veterans, RCMP members, forces personnel and their families, and the wider public. Carries news, views, and opinions, and serious articles on issues of interest to veterans, seniors, and others. Subjects include defence, veteran affairs, health, and pensions. Also buys memoirs and nostalgia. Articles 600 to 2,200 words. Pays $150 to $1,200 on acceptance (fee determined after final edit). Query first. Sample copies available on request. Average assessment time 4 to 6 months.

McGill News
3605, rue de la Montagne, Montreal, Que. H3G 2M1
Phone: (514) 398-3552   Fax: (514) 398-7338
Contact: Victor Swoboda, editor
Circulation: 110,000
Published quarterly

Directed towards McGill University graduates. Features articles about current affairs, entertainment, the humanities, medicine, and science with a McGill connection, and profiles of graduates. Pays on acceptance for features of 1,000 to 2,000 words ($350 to $500 for 2,000 words). Also buys news stories of 200 to 600 words. Prospective contributors may write for a sample copy.

Monarchy in Canada
3050 Yonge Street, Suite 206, Toronto, Ont. M4N 2K4
Phone: (416) 482-4157   Fax: (416) 482-4157
Contact: Arthur Bousfield, editor
Circulation: 8,000
Published quarterly

Looks at the monarchy from a Canadian historical perspective and carries articles on constitutional, social, and political affairs. Also reviews books and profiles personalities associated with the monarchy. Sometimes pays for articles of 1,500 to 2,000 words. Welcomes submission inquiries.

New Internationalist

1011 Bloor Street W., Toronto, Ont. M6H 1M1
Phone: (416) 588-6478   Fax: (416) 537-6435
Contact: Richard Swift, co-editor
Circulation: 8,000 in Canada; 70,000 worldwide
Published monthly

An uncompromising international periodical providing information and analysis on the major issues concerning international development. Exposes the politics of aid, militarism, and national and multinational exploitation of the developing countries, and discusses racial, gender, and social politics in the developed and developing worlds. Issues are thematic. Articles 500 to 1,800 words. Pays $400 on publication for full-length article. Guidelines available.

New Maritimes

6106 Lawrence Street, Halifax, N.S. B3L 1J6
Phone: (902) 425-6622
Contact: Scott Milsom, editor
Circulation: 2,300
Published bimonthly

A radical regional commentary carrying some of Canada's best journalism. Highlights areas of interest to Maritimers, addressing issues such as politics, labour, culture, history, social justice, environmentalism, feminism, and minority and welfare rights from an alternative viewpoint. Regularly reviews books relating to the Maritimes. Occasionally includes fiction and poetry. Can rarely pay contributors. Guidelines available.

NeWest Review

P.O. Box 394, R.P.O. University, Saskatoon, Sask. S7N 9Z9
Phone: (306) 934-1444   Fax: (306) 966-8839
Contact: Gail Youngberg, editorial co-ordinator
Circulation: 1,000
Published bimonthly

Carries news and opinion on Western Canadian cultural, social, and political issues. Reviews books and theatre, and carries some fiction and poetry. Articles/stories 1,500 to 2,500 words. Pays $100 for 2,000 words; $25 for reviews; $60 for gazette items (800 words). Pays on publication. Prefers initial proposals. Guidelines available.

Our Family

P.O. Box 249, Battleford, Sask. S0M 0E0
Phone: (306) 937-7771   Fax: (306) 937-7644
Contact: Nestor Gregoire, editor
Circulation: 10,000
Published monthly

A Christian general interest magazine. Buys photo stories on personalities, events, and issues mostly with religious themes. Pays 7¢ to 11¢/word on acceptance for pieces from 1,000 to 3,000 words. Guidelines available.

Our Times

390 Dufferin Street, Toronto, Ont. M6K 2A3
Phone: (416) 531-5762   Fax: (416) 533-2397
Contact: Lorraine Endicott, editor
Circulation: 4,000
Published bimonthly

Produced by a unionized, worker-owned co-operative to focus on current issues vital to today's labour movement. Most contributions written by labour activists to be used as educational tools. Pays small honoraria ($25 for book reviews; $75 to $200 for features of 1,500 to 2,500 words) on acceptance. Guidelines available.

Peace Magazine

736 Bathurst Street, Toronto, Ont. M5S 2R4
Phone: (416) 533-7581   Fax: (416) 531-6214
Contact: Metta Spencer, editor
Published bimonthly

A magazine providing interviews, commentary, and topical features relating to multilateral disarmament and non-violent conflict resolution. Covers domestic and world issues. Cannot pay but welcomes submission inquiries.

Perception

55 Parkdale Avenue, P.O. Box 3505, Station C, Ottawa,
   Ont. K1Y 4G1

Phone: (613) 728-1865   Fax: (613) 728-9387
Contact: Nancy Perkins, communications co-ordinator
Circulation: 3,500
Published quarterly

A bilingual magazine providing information and analysis on issues of social development, including income security, employment, health and social services, and aboriginal concerns. Articles 700 to 1,500 words. Cannot pay but welcomes submission inquiries. Guidelines available.

Policy Options

1470, rue Peel, Bureau 200, Montreal, Que. H3A 1T1
Phone: (514) 985-2461   Fax: (514) 985-2559
Contact: Mathew Horsman, editor
Circulation: 3,000
Published 10 times a year

Published by the Institute for Research on Public Policy, a national, independent, not-for-profit think tank. Carries analyses of public policy so as to encourage wide debate of major policy issues. Articles 1,500 to 2,500 words. Contributors are unpaid, but submission inquiries by qualified writers welcome. Guidelines avaiable.

This Magazine

16 Skey Lane, Toronto, Ont. M6J 3S4
Phone: (416) 588-6580
Contact: Moira Farr, managing editor
Circulation: 8,000
Published 8 times a year

A radical alternative news and opinion magazine carrying investigative features and researched commentary on culture, politics, labour, and other issues. Features of 1,000 to 3,000 words are paid a negotiated fee of between $100 and $500 on publication. "We prefer clearly focused, thoroughly researched, and sharply written material on topics the mainstream media ignore." Guidelines available.

The United Church Observer

84 Pleasant Boulevard, Toronto, Ont. M4T 2Z8
Phone: (416) 960-8500   Fax: (416) 960-8477

Contact: Muriel Duncan, editor
Circulation: 165,000
Published monthly

Provides news of the church, the nation, and the world, while maintaining an independent editorial policy. Prints serious articles on issues such as human rights, social justice, and Christian faith in action, and stories of personal courage – all with a Christian perspective. Also covers the religious dimension of art, literature, and theatre. Articles 850 to 1,000 words. Uses freelancers infrequently. Fees negotiable, paid on publication. Personal stories are paid at lower rates. Guidelines available.

Windspeaker

15001 – 112th Avenue, Edmonton, Alta. T5M 2V6
Phone: (403) 455-2700   Fax: (403) 455-7639
Contact: Linda Caldwell, editor
Circulation: 15,000
Published biweekly

A national First Nations newspaper with a regional section focusing on local issues. Includes columns and features of 300 to 800 words. Welcomes stories and profiles on issues of concern to Native peoples and those who work with them. Pays $3.60 per column inch for multi-source stories, $3.00 per inch for profiles, on publication. Guidelines available.

Special Interest

The Atlantic Co-operator

P.O. Box 1386, Antigonish, N.S. B2G 2L7
Phone: (902) 863-2776   Fax: (902) 863-8077
Contact: Brenda MacKinnon, editor
Circulation: 60,000
Published monthly

An educational resource for co-ops and credit unions throughout Atlantic Canada. Pays about 20¢/word on acceptance for pieces of between 600 and 800 words. Guidelines available.

CM: A Reviewing Journal of Canadian Materials for Young People

200 Elgin Street, Suite 602, Ottawa, Ont. K2P 1L5
Phone: (613) 232-9625, ext. 322   Fax: (613) 563-9895
Contact: Elizabeth Morton, editor
Circulation: 1,700
Published bimonthly

Published by the Canadian Library Association for educators and librarians, to evaluate books, magazines, videos, games, and education kits produced for children and young adults. Pays 5¢/word on publication for articles of 1,000 to 1,500 words.

Communicating Together

P.O. Box 986, Thornhill, Ont. L3T 4A5
Phone: (416) 771-1491
Contact: Shirley McNaughton, editor
Circulation: 800
Published quarterly

Published as a forum for those interested in the experiences, the systems, and the technology relating to non-speaking people. Its purpose: to share the life experiences and communication systems of augmentative communicators, their families, and those who work with them. "We have eight associate editors who either write articles or invite others to write them."

Companion Magazine

P.O. Box 535, Station F, Toronto, Ont. M4Y 2L8
Phone: (416) 591-5442   Fax: (416) 463-4392
Contact: Friar Richard Riccioli, editor
Circulation: 4,200
Published monthly

A Catholic inspirational magazine whose purpose is to "build community, foster renewal, and provide hope for our readers." Prefers strong human-interest feature articles that are "positive, upbeat, brief, and from a first-hand point of view." Pays 6¢/word on publication for 600 to 1,200 words. Guidelines available.

Computing Now!

Moorshead Publications, Mony Life Building, 10th Floor, 797
Don Mills Road, North York, Ont. M3C 3S5

Phone: (416) 696-5488   Fax: (416) 696-7395
Contact: Jeff Evans, editor
Circulation: 20,000
Published monthly

Helps users of personal and small business micro-computers to better understand computer technology. Includes market surveys, industry news, and product reviews – short reviews 900 words, feature reviews 1,800 words, feature articles 2,500 to 2,700 words. Pays 14¢/word. Interested in submissions on computer technology as it relates to education, telecommunications, multimedia, mobile computing, and health and safety. Send sample. Prefers writers with genuine interest in technology and technical writing experience.

Detective Files Group

1350 Sherbrooke W., Suite 600, Montreal, Que. H3G 2T4
Phone: (514) 849-7733   Fax: (514) 849-8330
Contact: Dominick Merle, editor-in-chief
Circulation: 100,000/month
Published bimonthly

A stable of six bimonthly true crime magazines. Stories from 3,500 to 6,000 words. Pays on acceptance $250 to $350 per article including photos. "Over 90 per cent of our readership is in the United States, but we welcome queries on Canadian cases as well." No phone queries. Guidelines available.

Disability Today

P.O. Box 237, Grimsby, Ont. L3M 4A3
Phone: (905) 945-5577   Fax: (905) 945-0818
Contact: Jeff Tressen, editor
Circulation: 25,000
Published quarterly

An access and awareness magazine aimed at better informing readers about physical disabilities and opportunities that exist for this population. Directed particularly towards educators, employers, and advocates. Articles are 1,000 to 3,000 words. Pays about $300 on publication. Guidelines available.

Dogs in Canada

43 Railside Road, Don Mills, Ont. M3A 3L9

Phone: (416) 441-3228   Fax: (416) 441-3212
Contact: Susan Pearce, editor
Circulation: 22,000
Published monthly

Geared towards the dog breeder and exhibitor. (A separate annual issue is broadened to appeal to all dog-owners, with complete information on selecting, caring for, and training a pet.) Articles 800 to 2,000 words. Pays $100 and up for 1,000+ words, on publication. "The monthly is quite specialized and the annual has a definite formula. Query in detail before submitting." Brief guidelines available.

Emergency Librarian

P.O. Box 284 – 810 West Broadway, Vancouver, B.C. v5z 4c9
Phone: (604) 925-0266   Fax: (604) 925-0566
Contact: Michele Farquharson, associate editor
Circulation: 12,000
Published 5 times a year

Canada's independent library journal. Lively, provocative articles (1,000 to 4,000 words) address all aspects of library services for children and young adults. Designed for school and public librarians. Pays a small honorarium on publication. Guidelines available.

Pets Magazine

797 Don Mills Road, North York, Ont. m3c 3s5
Phone: (416) 696-5488   Fax: (416) 696-7395
Contact: Edward Zapletel, editor
Circulation: 56,000
  bimonthly

Offers advice and guidance to Canadian pet owners, including general pet care, human interest (working dogs), obedience and training, grooming, and breeding. Preferred length 500 to 1,500 words. No fiction or poetry. First send one-page outline. No U.S. postage on SASES – only international postage coupons. Pays 12¢ to 15¢/word on publication. Guidelines available.

Photo Life

130 Spy Court, Markham, Ont. l3r 5h6
Phone: (905) 475-8440   Fax: (905) 475-9560
Contact: J. Kobalenko, editor

Circulation: 40,000
Published 8 times a year

Caters to the interests of Canadian photographers, both amateur and seasoned professional. Profiles, pieces on film and video techniques, equipment reviews, and general stories of interest to advanced amateur and professional photographers. Prints pieces from 100 to 2,500 words. Pays around $150 on acceptance, depending on length, amount of research, and rewriting necessary.

The Social Worker

383 Parkdale Avenue, Suite 402, Ottawa, Ont. K1Y 4R4
Phone: (613) 729-6668   Fax: (613) 729-9608
Contact: Penny Sipkes, managing editor
Circulation: 13,500
Published quarterly

A bilingual forum in which social workers and researchers share their knowledge, skills, and information with the general public. Articles 1,000 to 2,500 words. Cannot pay but welcomes submission inquiries. Guidelines available.

Teaching Today Magazine

P.O. Box 68149, 70 Bonnie Doon Mall, Edmonton, Alta. T6C 4N6
Phone: (403) 462-0585   Fax: (403) 468-0099
Contact: Andrea Carter, publisher/editor
Circulation: 10,000
Published 5 times a year

A resource for classroom teachers and administrators providing current information on educational issues and practical new ideas for classroom use. Pays 10¢/word on publication for articles of 250 to 1,200 words, $25 per photo published with article. "Articles that provide solutions to teaching problems and creative ideas based on experience are most welcome." Guidelines available.

Toronto Computes!

60 St. Clair Avenue W., Suite 5, Toronto, Ont. M4V 1M7
Phone: (416) 925-4533   Fax: (416) 925-7701
Contact: Mark Langton, editor
Circulation: 85,000
Published monthly

Runs articles and features about "low-end" personal computers and related technologies, with regular software reviews and an emphasis on local events. Pays 30 days after publication for articles of between 100 and 5,000 words. Fees negotiable. Inquiries first, please. Guidelines available.

Wine Tidings

5165 Sherbrooke Street W., Suite 414, Montreal, Que. H4A 1T6
Phone: (514) 481-5892   Fax: (514) 481-9699
Contact: Barbara Leslie, editor
Circulation: 20,000
Published 8 times a year

A magazine for discerning wine lovers. Reports on price trends and vintages, offers recipes, and profiles well-known wine cellars. Also compares wines and grape types, and reviews developments in the Canadian wine industry. Article length varies from 500 to 1,500 words, the longer paying $200. Pays on publication. "Advanced knowledge of wine and wine tasting is a prerequisite."

World of Wheels

1200 Markham Road, Suite 220, Scarborough, Ont. M1H 3C3
Phone: (416) 438-7777   Fax: (416) 438-5333
Contact: Joe Duarte, editor
Circulation: 100,000
Published bimonthly

A magazine for auto enthusiasts, and for those interested in develoments in the auto industry and their impact on Canada. Evaluates and compares the latest in cars, light pickup trucks, vans, and sport-utility vehicles. Pays 30¢/word on publication for articles of between 400 and 2,500 words.

Sports & Outdoors

Athletics

1220 Sheppard Avenue E., Willowdale, Ont. M2K 2X1
Phone: (416) 495-4055   Fax: (416) 495-4052
Contact: Cecil Smith, publisher
Circulation: 7,000

Published 9 times a year

Canada's national track and field/running magazine. Includes interviews, profiles, coverage of events, results, rankings, and fixture schedules. Prefers articles of 700 to 1,000 words. Writers must have a clear understanding of the sports they cover. Fees negotiable, paid on acceptance.

The Atlantic Salmon Journal

P.O. Box 429, St. Andrews, N.B. E0G 2X0
Phone: (506) 529-4581   Fax: (506) 529-4985
Contact: Harry Bruce, editor
Circulation: 13,000
Published quarterly

A glossy, full-colour magazine for serious anglers who fly fish and Atlantic salmon conservationists. Carries articles on researching salmon and where to catch them, and focuses on angling adventures and conservation. Knowledgeable, lucid, and lively prose as well as superior photography and art. Pays $300 to $500 on publication for articles of 1,500 to 2,500 words, $50 to $100 for short items, including book reviews. "We normally expect writers to provide photos for their stories." Guidelines available.

B.C. Outdoors

1132 Hamilton Street, Suite 202, Vancouver, B.C. V6B 2S2
Phone: (604) 687-1581   Fax: (604) 687-1925
Contact: Karl Bruin, editor
Circulation: 40,000
Published 8 times a year

Carries articles on outdoor recreation and conservation – wildlife, camping, hunting, sports shooting, and saltwater and freshwater fishing. Articles up to 2,000 words. Pays 27¢/word on publication for articles accompanied by photos. Guidelines available.

B.C. Sport Fishing

909 Jackson Crescent, New Westminster, B.C. V3L 4S1
Phone: (604) 683-4871
Contact: Rikk Taylor, editor
Circulation: 26,000
Published bimonthly

Runs well-illustrated saltwater and freshwater fishing adventures for those looking for the best fishing opportunities in major British Columbia resort areas. Pays on publication for articles of 1,500 to 2,500 words. Fees negotiable. Phone inquiries welcome.

Camping Canada
2585 Skymark Avenue, Suite 306, Mississauga, Ont. L4W 4L5
Phone: (905) 624-8218   Fax: (905) 624-6764
Contact: Diane Batten, editor
Circulation: 43,000
Published bimonthly

Focuses on recreational vehicle lifestyle articles featuring travel routes, destinations, and technical information on motor homes, wide-body vans, trailers, and trailer homes. Accepts articles of 1,500 to 3,000 words on RV camping in Canada. Destinations stories should have photos/slides with credits. Fees negotiable, paid on publication. Guidelines available.

Canadian Biker
P.O. Box 4122, Victoria, B.C. v8x 3x4
Phone: (604) 384-0333   Fax: (604) 384-1832
Contact: Frank Hilliard, co-editor
Circulation: 18,000
Published 8 times a year

Carries a variety of articles and columns for sport and touring motorcycle enthusiasts. Preferred length 750 to 1,500 words. "Articles paid according to quality rather than quantity; preferred with photos." Preference given to work sent on 3 1/2 in. computer disk with hard copy. Pays on publication. Guidelines available.

Canadian Horseman
225 Industrial Parkway S., P.O. Box 670, Aurora, Ont. L4G 4J9
Phone: (905) 727-0107   Fax: (905) 841-1530
Contact: Val Evans, managing editor
Circulation: 10,000
Published bimonthly

Profiles the Western rider, discussing everything from training and horse care to farm management. Interesting reading for horse enthusiasts of all disciplines, competitive and non-competitive. Fees negotiable. Guidelines available.

Canadian Rodeo News

2116 – 27th Avenue N.E., Suite 223, Calgary, Alta. T2E 7A6
Phone: (403) 250-7292   Fax: (403) 250-6926
Contact: Kirby Watt, editor
Circulation: 48,000
Published monthly

A tabloid of news, views, and opinions from the Canadian and U.S. rodeo circuit. Also accepts articles related to the West or to Canada's Western heritage. Pays $50 on publication for stories of 1,000 to 1,200 words, $25 for 500 to 600 words, $10 for photos. Phone editor with ideas before submitting. Guidelines available.

The Canadian Sportsman

P.O. Box 129, 25 Old Plank Road, Straffordville, Ont. N0J 1Y0
Phone: (519) 866-5558   Fax: (519) 866-5596
Contact: Gary Foerster, editor
Circulation: 5,500
Published biweekly

"The voice of harness racing since 1870." Carries features and news mostly about harness racing in Canada. Mail, phone, or fax inquiries welcome. Fees negotiable.

Canadian Thoroughbred

225 Industrial Parkway S., P.O. Box 670, Aurora, Ont. L4G 4J9
Phone: (905) 727-0107   Fax: (905) 841-1530
Contact: Susan Jane Anstey, publisher
Circulation: 5,000
Published monthly

Canada's national journal on thoroughbred racing features news and information on horses and their owners – pedigrees and stable product updates. Fees negotiable. A very specialist market, so always inquire first. Guidelines available.

Canadian Yachting

395 Matheson Boulevard E., Mississauga, Ont. L4Z 2H2

Phone: (905) 890-1846   Fax: (905) 890-5769
Contact: Iain MacMillan, editor
Circulation: 15,000
Published bimonthly
    Written for sailboat enthusiasts across Canada. Includes adventure, regattas, profiles, maintenance, boat reviews, news and gossip for cruisers, racers, keelboat and dinghy sailors. Features of 2,000 to 3,000 words earn $400 to $600; shorter pieces for departments (1,200 to 2,000 words) earn $200 to $250. Pays 60 days after publication. Send initial letter of inquiry.

Corinthian Horse Sport

225 Industrial Parkway S., P.O. Box 670, Aurora, Ont. L4G 4J9
Phone: (905) 727-0107   Fax: (905) 841-1530
Contact: Colette Hawkins, managing editor
Published monthly
    An authoritative equestrian periodical featuring articles on horse care, riding and training techniques, breeding, animal health, and the industry at large. Also covers the activities of the Canadian Equestrian Team. Pays on publication for articles of 700 to 1,500 words. Fees negotiable. Guidelines available.

Cycle Canada

86 Parliament Street, Suite 3B, Toronto, Ont. M5A 2Y6
Phone: (416) 362-7966   Fax: (416) 362-3950
Contact: Bruce Reeve, editor
Circulation: 31,000
Published 10 times a year
    A magazine written for Canadian motorcycle enthusiasts, with product tests and evaluations, technical information, and how-to maintenance articles, plus profiles in the world of biking. Pays on acceptance $50 for brief news items of about 100 words, $500 for a top feature up to 4,000 words plus photos.

Diver Magazine

10991 Shellbridge Way, Suite 295, Richmond, B.C. V6X 3C6
Phone: (604) 273-4333   Fax: (604) 273-0813
Contact: Peter Vassilopoulos, publisher/editor
Circulation: 20,000

Published 9 times a year

For North American sport divers. Carries regular articles on travel destinations and snorkelling, and scuba and deep-water diving. Also covers marine life and underwater photography. Articles range from 500 to 1,500 words. Pays $3/column inch after publication. Check guidelines before submitting material.

Equinews
R.R. 6, Site 15, Comp. 5, Vernon, B.C. V1T 6Y5
Phone: (604) 542-2002 or 545-3560   Fax: (604) 549-7099
Contact: John Whittle, owner/editor/publisher
Circulation: 10,000
Published monthly

An all-breed, all-discipline magazine. Covers equine events worldwide, with special emphasis on Western Canada. Profiles of trainers/riders and others involved in the horse world, news, and good-humoured stories. Welcomes unsolicited manuscripts. Fiction and non-fiction accepted. Payment varies. Request guidelines, as requirements are quite specific.

Explore: Canada's Outdoor Adventure Magazine
301 – 14th Street N.W., Suite 420, Calgary, Alta. T2N 2A1
Phone: (403) 270-8890   Fax: (403) 270-7922
Contact: Marion Harrison, editor
Circulation: 25,500
Published bimonthly

For people who enjoy self-propelled outdoor recreational activities such as backpacking, cycling, paddling, and backcountry skiing. Articles of 1,500 to 2,500 words cover adventure, outdoor equipment evaluations, new products, and environmental issues. Pays $350 for 2,000 words on publication. Guidelines available.

Formula: The International Autosport Magazine
395 Matheson Boulevard E., Mississauga, Ont. L4Z 2H2
Phone: (905) 890-1846   Fax: (905) 890-5769
Contact: Malcolm Elston, publisher
Circulation: 20,000
Published 10 times a year

Covers all forms and aspects of road racing, including Formula

One, Indy, and IMSA, as well as performance and luxury cars. Pays 30 days after publication for articles of 750 to 2,000 words. Fees 30¢/word and upwards. Query first.

Gam On Yachting

401 Richmond Street W., Suite 242, Toronto, Ont. M5V 1X3
Phone: (416) 599-4261   Fax: (416) 599-4264
Contact: Karin Larson, publisher/editor
Circulation: 20,000
Published 8 times a year

A magazine for the racing and cruising sailor, with how-to articles, upcoming events, harbour profiles, book reviews, safety information, and humour. Special issues coincide with Canadian boat shows. Pays on publication. Fees negotiable.

Horsepower

P.O. Box 670, Aurora, Ont. L4G 4J9
Phone: (905) 727-0107   Fax: (905) 841-1530
Contact: Susan Stafford, managing editor
Circulation: 6,000
Published bimonthly

Provides young riders and horse lovers with advice on horse care, feeding, and tips for riding and stable skills, plus profiles, puzzles, and contests. Pays $50 for 500 to 700 words, $75 for 1,000 words, on publication. "Our editorial focus is always on safety. Submissions must be horse-related (English or Western, all breeds), and suitable for pre-teens and young teens." Guidelines available.

Horses All

P.O. Box 9, Hill Spring, Alta. T0K 1E0
Phone: (403) 626-3613   Fax: (403) 626-3600
Contact: Ranae French, editor
Circulation: 10,000
Published monthly

A tabloid carrying stories about Canadian horses and their owners, with a special section devoted to young riders. Pays on acceptance. Submissions are edited to fit the need. Fee offered is decided by editor, who sends a cheque. Writers who cash their cheques have accepted the terms – a simple system!

Hot Water

2585 Skymark Avenue, Unit 306, Mississauga, Ont. L4W 4L5
Phone: (905) 624-8218   Fax: (905) 624-6764
Contact: Pam Cottrell, editor
Circulation: 15,000
Published quarterly

For personal watercraft owners. Carries features on newest PWC models and other jet-driven boats plus all accessories that contribute to their enjoyment. Also covers technical aspects of the sport, racing and other events, and destination stories. Preferred feature length 1,500 to 3,000 words. Pays $350 for 2,000 words plus photos, on publication. A new magazine looking for writers with an interest and knowledge of watersports.

Impact Magazine

908 – 17th Avenue S.W., Suite 312, Calgary, Alta. T2T 0A3
Phone: (403) 228-0605   Fax: (403) 228-0627
Contact: Heather Ellwood-Wright, editor
Circulation: 30,000
Published bimonthly

Features health, fitness, and sports for the active and physically fit of Calgary. All content focused on Calgary and surrounds. Articles 750 to 1,000 words. Query all ideas by phone or letter before submitting. "Our budget is very limited and we pay accordingly."

Ontario Out of Doors

227 Front Street E., Suite 100, Toronto, Ont. M5A 1E8
Phone: (416) 368-0185   Fax: (416) 941-9113
Contact: Burt Myers, editor
Circulation: 88,000
Published 10 times a year

A magazine for Ontario's hunters and anglers. Carries how-to and where-to articles on topics such as boating, firearms, archery, and backroad touring. Regular columns on hunting, fishing, wildlife, camp cooking, dogs, fly fishing, scientific research, and new products. Pays on acceptance for articles of 500 to 1,500 words. Fees negotiated; average feature earns $350 to $500. Pays $500 to $700 for cover photo. Guidelines available.

Ontario Snowmobiler

18540 Centre Street, R.R. 3, Mount Albert, Ont. LOG 1MO
Phone: (905) 473-7009　Fax: (905) 473-5217
Contact: Terrence Kehoe, publisher
Circulation: 60,000
Published quarterly

Informs Ontario snowmobilers of industry developments, snowmobile people, clubs, programs, and travel. Pays $75 to $100 on acceptance for 400 to 800 words. Uses freelancers infrequently.

Outdoor Canada

703 Evans Avenue, Suite 202, Toronto, Ont. M9C 5E9
Phone: (416) 695-0311　Fax: (416) 695-0382
Contact: Teddi Brown, editor
Published 9 times a year

A magazine dedicated to the use and conservation of Canada's outdoors. Carries articles on fishing, boating, hunting, cross-country skiing, canoeing, hiking, outdoor photography, and camping. Invites on-spec submissions. Pays on publication.

The Outdoor Edge

6922 – 104th Street, Edmonton, Alta. T8A 0H3
Phone: (403) 448-0381　Fax: (403) 438-3244
Contact: Ken Bailey, editor
Circulation: 65,000
Published bimonthly

Circulated to members of the Fish & Game Association and Wildlife Federations in the North and West. Articles 800 to 1,600 words. Pays $150 to $300 on publication for features. Query in writing. Relevant photo coverage important. Guidelines available.

Pacific Yachting

1132 Hamilton Street, Suite 202, Vancouver, B.C. V6B 2S2
Phone: (604) 687-1581　Fax: (604) 687-1925
Contact: John Shinnick, editor
Circulation: 25,000
Published monthly

Stories written from first-hand experience relating to boating on Canada's West Coast for Western Canada's sailboat and powerboat owners. Carries racing reports, adventure, and articles (800 to 2,000 words) on coastal and offshore cruising, powerboat handling, and the latest technical information. "Writers must be familiar with our special-interest viewpoint, language, and orientation." Buys photos and stories together. Pays on publication.

Power Boating Canada
2585 Skymark Avenue, Suite 306, Mississauga, Ont. L4W 4L5
Phone: (905) 624-8218   Fax: (905) 624-6764
Contact: Pam Cottrell, editor
Circulation: 40,000
Published bimonthly

Carries stories on powerboat performance and evaluates new equipment and boating techniques. Also covers waterskiing. Pays around $350 on publication for a feature of 1,500 to 2,000 words with photos. Query first with ideas.

Score: Canada's Golf Magazine
287 MacPherson Avenue, Toronto, Ont. M4V 1A4
Phone: (416) 928-2909   Fax: (416) 928-1357
Contact: Bob Weeks, managing editor
Circulation: 145,000
Published 7 times a year

A national golf magazine with regional inserts (Ontario and Western Canada). Profiles prominent golfers and golfing personalities, and reviews courses, clubs, and equipment. Also carries articles on travel and international competitions, and instructional pieces. Pays 50¢/word on acceptance for articles of 750 to 1,750 words – sometimes more for more detailed stories. Guidelines available.

Ski Canada
10 Pote Avenue, Toronto, Ont. M4N 2S7
Phone: (416) 322-9606   Fax: (416) 322-9607
Contact: Cathy Carl, editor
Circulation: 55,000
Published 7 times a year

Published during the ski season, with a balanced mix of entertainment and information for both the experienced and the novice-intermediate skier. Tests equipment and new products, and offers articles on instruction, ski resorts, competitions, fashion, and prominent people in the business. Articles vary from 600 to 2,000 words. Pays between $300 and $800, depending on type and length of article, research necessary, and writer's experience.

The Standardbred News

P.O. Box 150, Acton, Ont. L7J 2M3
Phone: (519) 853-5100 Fax: (519) 853-5040
Contact: Paul Nolan, editor
Circulation: 5,000
Published biweekly

Covers news and developments on the Canadian harness-racing scene from coast to coast. Readers are owners, trainers, drivers, and breeders. Carries articles on sales results, market analysis, bloodlines, training reports, and animal health. Query by mail or fax with story ideas. Fees negotiable.

Western Skier

P.O. Box 430, 1132 – 98th Street, North Battleford, Sask. S9A 2Y5
Phone: (306) 445-7477 Fax: (306) 445-1977
Contact: Rod McDonald, publisher
Circulation: 28,000
Published 6 times a year (October to March)

A magazine targeting ski enthusiasts from Manitoba to B.C. Articles to inform and entertain family-oriented skiers and junior and recreational racers. Covers resorts, equipment, and fashions, with fiction and racing features. Circulated to provincial alpine associations and by subscription. Pays 20¢/word on publication for articles of 1,500 to 2,500 words. Guidelines available.

Western Sportsman

P.O. Box 737, Regina, Sask. S4P 3A8
Phone: (306) 352-2773 Fax: (306) 565-2440
Contact: Brian Bowman, editor
Circulation: 26,000
Published bimonthly

Provides residents of Alberta, Saskatchewan, and Manitoba with news and features on hunting, fishing, wildlife, camping, backpacking, canoeing, and other outdoor activities. Prefers articles of 1,800 to 2,500 words. Pays up to $300 on publication with photos. "Our requirements are seasonal and regional – hunting stories for fall, fishing stories for spring, all focusing on the Prairie experience. Stories generally relate to personal experience rather than 'how-to' or 'where-to'." Guidelines available.

Whistler Answer

P.O. Box 587, Whistler, B.C. VON 1B0
Phone: (604) 932-4114   Fax: (604) 932-1176
Contact: Bob Colebrook, editor
Circulation: 4,000
Published monthly

A magazine reflecting, often with humour, an active and dynamic mountain lifestyle and culture, including stories and features on outdoor recreation and adventure. Preferred length 750 to 1,300 words. Pays $75 to $125 on publication for features.

Women's

BC Woman

704 Clarkson Street, New Westminster, B.C. V3M 1E2
Phone: (604) 540-8448   Fax: (604) 524-0041
Contact: Anne Brennan, editor
Circulation: 33,000
Published monthly

Designed to inspire and celebrate the achievements of B.C. women, to inform, entertain, and provide a forum for discussion of issues of importance to B.C. women. Pays 10¢ to 30¢/word for articles of 800 to 1,500 words. "We negotiate a flat fee for each story, based on length, research required, complexity of topic, and writer's skill level. Send written queries. All stories must be targeted to the B.C. market. Spec. manuscripts are welcome, though it sometimes takes several months to respond." Guidelines available.

Best Wishes

37 Hanna Avenue, Unit 1, Toronto, Ont. M6K 1X1
Phone: (416) 537-2604   Fax: (416) 538-1794
Contact: Bettie Bradley, editor

Circulation: 170,000
Published twice a year
Published by Family Communications Inc., and designed to meet the needs of women following childbirth. Articles on mother-care and baby care, written mostly by healthcare professionals. Pays on publication.

Canadian Living
50 Holly Street, Toronto, Ont. M4S 3B3
Phone: (416) 482-8600   Fax: (416) 482-2252
Contact: Bonnie Cowan, editor
Circulation: 600,000
Published 13 times a year
A vastly popular mass-market magazine emphasizing practical information to help Canadian women better cope with today's changing world as it relates to themselves and their families. Also carries articles on food, beauty, fashion, decorating, crafts, contemporary living, health, and fitness. Prefers original manuscripts of 300 to 2,000 words. Pays on acceptance. Fee depends on kind of article and writer's experience. Guidelines available.

Chatelaine
777 Bay Street, 8th Floor, Toronto, Ont. M5W 1A7
Phone: (416) 596-5425   Fax: (416) 596-5516
Contact: Mildred Istona, editor
Circulation: 900,000
Published monthly
High-quality glossy magazine addressing the needs and preferences of Canadian women. Covers current issues, personalities, lifestyles, health, relationships, travel, and politics. Runs features of 1,500 to 2,500 words (pay rate starts at $1,250), and regular 500-word "upfront" columns on parenting, health, nutrition, and fitness (fees start at $350). "For all serious articles, deep, accurate, and thorough research and rich details are required. Features on beauty, food, fashion, and home decorating are supplied by staff writers and editors only." Buys first North American serial rights in English and French (to cover possible use in French-language edition). Pays on acceptance. Query first with brief outline.

Focus on Women
1218 Langley Street, Victoria, B.C. v8w 1w2
Phone: (604) 388-7231   Fax: (604) 383-1140
Contact: Leslie Campbell, editor/publisher
Circulation: 30,000
Published monthly

A magazine serving Victoria women. Covers health, social issues, local news, and local profiles. All features have a local angle. Pays on publication $175 to $250 for features (2,500 to 3,000 words); $100 for profiles of Victoria women; $50 for essays, opinion, humour, and short stories. "We work mostly with freelancers we know. We do not accept queries – only articles on spec. Allow four weeks for response."

Homemaker's Magazine
50 Holly Street, Toronto, Ont. m4s 3b3
Phone: (416) 482-9399   Fax: (416) 482-8153
Contact: Sally Armstrong, editor-in-chief
Published 8 times a year

Directed towards women aged 25 to 54 with children at home. Feature articles, which average 3,000 words, address issues of particular concern to women, their families, and communities. There is a strong emphasis on relationships. Also published in French as *Madame au Foyer*. Pays on acceptance.

Today's Bride
37 Hanna Avenue, Unit 1, Toronto, Ont. m6k 1x1
Phone: (416) 537-2604   Fax: (416) 538-1794
Contact: Shirley-Anne Bickley, assistant editor
Circulation: 100,000
Published twice a year

Complete how-to advice on planning and co-ordinating formal weddings. Pays $200 to $300 on acceptance for 800 to 1,500 words. "Concentrate on anecdotal or unique wedding-related articles. All travel and standard planning pieces written in-house."

Toronto Life Fashion
59 Front Street E., Toronto, Ont. m5e 1b3

Phone: (416) 364-3333   Fax: (416) 594-3374
Contact: Joan Harting Barham, editor
Circulation: 135,000
Published bimonthly

A glossy women's magazine providing entertaining news and views on health, fitness, beauty, and fashion. Pays $1/word on acceptance for feature articles of 2,000 to 2,500 words.

You/Verve Magazine
37 Hanna Avenue, Unit 1, Toronto, Ont. M6K 1X1
Phone: (416) 537-2604   Fax: (416) 538-1794
Contact: Bettie Bradley, editor/general manager
Circulation: 205,000
Published quarterly

A magazine for the woman of the nineties who cares about how she looks, how she feels, how she eats, and her level of fitness. Pays $300 on acceptance for feature articles of 1,200 to 1,500 words.

Youth & Children's

Chickadee
56 The Esplanade, Suite 306, Toronto, Ont. M5E 1A7
Phone: (416) 868-6001   Fax: (416) 868-6009
Contact: Lizann Flatt, editor
Circulation: 150,000
Published 10 times a year

A magazine focusing on science and nature that offers 3- to 9-year-olds a bright, lively look at the world. Designed to entertain and educate, each issue contains photographs, illustrations, an animal story, puzzles, a science experiment, and a pullout poster. Pays $250 on acceptance for stories of between 300 to 800 words. "Avoid anthropomorphic material. Keep in mind the age range of readers, but do not talk down to them." Guidelines available.

Kids Toronto
540 Mount Pleasant Road, Suite 201, Toronto, Ont. M4S 2M6
Phone: (416) 481-5696   Fax: (416) 481-3883
Contact: Leslie Garrett, managing editor

Circulation: 60,000

Published monthly

Carries stories on topical issues of interest and concern to parents of children aged 2 to 14. Highlights events and activities for Toronto families. Pays 10¢/word on acceptance for articles of 800 to 1,800 words. Guidelines available.

Kids World Magazine

108 – 93 Lombard Avenue, Winnipeg, Man. R3B 3B1

Phone: (204) 942-2214   Fax: (204) 943-8991

Contact: Stuart Slayen, editor

Circulation: 200,000

Published 5 times a year

A general interest magazine for elementary students, grades 4 to 6, distributed nationally through schools, with a special emphasis on entertainment and motivation. Articles 400 to 1,200 words. Pays about 17¢/word, or $125 for 700 words, on publication. "Rates vary, depending on story. Writers are encouraged to phone editor to discuss story ideas before submitting." Guidelines available.

OWL

56 The Esplanade, Suite 306, Toronto, Ont. M5E 1A7

Phone: (416) 868-6001   Fax: (416) 868-6009

Contact: Nyla Ahmad, managing editor

Circulation: 100,000

Published 10 times a year

A discovery magazine for 8- to 12-year-olds. Sparks children's curiosity about the world around them and encourages them to become involved in caring for the environment. Pays around $200 on publication for 500 to 800 words. Prefers submission inquiries. Strongly recommends writers check back issues (available in libraries) for a sense of *OWL*'s approach.

TG Magazine: Voices of Today's Generation

202 Cleveland Street, Toronto, Ont. M4S 2W6

Phone: (416) 487-3204

Contact: Donna Douglas, editor

Circulation: 165,000

Published bimonthly

A magazine for Canadian teenagers, carrying articles on fashion, sports, fitness, nutrition, careers, as well as profiles of people of importance to teens. Also prints fiction. Concerned with issues of head and heart, promoting youth empowerment, and publishing student work: 40 per cent of it is written, photographed, or produced by high school students. Articles/stories 500 to 800 words. Pays $80 for 500 words on acceptance. Guidelines available.

What! A Magazine

108 – 93 Lombard Avenue, Winnipeg, Man. R3B 3B1
Phone: (204) 942-2214   Fax: (204) 943-8991
Contact: Stuart Slayen, editor
Circulation: 200,000
Published bimonthly

A general interest magazine directed towards high school students, grade 9 and up, distributed nationally through high schools, covering a mix of social issues and entertainment. Articles 700 to 2,000 words. Pays about 17¢/word, or $350 for 2,000 words, on publication. "Rates are negotiable, depending on story. Writers are encouraged to phone the editor to discuss story ideas before submitting." Guidelines available.

2

LITERARY & SCHOLARLY

It's ironic that literary and scholarly journals, among the most prestigious outlets for a writer's work, can usually afford to pay their contributors the least. Many journals rely on funding from arts councils, or academic or professional sources, and still run at a loss. They have relatively small subscription lists and perhaps one or two unpaid or part-time staff, and they attract little advertising support. The upshot is that they can rarely afford to pay their contributors much. In many cases, modest funding and low revenues preclude payment altogether, or limit it to small honoraria or free copies. Contributors to scholarly journals are frequently salaried academics or professionals, who draw on current areas of research.

Writers would be unwise to look to this sector of publishing as a significant source of income. Qualified writers would be just as unwise to neglect it because of this. Publishing your work in a distinguished literary or scholarly journal can add immeasurably to your reputation, and may well open up other publishing opportunities. This chapter lists many of Canada's most notable journals and literary magazines. Use the information presented in each entry to help you choose the most appropriate publications to approach.

Before you make your submission, familiarize yourself thoroughly with the journal to which you hope to contribute. Editors take a dim view of submissions from writers who are demonstrably unfamiliar with their periodical. Study several recent issues, or better still, subscribe. Learn what you can of the editors' approach and point of view and the kind of work they favour. Determine who their readers are. Always request writer's guidelines, if they are available, and follow these closely to ensure you meet the editor's needs. Refereed journals will require several copies of your submission. Scholarly articles should be accompanied by full documentation. Fiction, poetry, reviews, and criticism must be carefully targeted and professionally presented. The extra care and attention will pay dividends.

ARC

P.O. Box 7368, Ottawa, Ont. KIL 8E4
Contact: Maria Stewart, associate editor
Circulation: 600
Published twice a year

Publishes poetry from Canada and abroad, as well as reviews, interviews, and articles about aspects of Canadian poetry and Canada's poetry community. Poetry submissions must be typed and include 5 to 8 unpublished poems. Reviews, interviews, and other articles must be queried first. Pays $30 per published page on publication. Guidelines available.

Acadiensis: Journal of the History of the Atlantic Region

University of New Brunswick, Campus House, Fredericton,
    N.B. E3B 5A3
Phone: (506) 453-4978
Contact: David Frank, editor
Circulation: 850
Published twice a year

Includes original academic research, review articles, documents, notes, and a running bibliography compiled by librarians in the four Atlantic provinces. Published in English and in French. Cannot pay but welcomes submission inquiries. Guidelines available.

The Antigonish Review

St. Francis Xavier University, P.O. Box 135, Antigonish,
    N.S. B2G 1C0
Phone: (902) 867-3962   Fax: (902) 867-5153
Contact: George Sanderson, editor
Circulation: 1,000
Published quarterly

A creative literary review featuring poetry, fiction, and critical articles from Canada and abroad. Preferred length 1,500 to 3,000 words. Pays up to $150, depending on the article, on publication. Rights remain with author. Guidelines available.

Arachnē: A Journal of Language and Literature

Laurentian University, Ramsey Lake Road, Sudbury,
　　Ont. P3E 2C6
Phone: (705) 675-1151, ext. 4271   Fax: (705) 675-4836
Contact: Dr. David Darby, assistant professor, modern languages
Published twice a year

A new interdisciplinary journal that seeks to gauge the status quo of disciplines such as literature, film, philosophy, religion, art history, law, classics, history, and rhetoric, and to play an active role in bringing these disciplines into dialogue. Articles from 5,000 to 7,500 words. Cannot pay but welcomes submission inquiries. "Freelancers will always receive more than a form letter from *Arachnē*." Guidelines available.

Atlantic Books Today

2085 Maitland Street, 2nd Floor, Halifax, N.S. B3K 2Z8
Phone: (902) 429-4454   Fax: (902) 429-4454
Contact: Elizabeth Eve, managing editor
Circulation: 32,000
Published quarterly

Formerly the *Atlantic Provinces Review*. Features books, writing, and related issues of the Atlantic region. Pays 20¢/word on publication for short pieces of 250 to 350 words. Welcomes inquiries by mail, fax, or phone.

B.C. Bookworld

3516 West 13th Avenue, Vancouver, B.C. V6R 2S3
Phone: (604) 736-4011   Fax: (604) 736-4011
Contact: Alan Twigg, publisher
Circulation: 50,000
Published quarterly

Promotes B.C. books and authors. Preferred length 500 to 800 words. All fees negotiated on assignment. "Please phone or write first. We usually assign articles."

BC Studies: A Quarterly Journal of the Humanities and Social Sciences

University of British Columbia, 2029 West Mall, Vancouver,
    Suite 218, B.C. V6T 1Z2
Phone: (604) 822-3727   Fax: (604) 822-9452
Contact: Henry Winterton, editorial assistant/business manager
Circulation: 800
Published quarterly

An award-winning journal addressing all aspects of human history in British Columbia. Articles (500 to 750 words) cover a wide range of subjects including resource management, politics, history, anthropology, literature, economics, archaeology, and history. Cannot pay but welcomes submission inquiries. Guidelines available.

Blood & Aphorisms

456 College Street, Suite 711, Toronto, Ont. M6G 4A3
Phone: (416) 972-0637
Contact: Hilary G. Clark, fiction editor
Circulation: 800
Published quarterly

A literary journal carrying fresh, exciting fiction by new and established writers along with reviews and interviews with emerging writers. A great market for innovative newcomers. Articles between 500 and 4,000 words. Contributors receive a one-year subscription. Guidelines available.

Books in Canada

130 Spadina Avenue, Suite 603, Toronto, Ont. M5V 2L4
Phone: (416) 601-9880
Contact: Paul Stuewe, editor
Circulation: 10,000
Published 9 times a year

An award-winning magazine providing commentary on the world of books and related cultural fields. Carries reviews by some of the country's best-known writers and critics. Interviews and profiles authors and entertains the literate reader. Pays 12¢/word on publication. No unsolicited submissions. "All reviews and articles are assigned to our pool of freelancers. So query first, always. Don't contact us if you've never read *BiC* – we're a very specialized market."

Border/Lines

The Orient Building, 183 Bathurst Street, Suite 301, Toronto,
  Ont. M5T 2R7
Phone: (416) 360-5249   Fax: (416) 360-0781
Contact: Julie Jenkinson, managing editor
Circulation: 1,300
Published quarterly

An interdisciplinary magazine exploring all aspects of culture. Features articles, reviews, and visual pieces on the theory and practice of popular culture, including film, art, music, the landscape, mass communications, and political culture. Articles are between 500 and 4,000 words. Pays $50 to $250 on publication for features. Guidelines available.

CCL: Canadian Children's Literature

Department of English, University of Guelph, Guelph,
  Ont. N1G 2W1
Phone: (519) 824-4120, ext. 3189   Fax: (519) 837-1315
Contact: Barbara Conolly, administrator
Circulation: 1,000
Published quarterly

Presents in-depth criticism of Canadian literature for young people. Directed towards teachers, librarians, academics, and parents. Scholarly articles and reviews are supplemented by graphics, photographs, and interviews with authors of children's books. Cannot pay but welcomes submissions. Guidelines available.

Canadian Author

P.O. Box 351, Ailsa Craig, Ont. N0M 1A0
Phone: (519) 293-3579   Fax: (519) 293-3649
Contact: Gordon Symons, editor
Circulation: 3,500
Published quarterly

Canada's oldest, most respected national writers' magazine, owned by the Canadian Authors Association but with an independent editorial policy. Features profiles and interviews with people who influence Canadian literature. Also publishes fiction and poetry. A valuable resource for writers. Pays $125 for fiction, $30 to $60 per published page for all other material, on publication. Written queries only. Guidelines available.

Canadian Ethnic Studies

Research Unit for Canadian Ethnic Studies, University of Calgary,
2500 University Drive N.W., Calgary, Alta. T2N 1N4
Phone: (403) 220-7257   Fax: (403) 282-8606
Contact: Dr. J.S. Frideres, co-editor, or Sandra Demchuk,
assistant to the editors
Circulation: 700
Published 3 times a year

An interdisciplinary journal devoted to the study of ethnicity,
immigration, inter-group relations, and the history and cultural life
of ethnic groups in Canada. Also carries book reviews, opinions,
memoirs, creative writing, and poetry, and has an ethnic voice section. All material should address Canadian ethnicity. Contributors
are not paid. Guidelines available.

Canadian Fiction Magazine

P.O. Box 1061, 221 King Street E., Kingston, Ont. K7L 4Y5
Phone: (613) 548-8429   Fax: (613) 548-1556
Contact: managing editor, Quarry Press
Circulation: 2,000
Published quarterly

Now in partnership with Quarry Press, through whom all inquiries should be made. Dedicated for 25 years to new Canadian fiction,
including translations from Québécois and other languages spoken
in Canada. Publishes short stories and novel extracts, and is especially interested in innovative and experimental fiction. Also buys
book reviews, interviews, manifestos, graphics, and some photos.
Pays $10 per printed page on publication. Guidelines available.

Canadian Journal of Philosophy

Department of Philosophy, University of Alberta, Edmonton,
Alta. T6G 2E5
Phone: (403) 492-4103   Fax: (403) 492-9160
Contact: Dr. Mohan Matthen, board co-ordinator
Circulation: 1,300
Published quarterly

A leading Canadian philosophical journal, which investigates
and contributes to the scholarship, teaching, and research of the

country's major philosophers. Publishes work of high quality in any field of philosophy. Articles 10 to 25 pages. Contributors are unpaid. Guidelines available.

Canadian Literature

University of British Columbia, 2029 West Mall, Suite 223,
    Vancouver, B.C. V6T 1Z2
Phone: (604) 822-2780   Fax: (604) 822-9452
Contact: W.H. New, editor
Published quarterly

Devoted to studying all aspects of Canadian literature: fiction, non-fiction, poetry, and drama. For students and academics at all levels as well as general readers. Articles/stories 3,000 to 6,000 words. Pays $5 per printed page, $10 per poem, on publication; no payment for reviews.

Canadian Modern Language Review

237 Hellems Avenue, Welland, Ont. L3B 3B8
Phone: (905) 734-3640   Fax: (905) 734-3640
Contact: Sally Rehorick and Viviane Edwards, editors
Circulation: 2,100
Published quarterly

Publishes literary, linguistic, and pedagogical articles, book reviews, current advertisements, and other material of interest to teachers of French, German, Italian, Russian, Spanish, Ukrainian, and English as a second language, at all levels of instruction. Published since 1944. All articles are voluntarily submitted rather than assigned, and are refereed. Length should not exceed 6,500 words. Contributors are not paid, but submissions are welcomed. Consult "Guide to Authors" in each issue and write to editors for further information.

Canadian Notes & Queries

P.O. Box 367, Station F, Toronto, Ont. M4Y 2L8
   Fax: (416) 538-3317
Contact: Douglas Fetherling, editor
Circulation: 1,200
Published irregularly (2 to 3 times a year)

A journal of ideas for the educated reader; a forum for current research and reviews in Canadian literature and the humanities. Publishes essays, reviews, memoirs, and articles of interest to teachers, students, historians, and other scholars. Pays modestly on publication. "We welcome submission inquiries, but potential contributors simply *must* be familiar with *CNQ*. Amateur freelance writers without roots in our field are discouraged from giving us a try."

Canadian Poetry: Studies, Documents, Reviews

University of Western Ontario, Department of English, London,
    Ont. N6A 3K7
Phone: (519) 661-3403   Fax: (519) 661-3640
Contact: D.M.R. Bentley, editor
Circulation: 400
Published twice a year

A scholarly and critical journal devoted to the study of poetry from all periods and regions of Canada. Also prints articles, reviews, and documents directed towards university and college students and teachers. No original poetry. Cannot pay but welcomes submissions of 500 to 5,000 words. Follow *MLA Handbook* for style.

Canadian Public Administration

150 Eglinton Avenue E., Suite 305, Toronto, Ont. M4P 1E8
Phone: (416) 932-3666   Fax: (416) 932-3667
Contact: V. Seymour Wilson, editor
Circulation: 4,200
Published quarterly

A refereed journal that examines structures, processes, and outcomes of public policy and public management related to executive, legislative, judicial, and quasi-judicial functions in municipal, provincial, and federal spheres of government. Guidelines available.

Canadian Woman Studies Journal

212 Founders College, York University, 4700 Keele Street, North
    York, Ont. M3J 1P3
Phone: (416) 736-5356   Fax: (416) 736-5765
Contact: Luciana Ricciutelli, managing editor
Circulation: 4,000
Published quarterly

A bilingual journal featuring current writing and research on a wide variety of feminist topics. Welcomes creative writing, experimental articles, and essays of 500 to 2,000 words, as well as book, art, and film reviews. Contributors are unpaid. Guidelines available.

The Capilano Review

2055 Purcell Way, North Vancouver, B.C. v7J 3H5
Phone: (604) 984-1712
Contact: Robert Sherrin, editor
Circulation: 1,000
Published 3 times a year

Features poetry, prose, and fine art by some of Canada's most innovative writers and artists *before* they become famous. Pays $40 per page, to a maximum of $160, on publication. Carries stories up to 6,000 words. Guidelines available.

The Claremont Review

4980 Wesley Road, Victoria, B.C. v8Y 1Y9
Phone: (604) 658-5221   Fax: (604) 658-5037
Contact: Terence Young, co-editor
Circulation: 350
Published twice a year

Dedicated to publishing the fiction, poetry, and short drama of emerging young writers aged 13 to 19. Introduces some of the best student writing in Canada. Submissions should be between 1,500 and 5,000 words. Offers an honorarium of $5 per page. "Our editorial board responds to all submissions with a critical evaluation." Guidelines available.

Dalhousie Review

Dalhousie University, Sir James Dunn Building, Room 314,
    Halifax, N.S. B3H 3J5
Phone: (902) 494-2541   Fax: (902) 494-2319
Contact: Dr Alan Andrews, editor
Circulation: 750
Published quarterly

Invites contributions of articles up to 5,000 words in such fields as history, literature, political science, and philosophy, as well as prose fiction and poetry from both new and established writers. Also carries book reviews. Prefers poetry of less than 40 lines. Contributors to this distinguished quarterly, first published in 1921, are not usually paid. Guidelines available.

Dandelion

922 – 9th Avenue S.E., Calgary, Alta. T2G 0S4
Phone: (403) 265-0524
Contact: Barbara Kermode-Scott, managing editor
Circulation: 1,000
Published twice a year

International journal of poetry and fiction from writers across Canada, plus interviews, reviews, and articles (1,000 to 2,500 words) about the regional literary scene and local visual art. Pays on publication $125 per story, $50 per review, $15/page for poetry. Guidelines available.

Descant

P.O. Box 314, Station P, Toronto, Ont. M5S 2S8
Phone: (416) 603-0223
Contact: Elizabeth Mitchell, managing editor
Circulation: 1,200
Published quarterly

A literary journal publishing poetry, prose, fiction, interviews, travel pieces, letters, photographs, engravings, art, and literary criticism. Pays an honorarium of $100 on publication to all contributors. "Our purpose is the critical reading of manuscripts of new and established writers. We ask for one-time publishing rights, and only use unpublished work. Turnaround time for manuscripts can be up to 4 months. Each manuscript is read three times before acceptance." Guidelines available.

ENVIRONMENTS: A Journal of Interdisciplinary Studies

University of Waterloo, Faculty of Environmental Studies,
  Waterloo, Ont. N2L 3G1
Phone: (519) 885-1211, ext. 3586   Fax: (519) 746-2031
Contact: Catherine Elstone, managing editor
Circulation: 500

Published 2 to 3 times a year

A refereed journal for scholars and practitioners that seeks to integrate the fields of environment, development, and design. For more information, check inside front cover. Cannot pay but welcomes submission inquiries. Guidelines available.

Essays on Canadian Writing

1980 Queen Street E., Toronto, Ont. M4L 1J2
Phone: (416) 694-3348   Fax: (416) 698-9906
Contact: Jack David and Robert Lecker, editors
Circulation: 1,000
Published 3 times a year

Devoted to criticism of Canadian writers and their works. Concentrates on essays featuring contemporary authors and current critical approaches. Publishes bibliographies, interviews, and full-length book reviews of fiction, poetry, and criticism. Pays $75 to $100 on acceptance for 4,000 to 11,000 words. Author retains all rights. Guidelines available.

Event: The Douglas College Review

Douglas College, P.O. Box 2503, New Westminster, B.C. V3L 5B2
Phone: (604) 527-5293   Fax: (604) 527-5095
Contact: Dale Zieroth, editor
Circulation: 3,000
Published 3 times a year

Presents new and established Canadian and international writers through their fiction and poetry, and reviews of their work. (Features an annual $500 Creative Non-Fiction Contest each spring.) Stories to a maximum of 5,000 words or up to 8 poems may be submitted. Pays $22/page on publication. Guidelines available.

Exile

P.O. Box 67, Station B, Toronto, Ont. M5T 2C0
Phone: (416) 922-8221
Contact: Barry Callaghan, editor
Circulation: 1,200
Published quarterly

Devoted to fine fiction, poetry, drama, painting, and drawing from Canada and abroad. Pays sometimes on acceptance, sometimes on publication. Mail typed inquiries. Study journal first.

The Fiddlehead

Campus House, University of New Brunswick, P.O. Box 4400,
   Fredericton, N.B. E3B 5A3
Phone: (506) 453-3501   Fax: (506) 453-4599
Contact: Don McKay, editor
Circulation: 900
Published quarterly

A highly respected literary journal, established in 1945, publishing fine poetry, prose, book reviews, and art work, with a focus on freshness and vitality. While retaining a special interest in writers of Atlantic Canada, it is open to outstanding work from all over the country. Prose submissions may be 100 up to 4,000 words ($10/page). Poetry submissions, 3 to 10 poems. Pays on publication.

Grain

P.O. Box 1154, Regina, Sask. S4P 3B4
Phone: (306) 244-2828   Fax: (306) 565-8554
Contact: Geoffrey Ursell, editor
Circulation: 2,000
Published quarterly

A literary journal of national and international scope published by the Saskatchewan Writers' Guild. Prints high-quality literary and visual art, both traditional and experimental, with the aim of challenging its readers and encouraging promising new writers. Original fiction and poetry, creative non-fiction, songs, and excerpts from produced plays considered. Pays $30 to $100 on publication for poetry and fiction. Guidelines available.

Journal of Canadian Studies

Trent University, P.O. Box 4800, Peterborough, Ont. K9J 7B8
Contact: Michael Peterman, editor
Circulation: 1,400
Published quarterly

Publishes a variety of scholarly articles, critical comment, and book reviews pertaining to Canadian history, politics, the economy, education, literature and the arts, public policy, communications, anthropology, and sociology. Accepts articles of between 3,000 and 10,000 words. Cannot pay but welcomes submission inquiries. Guidelines available.

Labour/Le travail
Memorial University, Department of History, St John's,
   Nfld. A1C 5S7
Phone: (709) 737-2144   Fax: (709) 737-2146
Contact: G.S. Kealey, editor; I.A. Whitefield, managing editor
Circulation: 1,150
Published twice a year
   A bilingual, interdisciplinary, historical journal concerned with work, workers, and the labour movement. Includes articles, book notes, archival notes, and an annual bibliography of Canadian labour studies. Contributors are not paid.

The Literary Review of Canada
3266 Yonge Street, P.O. Box 1830, Toronto, Ont. M4N 3P6
  Fax: (416) 322-4852
Contact: Pat Dutil, editor
Circulation: 1,200
Published 11 times a year
   A scholarly tabloid, in the style of *The New York Review of Books*, carrying substantive book reviews of Canadian non-fiction. Intriguing, incisively written, and informative, it attracts a highly educated readership. Contributors must be fluent in the symbols of Canada. Reviews are 3,000 to 5,000 words. Cannot yet pay contributors, but hopes to in the future. Warmly welcomes faxed or mailed proposals and outlines. Do not submit before studying the review.

The Malahat Review
University of Victoria, P.O. Box 1700, MS 8524, Victoria,
   B.C. V8W 2Y2
Phone: (604) 721-8524   Fax: (604) 721-7212
Contact: Derk Wynand, editor
Circulation: 1,800
Published quarterly
   A distinguished, award-winning literary journal publishing

Canada's best poets and short story writers. Pays $25 per estimated published page on acceptance. Don't send queries first. For poetry, submit 6 to 10 pages of poems; for fiction, send one complete story.

Material History Review

National Museum of Science & Technology, P.O. Box 9724,
    Ottawa Terminal, Ottawa, Ont. KIG 5A3
Phone: (613) 990-7529   Fax: (613) 990-3636
Contact: Wendy McPeake, director of publishing and marketing
Circulation: 1,400
Published biannually

Encourages new methods of research through the documentation of cultural artifacts in studying history from a variety of fields, including social history, history of technology and architecture, anthropology, geography, and art history. Contributors are unpaid. Contact for author's guidelines.

Matrix

C.P. 100, Ste.-Anne-de-Bellevue, Que. H9X 3L4
Phone: (514) 426-8654   Fax: (514) 426-8658
Contact: Linda Leith and Kenneth Radu, co-editors
Circulation: 2,000
Published 3 times a year

A literary/cultural magazine rooted in Quebec but open to writers from across Canada, the United States, and abroad. Described by Bill Katz, in *Library Journal,* as "a northern combination of *The New Yorker* and *Atlantic Monthly.*" Publishes original prose and poetry by new and established writers. Preferred length 3,000 to 5,000 words. Articles/fiction receive $50 to $100; poetry $20 to $50; reviews $40. Pays on publication. Guidelines available.

McGill Street Magazine

193 Bellwoods Avenue, Toronto, Ont. M6J 2P8
Phone: (416) 860-0204
Contact: Alexandra Soiseth, co-editor
Circulation: 400
Published quarterly

A new magazine dedicated to publishing the work of emerging

writers, including poetry, short stories, and excerpts from longer works and plays (to a maximum 4,000 words). Pays two copies only. Submissions welcome. Guidelines available.

Modern Drama

Graduate Centre for Study of Drama, 214 College Street, Toronto, Ont. M5T 2Z9
Phone: (416) 978-7984   Fax: (416) 971-1378
Contact: Dorothy Parker, editor
Published quarterly

A scholarly journal focusing exclusively on world drama from 1850 to the present. Carries essays and interviews with famous theatrical creators, critics, and scholars. Contributors are unpaid.

Mosaic: A Journal for the Interdisciplinary Study of Literature

208 Tier Building, University of Manitoba, Winnipeg, Man. R3T 2N2
Phone: (204) 474-9763   Fax: (204) 261-9086
Contact: Dr. Evelyn J. Hinz, editor
Circulation: 1,000
Published quarterly

For scholars, educators, students, and the sophisticated general reader. Combining reader-friendly prose and current research, essays use insights from a wide variety of disciplines to highlight the practical and cultural relevance of literary works. Essays are 5,000 to 6,000 words. Contributors are unpaid. Submission inquiries welcome. "We strongly encourage potential contributors to subscribe to *Mosaic* in order to become familiar with our format, editorial mandate, and interdisciplinary requirements." Guidelines available.

The Muse Journal

226 Lisgar Street, Toronto, Ont. M6J 3G7
Phone: (416) 539-9517   Fax: (416) 539-0047
Contact: Emanuel Goncalves, editor
Circulation: 1,000
Published monthly

A journal for writers, poets, and visual artists open to all topics,

themes, and genres but emphasizing the metaphysical, philosophical, and humorous. Preferred length 500 to 1,200 words. Generally
only pays for solicited works. "*The Muse Journal* serves, supports,
and publishes poets, writers, and artists of exceptional talent,
whether they are known or unknown." Guidelines available.

The New Quarterly

University of Waterloo, English Language Proficiency Program,
   PAS 2082, Waterloo, Ont. N2L 3G1
Phone: (519) 885-1211, ext. 2837
Contact: Mary Merikle, managing editor
Circulation: 500

   Publishes poetry, short fiction, and excerpts from novels, while
encouraging "new voices and directions" in Canadian writing. Prose
should be about 20 pages. Pays $100 for a short story or novel
extract, $20 for a poem, on publication. Guidelines available.

ON SPEC: The Canadian Magazine of Speculative Writing

P.O. Box 4727, Edmonton, Alta. T6E 5G6
Phone: (403) 432-7927
Contact: Cath Jackel, administrator
Circulation: 2,000
Published quarterly

   Specializes in Canadian science fiction, fantasy, horror, and
magic realism in stories and poetry. Stories 1,000 to 6,000 words
(paid 2¢/word), poems up to 100 lines ($15 per poem). Pays on
acceptance. "Read a copy of the magazine, and send for guidelines
before submitting – we have unusual format requirements."

Ontario History

5151 Yonge Street, Willowdale, Ont. M2N 5P5
Phone: (416) 226-9011   Fax: (416) 226-2740
Contact: Jean Burnet, editor
Circulation: 1,200
Published quarterly

   A regional journal of current scholarly writing on various aspects
of the province's past, directed towards academics, professional and
amateur historians, libraries, and universities. Articles should be

6,000 to 7,000 words. Cannot pay but welcomes submission inquiries. Guidelines available.

Pacific Affairs

University of British Columbia, 2029 West Mall, Vancouver,
  B.C. V6T 1Z2
Phone: (604) 822-6504   Fax: (604) 822-9452
Contact: Bernie Chisholm, business manager
Circulation: 2,800
Published quarterly

A source of scholarly insight into the social, cultural, political, and economic issues of the Pacific region, directed towards universities, institutions, embassies, and consulates. Runs articles, review articles, and research notes contributed by authors from around the world. Also reviews about 60 books each issue. Preferred length 6,000 to 6,250 words. Contributors are not paid. Submission inquiries welcome. See inside back cover for guidelines.

Paragraph

P.O. Box 794, Station P, Toronto, Ont. M5S 2Z1
Contact: Daniel Jones, editor
Circulation: 1,500
Published quarterly

Explores Canadian contemporary fiction. Includes interviews, essays, criticism, fiction, and a substantial reviews section. Accepts suitable fiction submissions up to 2,000 words. Inquire first concerning non-fiction (up to 3,500 words). Fees vary and are paid on publication. Guidelines available.

Poetry Canada

P.O. Box 1061, Kingston, Ont. K7L 4Y5
Phone: (613) 548-8429   Fax: (613) 548-1556
Contact: Melanie Dugan, managing editor
Circulation: 1,500
Published quarterly

The nation's only magazine devoted entirely to publishing poetry, criticism of poetry, and poetry news. Carries about 30 poems each issue, some by Canada's best poets, others by new writers. Aims to discover the best new work by established and emerging poets in

Canada. Includes essays and in-depth interviews of 1,750 to 3,500 words. Pays $20/poem, $100/page, $50/review, after publication. "Please read the magazine first to get a sense of what we publish."

Possibilitiis Literary Arts Magazine

109 – 2100 Scott Street, Ottawa, Ont. K1Z 1A3
Phone: (613) 761-1177
Contact: Maureen Henry, administrator
Circulation: 600
Published quarterly

A new periodical that aims to provide a forum for emerging and established writers of colour or those writing from particular minority cultural perspectives. Seeks adult and children's fiction, poetry, stories, and other creative work written from the writer's distinct cultural perspective. Preferred length 1,000 to 2,500 words. A short (50-word) abstract and a brief biographical note should accompany submissions. Preference given to previously unpublished material. Guidelines available.

Prairie Books Now

P.O. Box 269, Milk River, Alta. T0K 1M0
Phone: (403) 647-2226   Fax: (403) 647-3562
Contact: Les Miller, publisher
Circulation: 30,000
Published quarterly

Promotes books, publishers, writers, and booksellers in the Prairie provinces. Preferred length of articles/reviews 200 to 500 words. Pays on publication. Query first.

Prairie Fire

100 Arthur Street, Suite 423, Winnipeg, Man. R3B 1H3
Phone: (204) 943-9066   Fax: (204) 942-1555
Contact: Andris Taskans, managing editor
Circulation: 1,500
Published quarterly

Publishes poetry, fiction, essays, interviews, reviews, commentary, satire, and literary and other arts criticism. Submissions may be from 200 to 4,000 words. Pays on publication: for fiction, $45/first page, then $30/page; for articles, $40/first page, then $25/page; for reviews/interviews, $30/first page, then $15/page. Guidelines and full payment schedule available.

PRISM international

Department of Creative Writing, University of British Columbia,
    1866 Main Mall, Buch E462, Vancouver, B.C. v6T 1w5
Phone: (604) 822-2514   Fax: (604) 228-6096
Contact: Anna Nobile, editor
Circulation: 1,100
Published quarterly

Features contemporary fiction, poetry, drama, non-fiction, and translation from Canadian and international authors. The oldest literary journal on the West Coast. Welcomes submissions from both established and unknown writers. "We are looking for exciting, original writing in all genres." Send original, unpublished material – no multiple submissions. Pays $20 per published page plus one year's subscription on publication. Guidelines available.

Public

192 Spadina Avenue, Suite 307, Toronto, Ont. M5T 2C2
Phone: (416) 868-1161   Fax: (416) 868-1161
Contact: Tom Taylor, collective member
Circulation: 1,500
Published twice a year

An interdisciplinary journal combining scholarly and critical writing in cultural studies, focusing on the visual arts, performance, and literature. Dedicated to providing a forum in which artists, critics, and theorists exchange ideas on topics previously segregated by ideological boundaries of discipline. Pays $500 on publication for contributions of 3,000 to 6,000 words.

Quarry

P.O. Box 1061, Kingston, Ont. K7L 4Y5
Phone: (613) 548-8429
Contact: Steven Heighton, editor
Circulation: 1,000
Published quarterly

For more than 40 years this literary magazine has been publishing new, innovative fiction, poetry, and essays by established and emerging Canadian writers. Also carries translations, travel writing, and reviews. Committed to dicovering talented new writers. Pays $10 per published page for fiction, $15 per poem, after publication.

Queen's Quarterly

184 Union Street, Kingston, Ont. K7L 3N6
Phone: (613) 545-2667   Fax: (613) 545-6822
Contact: Boris Castel, editor
Circulation: 2,700
Published quarterly

A distinctive and authoritative university-based review with a Canadian focus and an international outlook. First published in 1893. Features scholarly articles of general interest on politics, history, science, the humanities, and arts and letters, plus regular music and science columns, original poetry, fiction, and extensive book reviews. Pays on publication. Guidelines available.

Quill & Quire

70 The Esplanade, 4th Floor, Toronto, Ont. M5E 1R2
Phone: (416) 360-0044   Fax: (416) 360-8745
Contact: Ted Mumford, editor/co-publisher
Circulation: 7,000
Published monthly

The news journal of the Canadian book trade – for booksellers, librarians, educators, publishers, and writers. Prints news, reviews, lists of recently published and upcoming books, and profiles of authors, and publishing houses. Includes the biannual supplement, *Canadian Publishers Directory*. Pays a variable fee on acceptance.

Raddle Moon

2239 Stephens Street, Vancouver, B.C. V6K 3W5
Contact: Susan Clark, Catriona Strang, and Lisa Robertson,
    editors
Published twice a year

An international literary review featuring mostly Canadian and U.S. poetry and criticism as well as previously untranslated writing from many countries. Welcomes submission inquiries from those who have familiarized themselves with the journal.

Rampike
95 Rivercrest Road, Toronto, Ont. M6S 4H7
Phone: (416) 767-6713
Contact: Karl Jirgens, publisher
Published twice a year

Features poetry, fiction, one-act plays, and cinema and video scripts. Innovative work by writers, theorists, and artists from around the world. There's never a shortage of stimulating contributors to this visually arresting and highly regarded magazine. But contact editors regarding upcoming themes and you may be able to offer them something they need. Pays a nominal fee.

Resources for Feminist Research
OISE, 252 Bloor Street W., Toronto, Ont. M5S 1V6
Phone: (416) 923-6641, ext. 2277   Fax: (416) 926-4725
Contact: Philinda Masters, co-ordinating editor
Circulation: 2,000
Published quarterly

A journal of feminist scholarship containing papers, abstracts, reviews, reports of work in progress, and bibliographies. Preferred length 3,000 to 5,000 words. Cannot pay but welcomes submissions. Guidelines are outlined on inside back cover.

Room of One's Own
P.O. Box 46160, Station D, Vancouver, B.C. V6J 5G5
Contact: editorial collective
Circulation: 900
Published quarterly

Solicits fine writing and editing from Canada's best women authors, both well-known and unknown. Features original poetry, fiction, criticism, and reviews. Contributors receive free copies and honorarium. Guidelines are available, but reading recent back issues will provide best guidance. An irregular quarterly.

Rotunda
Royal Ontario Museum, 100 Queen's Park, Toronto,
    Ont. M5S 2C6
Phone: (416) 586-5590   Fax: (416) 586-5827
Contact: Sandra Shaul, executive editor

Circulation: 25,000
Published quarterly

A semi-scholarly magazine, published by the Royal Ontario Museum, carrying authoritative pieces on art, archaeology, the earth and life sciences, astronomy, and museology, addressing the research of ROM scholars and their associates worldwide. Preferred length 2,000 to 2,500 words. Pays professional journalists $375 on acceptance for articles from 1,500 to 2,500 words. Academics receive honoraria.

Scholarly Publishing

University of Toronto Press, 10 St. Mary Street, Suite 700,
    Toronto, Ont. M4Y 2W8
Phone: (416) 978-2232   Fax: (416) 978-4738
Contact: Hamish Cameron, editor
Circulation: 2,000
Published quarterly

Concerned with the "pleasure and perils" of publishing. Coverage ranges from the classic concerns of manuscript editing and list building to such contemporary issues as on-demand publishing and computer applications. Also explores the delicate balance of author–editor relations, and the intricacies of production and budgeting. Carries articles with a unique blend of philosophical analysis and practical advice. Contributors unpaid, but submission inquiries welcome. Guidelines available.

Studies in Canadian Literature

University of New Brunswick, English Department, P.O. Box
    4400, Fredericton, N.B. E3B 5A3
Phone: (506) 453-4676   Fax: (506) 453-5069
Contact: Kathleen Scherf, editor
Circulation: 575
Published twice a year

A bilingual, refereed journal of Canadian literary criticism. Carries essays of 8,000 to 10,000 words. Contributors are not paid. Guidelines in journal. Use *MLA Handbook* for style.

Studies in Political Economy

Social Sciences Research Building, Room 303, Carleton
    University, 1125 Colonel By Drive, Ottawa, Ont. K1S 5B6

Phone: (613) 788-2600, ext. 6625
Contact: Emer Killean, editor
Published 3 times a year

Offers a multidisciplinary approach to contemporary and historical issues. Presents original research and theoretical work with a socialist perspective by Canadian and international authors. Covers key debates in public policy, workers' history, feminism, the labour movement, international affairs, economics, and the peace movement. Contributors are not paid.

sub-Terrain Magazine

175 East Broadway, Suite 204A, Vancouver, B.C. V5T 1W2
Phone: (604) 876-8710   Fax: (604) 879-2667
Contact: Brian Kaufman, managing editor
Circulation: 2,000
Published quarterly

Publishes new and established writers from across North America. Interested in contemporary fiction and poetry from original voices. Preferred length 1,000 to 2,500 words. Pays in copies. Read the magazine before submitting. Guidelines available.

Tessera

350 Stong College, York University, 4700 Keele Street, North
   York, Ont. M3J 1P3
Phone: (416) 929-5919
Contact: Barbara Godard, managing editor; Jennifer Henderson,
   editor
Circulation: 375
Published twice a year

A bilingual journal of experimental contemporary feminist theory and literary criticism. "We encourage play along borders, especially crossings of the boundary between creative and theoretical texts." Issues are organized by topic; consult the editors for forthcoming topics. Pays about $10/page on publication. Contributions, which should include a biographical note, must be supplied on diskette. Guidelines available.

TickleAce

P.O. Box 5353, St John's, Nfld. A1C 5W2

Phone: (709) 754-6610
Contact: Bruce Porter, managing editor
Circulation: 900
Published twice a year

A literary review publishing an eclectic blend of quality poetry, fiction, visual art, book reviews, and literary interviews. Favours Newfoundland- and Labrador-based contributors, but always includes work from elsewhere. Stories up to 5,000 words. Pays $15 per page to a maximum $150 on publication. Guidelines available.

The Toronto Review (of Contemporary Writing Abroad)

P.O. Box 6996, Station A, Toronto, Ont. M5W 1X7
Contact: Ms. Nurjehan Aziz, editorial board
Published 3 times a year

Carries poetry, fiction, drama, criticism, and book reviews by writers who originate from the Indian subcontinent, Africa, and the Caribbean. A bias towards diasporic and Third World subjects. Prose 2,000 to 4,000 words. Cash payment for solicited material only; other contributors receive free subscriptions. Published in English and in translation.

Urban History Review

36 Bessemer, Unit 3, Concord, Ont. L4K 3C9
Phone: (905) 669-5373   Fax: (905) 669-1927
Contact: John Becker, managing editor
Circulation: 500
Published twice a year

A bilingual interdisciplinary and refereed journal presenting lively articles covering such topics as architecture, heritage, urbanization, housing, and planning – all in a generously illustrated format. Regular features include in-depth articles, research notes, two annual bibliographies covering Canadian and international publications, comprehensive book reviews, and notes and comments on conferences, urban policy, and publications. Contributors are unpaid.

3

TRADE, BUSINESS, FARM, & PROFESSIONAL PUBLICATIONS

This is a potentially lucrative sector of the writer's market that is often ignored. Although trade publications rarely pay more than $500 for a full-length article, and usually less, the writing may require considerably fewer sources than are needed for consumer magazine features. An article can often be completed in a day or two, sometimes after research and interviews conducted solely by telephone. In terms of hours spent, therefore, the pay is generally relatively good. What's more, trade editors are often keen to find competent new writers. Writers living in remote areas can find themselves at an unexpected advantage, as editors seek regional balance, and copy can always readily be sent long distance.

The secret to making money from these publications is to work frequently for as many as possible, always bearing in mind that they may want a degree of technical detail that will inform readers already well acquainted with the specific fields they serve. Most trade periodicals, however, deliberately avoid becoming *too* technical, and aim to appeal to a wide readership. If you're not well informed on your subject, become so through research. It bears repeating that before submitting, you *must* familiarize yourself with the magazine thoroughly by reading back issues and related periodicals.

Magazines in each of the following categories carry pieces about new products and developments, unusual marketing and promotion ideas, innovative management techniques, and prominent people and events specific to the industry, trade, or profession they serve. In many cases, staff writers produce the bulk of the feature writing, and call on outside "experts" to provide specific material. But they will often utilize freelancers when there is an editorial shortfall. Some editors cultivate long-term relationships with regular freelancers, who produce much of their copy.

Often one editor is involved in several magazines, so that making yourself and your work known to him or her can lead to further commissions, especially if you show yourself to be reliable and adaptable. Chapter 10, Book Resources, lists some of the larger publishers of trade magazines in Canada, who can be contacted for a list of their publications. If you have an area of technical or specialist knowledge, you have a significant advantage. If not, you would do well to familiarize yourself with at least one trade or business area and the publications that serve it.

This chapter offers a broadly representative selection of trade publications across a wide range of industrial and professional areas, including many well-established, dependable employment sources, and provides a solid resource for the freelance writer looking to break into a new market. However, this is perhaps the most fluid sector in publishing: periodicals appear and disappear and editors move from job to job relatively often in response to industry and structural changes. For a monthly updated reference source, consult Maclean Hunter's *CARD* directory, or refer to *Matthews Media Directory*, published three times a year by Canadian Corporate News, at your library. Check *CARD*, too, for upcoming editorial themes, media profiles, circulation figures, and other useful information.

Advertising, Marketing, & Sales

Adnews
2 Lansing Square, Suite 801, Willowdale, Ont. M2J 4P8
Phone: (416) 498-5164   Fax: (416) 498-6845
Contact: Mike Deibert, managing editor
Published weekly

Canadian Direct Marketing News
1200 Markham Road, Suite 301, Scarborough, Ont. M1H 3C3
Phone: (416) 439-4083   Fax: (416) 439-4086

Contact: Cheryl Sandys, editor
Published monthly

Canadian Retailer
200 – 388 Donald Street, Winnipeg, Man. R3B 2J4
Phone: (204) 957-0265   Fax: (204) 957-0217
Contact: Andrea Kuch, editor
Published bimonthly

Government Purchasing Guide
797 Don Mills Road, 10th Floor, Don Mills, Ont. M3C 3S5
Phone: (416) 696-5488   Fax: (416) 696-7395
Contact: Edward Zapletel, editor
Published monthly

Marketing
777 Bay Street, Toronto, Ont. M5W 1A7
Phone: (416) 596-5835   Fax: (416) 593-3170
Contact: Wayne Gooding, editor
Published weekly

Marketing Edge
1497 Marine Drive, Suite 300, West Vancouver, B.C. V7T 1B8
Phone: (604) 926-8765   Fax: (604) 926-7326
Contact: Blake Desaulniers, editor
Published bimonthly

Marketnews
501 Oakdale Road, Downsview, Ont. M3N 1W7
Phone: (416) 746-7360   Fax: (416) 746-1421
Contact: Robert Franner, editor
Published monthly

Meetings Monthly
1055 Beaver Hall, Suite 400, Montreal, Que. H2Y 3H1
Phone: (514) 274-0004   Fax: (514) 274-5884
Contact: Guy Jonkman, publisher/editor
Published 10 times a year

Modern Purchasing
777 Bay Street, Toronto, Ont. M5W 1A7
Phone: (416) 596-5704   Fax: (416) 596-5866
Contact: Joe Terrett, editor
Published 10 times a year

Pool & Spa Marketing
270 Esna Park Drive, Unit 12, Markham, Ont. L3R 1H3
Phone: (905) 513-0090   Fax: (905) 513-1377
Contact: David Barnsley, editor
Published 7 times a year

Shows & Exhibitions
720 King Street W., 5th Floor, Toronto, Ont. M5V 2T3
Phone: (416) 867-9500   Fax: (416) 867-9330
Contact: Nancy Remnant, managing editor
Published twice a year

Strategy
366 Adelaide Street W., Suite 500, Toronto, Ont. M5V 1R9
Phone: (416) 408-2300   Fax: (416) 408-0870
Contact: Mark Smyka, editor
Published biweekly

Automotive (see also Transportation & Cargo)

Automotive Retailer
120 – 4281 Canada Way, Burnaby, B.C. V5G 4P1
Phone: (604) 432-7987   Fax: (604) 432-1756
Contact: Reg Romero, editor
Published monthly

Bodyshop
1450 Don Mills Road, Don Mills, Ont. M3B 2X7
Phone: (416) 445-6641   Fax: (416) 442-2213
Contact: Brian Harper, editor
Published bimonthly

Canadian Auto World

1200 Markham Road, Suite 220, Scarborough, Ont. M1H 3C3
Phone: (416) 438-7777   Fax: (416) 438-5333
Contact: Michael Goetz, editor
Published monthly

Canadian Automotive Fleet

152 Parliament St., Toronto, Ont. M5A 2Z1
Phone: (416) 864-1700   Fax: (416) 864-1498
Contact: Kevin Sheehy, managing editor
Published bimonthly

Canadian RV Dealer

2585 Skymark Avenue, Suite 306, Mississauga, Ont. L4W 4L5
Phone: (416) 624-8218   Fax: (416) 624-6764
Contact: Norm Rosen, editor
Published bimonthly

Corporate Fleet Management

777 Bay Street, Toronto, Ont. M5W 1A7
Phone: (416) 596-5704   Fax: (416) 596-5866
Contact: Joe Terrett, editor
Published quarterly

Jobber News

1450 Don Mills Road, Don Mills, Ont. M3B 2X7
Phone: (416) 442-4101   Fax: (416) 442-2077
Contact: Bob Blans, editor
Published monthly

Motorcycle Dealer & Trade

86 Parliament Street, Studio 3B, Toronto, Ont. M5A 2Y6
Phone: (416) 362-7966   Fax: (416) 362-3950
Contact: Hugh McLean, editor
Published bimonthly

Octane

1015 Centre Street N., Suite 200, Calgary, Alta. T2E 2P8
Phone: (403) 276-7881   Fax: (403) 276-5026

Contact: David Coll, editor
Published quarterly

Service Station & Garage Management
1450 Don Mills Road, Don Mills, Ont. M3B 2X7
Phone: (416) 445-6641   Fax: (416) 442-2077
Contact: Gary Kenez, editor
Published monthly

Taxi News
38 Fairmount Crescent, Toronto, Ont. M4L 2H4
Phone: (416) 466-2328   Fax: (416) 466-4220
Contact: John Q. Duffy, publisher
Published monthly

Thunder Bay Car & Truck News
1145 Barton Street, Thunder Bay, Ont. P7B 5N3
Phone: (807) 623-2348   Fax: (807) 623-7515
Contact: Scott Sumner, publisher
Published biweekly

Western Automotive Repair
P.O. Box 64011, Winnipeg, Man. R2K 2Z4
Phone: (204) 654-3573   Fax: (204) 667-8922
Contact: Dan Proudley, editor
Published 9 times a year

Aviation & Aerospace

Airforce
100 Metcalfe Street, Ottawa, Ont. KIP 5W6
Phone: (613) 992-5184
Contact: Doug Stuebing, editor
Published quarterly

Aviation & Aerospace
310 Dupont Street, Toronto, Ont. M5R IV9
Phone: (416) 968-7252   Fax: (416) 968-2377

Contact: Garth Wallace, editor
Published bimonthly

The Canadian Aircraft Operator
P.O. Box 149, Mississauga, Ont. L4W 1V5
Phone: (905) 625-9660   Fax: (905) 625-9604
Contact: Edward Belitsky, editor
Published twice a month

Canadian Flight
P.O. Box 563, Station B, Ottawa, Ont. K1P 5P7
Phone: (613) 236-4901   Fax: (613) 236-8646
Contact: Doris Ohlmann, managing editor
Published quarterly

Canadian General Aviation News
P.O. Box 563, Station B, Ottawa, Ont. K1P 5P7
Phone: (613) 236-4901   Fax: (613) 236-8646
Contact: Doris Ohlmann, managing editor
Published monthly

Helicopters
1224 Aviation Park N.E., Suite 158, Calgary, Alta. T2E 7E2
Phone: (403) 275-9457   Fax: (403) 275-3925
Contact: Paul Skinner, editor/publisher
Published quarterly

ICAO Journal
Published by the International Civil Aviation Organization, 1000
    Sherbrooke Street W., Suite 327, Montreal, Que. H3A 2R2
Phone: (514) 285-8222   Fax: (514) 288-4772
Contact: Eric MacBurnie, editor
Published 10 times a year

Wings Magazine
1224 Aviation Park N.E., Suite 158, Calgary, Alta. T2E 7E2
Phone: (403) 275-9457   Fax: (403) 275-3925
Contact: Paul Skinner, editor/publisher
Published bimonthly

Building, Engineering, & Heavy Construction

Alberta Construction
124 West 8th Street, North Vancouver, B.C. v7m 3h2
Phone: (604) 985-8711   Fax: (604) 985-7399
Contact: Jim Hutson, editor
Published quarterly

Alumi-News
P.O. Box 400, Victoria Station, Westmount, Que. h3z 2v8
Phone: (514) 489-4941   Fax: (514) 489-5505
Contact: Nachmi Artzy, publisher
Published bimonthly

Award
4180 Lougheed Highway, Suite 401, Burnaby, B.C. v5c 6a7
Phone: (604) 299-7311   Fax: (604) 299-9188
Contact: Marisa Paterson, editor
Published 5 times a year

The B.C. Professional Engineer
6400 Roberts Street, Burnaby, B.C. v5g 4c9
Phone: (604) 929-6733   Fax: (604) 929-6753
Contact: Colleen Chen, editor
Published 10 times a year

Building Management & Design
1450 Don Mills Road, Don Mills, Ont. m3b 2x7
Phone: (416) 442-2166   Fax: (416) 442-2214
Contact: Cindy Woods, publisher/editor
Published 7 times a year

The Canadian Architect
1450 Don Mills Road, Don Mills, Ont. m3b 2x7
Phone: (416) 445-6641   Fax: (416) 442-2077
Contact: Bronwen Ledger, managing editor
Published monthly

Canadian Consulting Engineer
1450 Don Mills Road, Don Mills, Ont. M3B 2X7
Phone: (416) 445-6641   Fax: (416) 442-2214
Contact: Sophie Kneisel, editor
Published bimonthly

Canadian Industrial Equipment News
1450 Don Mills Road, Don Mills, Ont. M5B 2X7
Phone: (416) 445-6641   Fax: (416) 442-2214
Contact: Olga Markovich, editor
Published monthly

Canadian Masonry Contractor
1735 Bayly Street, Suite 7A, Pickering, Ont. L1W 3G7
Phone: (905) 831-4711
Contact: Tanja Nowotny, editor
Published quarterly

Canadian Roofing Contractor
1735 Bayly Street, Suite 7A, Pickering, Ont. L1W 3G7
Phone: (905) 831-4711
Contact: Tanja Nowotny, editor
Published quarterly

Civic Public Works
777 Bay Street, 5th Floor, Toronto, Ont. M5W 1A7
Phone: (416) 596-5953   Fax: (416) 593-3193
Contact: Fiona Hendry, editor
Published bimonthly

Construction Alberta News
10536 – 106th Street, Edmonton, Alta. T5H 2X6
Phone: (403) 424-1146   Fax: (403) 425-5886
Contact: Don Coates, editor
Published twice a week

Construction Canada
100 Lombard Street, Suite 200, Toronto, Ont. M5C 1M3

Phone: (416) 266-7009
Contact: Stuart Frost, editor
Published bimonthly

Construction Comment

920 Yonge Street, 6th Floor, Toronto, Ont. M4W 3C7
Phone: (416) 961-1028   Fax: (416) 924-4408
Contact: Gregory Kero, editor
Published twice a year

Daily Commercial News & Construction Record

280 Yorkland Boulevard, Willowdale, Ont. M2J 4Z6
Phone: (416) 494-4990   Fax: (416) 756-2767
Contact: Scott Button, editor

Design Engineering

777 Bay Street, Toronto, Ont. M5W 1A7
Phone: (416) 596-5833   Fax: (416) 596-5881
Contact: Steve Purwitsky, editor
Published monthly

Engineering Dimensions

1155 Yonge Street, Suite 101, Toronto, Ont. M4T 2Y5
Phone: (416) 961-1100   Fax: (416) 961-1499
Contact: Connie Mucklestone, managing editor
Published bimonthly

Hardware Merchandising Building Supply Dealer

777 Bay Street, Toronto, Ont. M5W 1A7
Phone: (416) 596-5259   Fax: (416) 593-3201
Contact: Michael McLarney, editor
Published 10 times a year

Heavy Construction News

777 Bay Street, Toronto, Ont. M5W 1A7
Phone: (416) 596-5844   Fax: (416) 593-3193
Contact: Russ Noble, editor
Published monthly

Northpoint
10 Four Seasons Place, Suite 404, Etobicoke, Ont. M9B 6H7
Phone: (416) 620-1885   Fax: (416) 621-8694
Contact: Robert Fowler, editor
Published quarterly

The Pegg
10060 Jasper Avenue, 15th Floor, Tower One, Scotia Place,
    Edmonton, Alta. T5J 4A2
Phone: (403) 426-3990   Fax: (403) 426-1877
Contact: Trevor Maine, managing editor
Published 10 times a year

Toronto Construction News
280 Yorkland Boulevard, Willowdale, Ont. M2J 4Z6
Phone: (416) 494-4990   Fax: (416) 756-2767
Contact: Randy Threndyle, managing editor
Published bimonthly

What's New in Welding
245 Fairview Mall Drive, Suite 500, Willowdale, Ont. M2J 4T1
Phone: (416) 490-0220   Fax: (416) 496-2625
Contact: Glen Alton, publisher (ph. 596-5000)
Published bimonthly

Business, Commerce, Banking, Law, Insurance, & Pensions

Arabusiness International
370 Queen Street E., Toronto, Ont. M5A 1T1
Phone: (416) 362-0304   Fax: (416) 861-0238
Contact: Salah Allam, publisher/editor
Published biweekly

Atlantic Chamber Journal
95 Foundry Street, Heritage Court, Suite 116, Moncton,
    N.B. E1C 5H7
Phone: (506) 858-8710   Fax: (586) 858-1707

Contact: Jerry Poirier, publisher
Published bimonthly

Benefits Canada
777 Bay Street, Toronto, Ont. M5W 1A7
Phone: (416) 596-5958   Fax: (416) 593-3166
Contact: Paul Williams, editor
Published 11 times a year

Benefits and Pensions Monitor
235 Yorkland Boulevard, 3rd Floor, North York, M2J 4Y8
Phone: (416) 494-1066   Fax: (416) 946-8931
Contact: Robin Schiele, managing editor
Published bimonthly

The Bottom Line
75 Clegg Road, Suite 200, Markham, Ont. L6G 1A1
Phone: (905) 415-5803   Fax: (905) 479-3758
Contact: Michael Lewis, editor
Published monthly

The Business Advocate
244 Pall Mall Street, P.O. Box 3295, London, Ont. N6A 5P6
Phone: (519) 432-7551   Fax: (519) 432-8063
Contact: John Redmond, editor
Published monthly

The Business & Professional Woman
95 Leeward Glenway, Unit 121, Don Mills, Ont. M3C 2Z6
Phone: (416) 424-1393   Fax: (416) 467-8262
Contact: Valerie Dunn, editor
Published quarterly

Business in Vancouver
1235 West Pender Street, Lower Floor, Vancouver, B.C. V6E 2V6
Phone: (604) 688-2398   Fax: (604) 688-1963
Contact: Peter Ladner, editor/publisher
Published weekly

Business Quarterly

University of Western Ontario, Western Business School, London,
Ont. N6A 3K7
Phone: (519) 661-3309   Fax: (519) 661-3838
Contact: Angela Smith, managing editor
Published quarterly

The Business Times

231 Dundas Street, Suite 203, London, Ont. N6A 1H1
Phone: (519) 679-4901   Fax: (519) 434-7842
Contact: David Helwig, editor
Published 13 times a year

CA Magazine

Published by The Canadian Institute of Chartered Accountants,
277 Wellington Street W., Toronto, Ont. M5V 3H2
Phone: (416) 977-3222   Fax: (416) 204-3409
Contact: Nelson Luscombe, editor/publisher
Published 10 times a year

CGA Magazine

Published by the Certified General Accountants' Association of
Canada, 1188 West Georgia Street, Suite 700, Vancouver,
B.C. V6E 4E2
Phone: (604) 669-3555   Fax: (604) 689-5845
Contact: Lesley Wood, editor
Published monthly

CMA Magazine

Published by the Society of Management Accountants of Canada,
P.O. Box 176, Hamilton, Ont. L8N 3C3
Phone: (905) 525-4100   Fax: (905) 525-4533
Contact: Kevin Graham, associate publisher
Published 10 times a year

Canada Japan Business Journal

220 Cambie Street, Suite 370, Vancouver, B.C. V6B 2M9
Phone: (604) 688-2486   Fax: (604) 688-1487

Contact: Taka Aoki, editor
Published monthly

Canadian Banker

P.O. Box 348, Commerce Court Postal Station, Toronto,
Ont. M5L 1G2
Phone: (416) 362-6092   Fax: (416) 362-5658
Contact: Bruce McDougall, editor
Published bimonthly

Canadian Bar Review

50 O'Connor Street, Suite 902, Ottawa, Ont. K1P 6L2
Phone: (613) 237-2925   Fax: (613) 237-0185
Contact: A. J. McClean, editor
Published quarterly

Canadian Insurance

111 Peter Street, Suite 202, Toronto, Ont. M5V 2H1
Phone: (416) 599-0772   Fax: (416) 599-0867
Contact: Sally Praskey, editor
Published monthly

The Canadian Manager

2175 Sheppard Avenue E., Suite 110, Willowdale, Ont. M2J 1W8
Phone: (416) 493-0155   Fax: (416) 491-1670
Contact: Ruth Max, editor
Published quarterly

Canadian Shareowner

1090 University Avenue W., Suite 204, Windsor, Ont. N9A 5S4
Phone: (519) 252-9965   Fax: (519) 252-9570
Contact: John T. Bart, editor
Published bimonthly

Canadian Underwriter

1450 Don Mills Road, Don Mills, Ont. M5B 2X7
Phone: (416) 445-6641   Fax: (416) 442-2213

Contact: Larry Welsh, managing editor
Published monthly

Charitable Business
4040 Creditview Road, Unit 11, P.O. Box 6900, Mississauga,
    Ont. L5C 3Y8
Phone: (905) 569-1800   Fax: (905) 569-1818
Contact: Terry Hrynyshyn, editor
Published bimonthly

Church Business
4040 Creditview Road, Unit 11, P.O. Box 6900, Mississauga,
    Ont. L5C 3Y8
Phone: (905) 569-1800   Fax: (905) 569-1818
Contact: Terry Hrynyshyn, editor
Published bimonthly

Commerce
P.O. Box 624, Lacombe, Alta. TOC 1S0
Phone: (403) 782-7356   Fax: (403) 782-7356
Contact: Ted Proud, publisher/editor
Published bimonthly

Commerce News
10123 – 99th Street, Suite 600, Edmonton, Alta. T5J 3G9
Phone: (403) 426-4620   Fax: (403) 424-7946
Contact: Gretchen Ziegler, editor
Published 10 times a year

Commercial News
201 Brownlow Avenue, Suite 33, Burnside Park, Dartmouth,
    N.S. B2Y 3Y5
Phone: (902) 468-2682   Fax: (902) 468-3996
Contact: Jim Gourlay, editor-in-chief
Published 9 times a year

Communication
Published by the Institute of Chartered Accountants of B.C., 1133

Melville Street, 6th Floor, Vancouver, B.C. V6E 4E5
Phone: (604) 681-3264   Fax: (604) 681-1523
Contact: Penelope Noble, editor
Published 11 times a year

Equity

1178 West Pender Street, Suite 200, Vancouver, B.C. V6E 2R5
Phone: (604) 684-1414   Fax: (604) 684-6907
Contact: David Hanley, editor
Published 10 times a year

Exchange

215 Fairway Road, Kitchener, Ont. N2G 4E5
Phone: (519) 894-1630; Toronto (416) 826-9182
     Fax: (519) 894-2173
Contact: Alan Howell, editor
Published monthly

The Financial Post

333 King Street E., Toronto, Ont. M5A 4N2
Phone: (416) 350-6000   Fax: (416) 350-6080
Contact: Diane Francis, editor
Published daily

Financial Times of Canada

440 Front Street W., Toronto, Ont. M5V 3E6
Phone: (416) 585-5555   Fax: (416) 585-5549
Contact: Steve Lawrence, editor
Published weekly

Government Business

4040 Creditview Road, Unit 11, P.O. Box 6900, Mississauga,
     Ont. L5C 3Y8
Phone: (905) 569-1800   Fax: (905) 569-1818
Contact: Terry Hrynyshyn, editor
Published monthly

Halton Business Journal

1439 Speers Road, Oakville, Ont. L6L 2X5

Phone: (905) 847-1404
Contact: Roy Wilson, editor
Published monthly

Hamilton Business Report
361 King Street W., Hamilton, Ont. L8P 1B4
Phone: (905) 522-6117   Fax: (905) 529-2242
Contact: Elizabeth Kelly, editor-in-chief
Published quarterly

Head Office at Home
145 Royal Crest Court, Unit 2, Markham, Ont. L3R 9Z4
Phone: (905) 477-4349
Contact: Elizabeth Harris, editor
Published bimonthly

Human Resources Professional
2 Bloor Street W., Suite 1902, Toronto, Ont. M4W 3E2
Phone: (416) 923-2324   Fax: (416) 923-7264
Contact: Joanne Eidinger, editor
Published monthly

Huronia Business Times
24 Dunlop Street E., 2nd Floor, Barrie, Ont. L4M 1A3
Phone: (705) 721-1450   Fax: (705) 721-1449
Contact: Rebecca Corbeil, editor
Published 10 times a year

In Business Windsor
4510 Rhodes Drive, Building 800, Suite 805, Windsor,
    Ont. N8W 5C2
Phone: (519) 974-2267   Fax: (519) 974-3867
Contact: Alan Halberstadt, editor
Published monthly

Journal of Commerce
4285 Canada Way, Burnaby, B.C. V5G 1H2
Phone: (604) 433-8164   Fax: (604) 433-9549

Contact: Frank Lillquist, editor
Published twice a week

Kootenay Business Journal
P.O. Box 784, Nelson, B.C. v1L 5P5
Phone: (604) 352-6397   Fax: (604) 352-2588
Contact: Jeff Shecter, publisher/editor
Published monthly

Kootenay Business Magazine
1510 – 2nd Street N., Cranbrook, B.C. v1C 3L2
Phone: (604) 489-3455
Contact: Daryl Shellborn, publisher
Published monthly

LUAC Forum
Published by The Life Underwriters' Association of Canada,
    41 Lesmill Road, Don Mills, Ont. M3B 2T3
Phone: (416) 444-5251   Fax: (416) 444-8031
Contact: Val Osborne, editor
Published 10 times a year

Law Times
240 Edward Street, Aurora, Ont. L4G 3S9
Phone: (905) 841-6481   Fax: (905) 841-5078
Contact: Paula Kulig, managing editor
Published weekly

The Lawyers Weekly
75 Clegg Road, Markham, Ont. L6G 1A1
Phone: (905) 415-5804   Fax: (905) 479-3758
Contact: Don Brillinger, editor

London Business Monthly Magazine
P.O. Box 7400, London, Ont. N5Y 4X3
Phone: (519) 472-7601   Fax: (519) 473-2256
Contact: Janine Foster, managing editor
Published monthly

Manitoba Business
470 River Avenue, 3rd Floor, Winnipeg, Man. R3L 0C8
Phone: (204) 477-4620   Fax: (204) 284-3255
Contact: Ritchie Gage, editor
Published 10 times a year

Mississauga Business Report Magazine
3145 Wolfedale Road, Mississauga, Ont. L5C 3A9
Phone: (905) 273-8104   Fax: (905) 273-9127
Contact: Jim Robinson, editor
Published 8 times a year

Mississauga Business Times
1606 Sedlescomb Drive, Unit 8, Mississauga, Ont. L4X 1M6
Phone: (905) 625-7070   Fax: (905) 625-4856
Contact: Adam Gutteridge, managing editor
Published 10 times a year

Montreal Business Magazine
275 St. Jacques Street W., Suite 43, Montreal, Que. H2Y 1M9
Phone: (514) 286-8038
Contact: Mark Weller, publisher
Published bimonthly

Muskoka Focus on Business
P.O. Box 1600, Bracebridge, Ont. P1L 1V6
Phone: (705) 645-4463   Fax: (705) 645-3928
Contact: Donald Smith, publisher
Published bimonthly

National (The Canadian Bar Association)
777 Bay Street, 5th Floor, Toronto, Ont. M5W 1A7
Phone: (416) 596-5247   Fax: (416) 593-3162
Contact: J. Stuart Langford, editor
Published 8 times a year

Northern Ontario Business
158 Elgin Street, Sudbury, Ont. P3E 3N5

Phone: (705) 673-5705   Fax: (705) 673-9542
Contact: Mark Sandford, publisher/editor
Published monthly

Office Productivity
777 Bay Street, Toronto, Ont, M5W 1A7
Phone: (416) 596-5920   Fax: (416) 593-3166
Contact: Tom Kelly, editor
Published 10 times a year

Okanagan Business Magazine
P.O. Box 1479, Station A, Kelowna, B.C. V1Y 7V8
Phone: (604) 861-5399   Fax: (604) 868-3040
Contact: J. Paul Byrne, publisher/managing editor
Published 10 times a year

Ontario Business Journal
100 Main Street E., 40th Floor, Hamilton, Ont. L8N 3W6
Phone: (905) 526-8600   Fax: (905) 0086
Contact: managing editor
Published monthly

Ottawa Business News
77 Auriga Drive, Unit 3, Nepean, Ont. K2E 7Z7
Phone: (613) 727-1400   Fax: (613) 727-1010
Contact: Mark Sutcliffe, editor
Published biweekly

Ottawa Business Quarterly
192 Bank Street, Ottawa, Ont. K2P 1W8
Phone: (613) 234-7751   Fax: (613) 234-9226
Contact: Rosa Harris-Adler, editor

Sports Business
501 Oakdale Road, Downsview, Ont. M3N 1W7
Phone: (416) 746-7360   Fax: (416) 746-1421
Contact: Melanie Franner, editor
Published 8 times a year

This Week in Business
250 St. Antoine Street W., Montreal, Que. H2Y 3R7
Phone: (514) 987-2512   Fax: (514) 987-2433
Contact: David Perks, publisher
Published weekly

Toronto Business Magazine
Zanny Ltd., 11966, Woodbine Avenue, Gormley, Ont. L0H 1G0
Phone: (905) 887-4813   Fax: (905) 479-4834
Contact: Janet Gardiner, publisher
Published bimonthly

Trade and Commerce
P.O. Box 6900, 1700 Church Avenue, Winnipeg, Man. R3C 3B1
Phone: (204) 632-2606   Fax: (204) 694-3040
Contact: Laura Jean Stewart, editor
Published 5 times a year

Western Commerce & Industry
945 King Edward Street, Winnipeg, Man. R3H 0P8
Phone: (204) 775-0387   Fax: (204) 775-7830
Contact: Kelly Gray, editor
Published bimonthly

World Business
1010 Polytek Street, Suite 13, Gloucester, Ont. K1J 9H9
Phone: (613) 747-2732   Fax: (613) 747-2735
Contact: Douglas MacArthur, publisher/editor
Published monthly

The York Region Business Journal
505 Hood Road, Unit 9, Markham, Ont. L3R 5V6
Phone: (905) 940-4922   Fax: (905) 940-4931
Contact: Angela Piper, publisher
Published monthly

Clothing, Accessories, & Footwear

Canadian Apparel Manufacturer
1, rue Pacifique, Ste.-Anne-de-Bellevue, Que. H9X 1C5
Phone: (514) 457-2347   Fax: (514) 457-2147
Contact: Kathryn Hanley, editor
Published monthly

Canadian Footwear Journal
1, rue Pacifique, Ste.-Anne-de-Bellevue, Que. H9X 1C5
Phone: (514) 457-2423   Fax: (514) 457-2577
Contact: Barbara McLeish, managing editor
Published 9 times a year

Canadian Jeweller
1448 Lawrence Avenue W., Suite 302, Toronto, Ont. M4A 2V6
Phone: (416) 755-5199   Fax: (416) 755-9123
Contact: Pat McLean, editor
Published bimonthly

Ego
254 Brighton Drive, Beaconsfield, Que. H9W 2L4
Phone: (514) 426-1446   Fax: (514) 426-1448
Contact: Lawrence Schwartz, editor-in-chief
Published quarterly

Elan
1620 Pine Avenue W., Montreal, Que. H3G 1B4
Phone: (514) 931-7322   Fax: (514) 931-0254
Contact: Eileen Collyer, editor
Published bimonthly

Footwear Forum
1448 Lawrence Avenue E., Suite 302, Toronto, Ont. M4A 2V6
Phone: (416) 755-5199   Fax: (416) 755-9123
Contact: Victoria Curran, editor
Published 7 times a year

Jewellery World
20 Eglinton Avenue W., Toronto, Ont. M4R 1K8
Phone: (416) 480-1450   Fax: (416) 480-2342
Contact: Jonathon Reid, editor
Published bimonthly

Luggage, Leathergoods & Accessories
501 Oakdale Road, Downsview, Ont. M3N 1W7
Phone: (416) 746-7360   Fax: (416) 746-1421
Contact: Virginia Hutton, publisher/editor
Published 5 times a year

Salon Magazine
146 Parliament Street, Toronto, Ont. M5A 2Z1
Phone: (416) 869-3131   Fax: (416) 869-3008
Contact: Greg Robins, editor
Published 5 times a year

Style
1448 Lawrence Avenue E., Suite 302, Toronto, Ont. M4A 2V6
Phone: (416) 755-5199   Fax: (416) 755-9123
Contact: Marsha Ross, editor
Published 16 times a year

Data Processing

CAD Systems
395 Matheson Boulevard E., Mississauga, Ont. L4Z 2H2
Phone: (905) 890-1846   Fax: (905) 890-5769
Contact: Graham Pitcher, editor
Published 7 times a year

Canadian Computer Reseller
777 Bay Street, Toronto, Ont. M5W 1A7
Phone: (416) 596-2640   Fax: (416) 596-5553
Contact: Kevin McKee, editor
Published twice a month

Computer Dealer News

2005 Sheppard Avenue E., 4th Floor, Willowdale, Ont. M2J 5B1
Phone: (416) 497-9562   Fax: (416) 497-9427
Contact: Paul Plesman, publisher
Published twice a month

The Computer Paper

3661 West 4th Avenue, Suite 8, Vancouver, B.C. V6R 1P2
Phone: (604) 733-5596   Fax: (604) 732-4280
Contact: Douglas Alder, publisher/editor
Published monthly

The Computer Post

P.O. Box 1481, Winnipeg, Man. R3C 2Z4
Phone: (204) 947-9766   Fax: (204) 947-9767
Contact: Robert Li, editor-in-chief
Published monthly

Computing Canada

2005 Sheppard Avenue E., 4th Floor, Willowdale, Ont. M2J 5B1
Phone: (416) 497-9562   Fax: (416) 497-9427
Contact: Gordon Campbell, editor
Published twice a month

Computerworld Canada

501 Oakdale Road, Downsview, Ont. M3N 1W7
Phone: (416) 746-7360   Fax: (416) 746-1421
Contact: Andrew White, publisher
Published twice a month

Government Computing Digest

132 Adrian Crescent, Markham, Ont. L3P 7B3
Phone: (905) 472-2801   Fax: (905) 472-3091
Contact: Gordon Campbell, editor
Published bimonthly

Hum Magazine: The Government Computing Magazine

202 – 557 Cambridge Street S., Ottawa, Ont. K1S 4J4
Phone: (613) 237-4862   Fax: (613) 237-4232

Contact: Lee Hunter, publisher
Published 11 times a year

Information Technology (I.T.) Magazine
777 Bay Street, Toronto, Ont. M5W 1A7
Phone: (416) 596-5908   Fax: (416) 593-3166
Contact: David Carey, editor
Published monthly

Info Canada
501 Oakdale Road, Downsview, Ont. M3N 1W7
Phone: (416) 746-7360   Fax: (416) 746-1421
Contact: John Pickett, editor-in-chief
Published monthly

Network World
501 Oakdale Road, Downsview, Ont. M3N 1W7
Phone: (416) 746-7360   Fax: (416) 746-1421
Contact: John Pickett, editor
Published monthly

Education & School Management

The ATA Magazine (Alberta Teachers' Association)
11010 – 142nd Street, Edmonton, Alta. T5N 2R1
Phone: (403) 453-2411
Contact: Timothy Johnston, editor
Published quarterly

The Canadian School Executive
P.O. Box 48265, Bentall Court, Vancouver, B.C. V7X 1A1
Phone: (604) 739-8600   Fax: (604) 739-8200
Contact: Dr. Joe Fris, editor
Published 10 times a year

Education Digest
Zanny Ltd., 11966 Woodbine Avenue, Gormley, Ont. L0H 1G0
Phone: (905) 887-4813   Fax: (905) 479-4834

Contact: Janet Gardiner, publisher
Published 5 times a year

Education Today
439 University Avenue, 18th Floor, Toronto, Ont. M5G 1V8
Phone: (416) 340-2540   Fax: (416) 340-7571
Contact: Heather Dion, editor
Published 5 times a year

Quebec Home & School News
3285 Cavendish Boulevard, Suite 562, Montreal, Que. H4B 2L9
Phone: (514) 481-5619
Contact: Charlene De Conde, editor
Published 5 times a year

The Reporter
65 St. Clair Ave. East, Toronto, Ont. M4T 2Y8
Phone: (416) 925-2493   Fax: (416) 925-7764
Contact: Aleda O'Connor, editor
Published 5 times a year

School Business
4040 Creditview Road, Unit 11, P.O. Box 6900, Mississauga,
    Ont. L5C 3Y8
Phone: (905) 569-1800   Fax: (905) 569-1818
Contact: Terry Hrynyshyn, editor
Published bimonthly

The School Trustee
2222 – 13th Avenue, Suite 400, Regina, Sask. S4P 3M7
Phone: (306) 569-0750
Contact: Leslie Anderson, editor
Published 5 times a year

University Affairs
151 Slater Street, Ottawa, Ont. K1P 5N1
Phone: (613) 563-1236   Fax: (613) 563-9745
Contact: Christine Tausig Ford, editor
Published 10 times a year

University Manager
388 Donald Street, Suite 200, Winnipeg, Man. R3B 2J4
Phone: (204) 957-0265   Fax: (204) 957-0217
Contact: Andrea Kuch, editor
Published quarterly

Electronics & Electrical

Canadian Electronics
135 Spy Court, Markham, Ont. L3R 5H6
Phone: (905) 447-3222   Fax: (905) 477-4320
Contact: Mark Langton, editor
Published monthly

ESE (Electrical Systems Engineer) Magazine
395 Matheson Boulevard E., Mississauga, Ont. L4Z 2H2
Phone: (905) 890-1846   Fax: (905) 890-5769
Contact: Hugh McBride, editorial director
Published quarterly

Electrical Business
395 Matheson Blvd. E., Mississauga, Ont. L4Z 2H2
Phone: (905) 890-1846   Fax: (905) 890-5769
Contact: Hugh McBride, editor
Published monthly

Electrical Equipment News
1450 Don Mills Road, Don Mills, Ont. M3B 2X7
Phone: (416) 445-6641   Fax: (416) 442-2214
Contact: Olga Markovich, editor/associate publisher
Published bimonthly

Electricity Today
900 McKay Road, Unit 3, Pickering, Ont. L1W 3X8
Phone: (905) 428-2299   Fax: (905) 428-7040
Contact: Randolph Hurst, publisher
Published 10 times a year

Electronic Products & Technology
1200 Aerowood Drive, Unit 27, Mississauga, Ont. L4W 2S7
Phone: (905) 624-8100   Fax: (905) 624-1760
Contact: David Kerfoot, editor
Published 8 times a year

Energy, Mining, Forestry, Lumber, Pulp & Paper, & Fisheries

Atlantic Fisherman
1869 Upper Water Street, 3rd Floor, Collins Bank Building,
    Halifax, N.S. B3J 1S9
Phone: (902) 422-4990   Fax: (902) 422-4728
Contact: John MacIntyre, editor
Published monthly

Canadian Forest Industries
1, rue Pacifique, Ste.-Anne-de-Bellevue, Que. H9X 1C5
Phone: (514) 457-2211   Fax: (514) 457-2558
Contact: Scott Jamieson, editor
Published 8 times a year

Canadian Mill Product News
1625 Ingleton Avenue, Burnaby, B.C. V5C 4L8
Phone: (604) 298-3004   Fax: (604) 291-1906
Contact: Toni Dabbs, editor
Published bimonthly

Canadian Mining Journal
1450 Don Mills Road, Don Mills, Ont. M3B 2X7
Phone: (416) 445-6641   Fax: (416) 442-2272
Contact: Patrick Whiteway, editor
Published bimonthly

Canadian Papermaker
777 Bay Street, Toronto, Ont. M5W 1A7
Phone: (416) 596-5832   Fax: (416) 593-3193
Contact: Wayne Karl, editor
Published monthly

Canadian Wood Processing
P.O. Box 14, Lachine, Que. H8S 4A5
Phone: (514) 333-1116   Fax: (514) 631-8858
Contact: Keith Fredericks, editor
Published bimonthly

Canadian Wood Products
1, rue Pacifique, Ste.-Anne-de-Bellevue, Que. H9X 1C5
Phone: (514) 457-2211   Fax: (514) 457-2558
Contact: Scott Jamieson, editor
Published bimonthly

Energy Processing/Canada
1600, 700 – 4th Avenue S.W., Calgary, Alta. T2P 3J4
Phone: (403) 263-6881   Fax: (403) 263-6886
Contact: Scott Jeffrey, publisher
Published bimonthly

The Fisherman
111 Victoria Drive, Suite 160, Vancouver, B.C. V5L 4C4
Phone: (604) 255-1366   Fax: (604) 255-3162
Contact: Sean Griffin, editor
Published monthly

The Forestry Chronicle
151 Slater Street, Suite 1005, Ottawa, Ont. K1P 5H3
Phone: (613) 234-2242   Fax: (613) 234-6181
Contact: J.H. Cayford, D. Burgess, editors
Published bimonthly

Hiballer Forest Magazine
106 – 14th Street E., Suite 11, North Vancouver, B.C. V7L 2N3
Phone: (604) 984-2002   Fax: (604) 984-2820
Contact: Paul Young, managing editor
Published bimonthly

Logging and Sawmilling Journal
1130 West Pender Street, Suite 900, Vancouver, B.C. V6E 4A4
Phone: (604) 683-8254   Fax: (604) 683-8202

Contact: Norm Poole, editor (ph. 462-7750)
Published 9 times a year

Mining Review
124 West 8th Street, North Vancouver, B.C. v7M 3H2
Phone: (604) 985-8711   Fax: (604) 985-7399
Contact: Jim Hutson, editor
Published quarterly

The Northern Miner
1450 Don Mills Road, Don Mills, Ont. M3B 2X7
Phone: (416) 445-6641   Fax: (416) 442-2272
Contact: John Cooke, publisher
Published weekly

Oil Patch Magazine
17560 – 107th Avenue, 2nd Floor, Edmonton, Alta. T5S 1E9
Phone: (403) 486-1295   Fax: (403) 484-0884
Contact: L.M. Hyman, publisher
Published bimonthly

Oilweek
110 – 6th Avenue S.W., Suite 2459, Calgary, Alta. T2P 3P4
Phone: (403) 266-8700   Fax: (403) 266-6634
Contact: David Coll, editor
Published weekly

Propane/Canada
700 – 4th Avenue S.W., Suite 1600, Calgary, Alta. T2P 3J4
Phone: (403) 263-6881   Fax: (403) 263-6886
Contact: Scott Jeffrey, publisher
Published bimonthly

Pulp & Paper Canada
3300 Côte Vertu, Suite 410, St. Laurent, Que. H4R 2B7
Phone: (514) 339-1399   Fax: (514) 339-1396
Contact: Susan Stevenson, editor
Published monthly

The Roughneck
700 – 4th Avenue S.W., 16th Floor, Calgary, Alta. T2P 3J4
Phone: (403) 263-6881   Fax: (403) 263-6886
Contact: Scott Jeffrey, publisher
Published monthly

Silviculture: Journal of the New Forest
1130 West Pender Street, Suite 900, Vancouver, B.C. V6E 4A4
Phone: (604) 683-8254   Fax: (604) 683-8202
Contact: Deborra Schug, editor
Published quarterly

The Sou'wester
P.O. Box 128, Yarmouth, N.S. B5A 4B1
Phone: (902) 742-7111   Fax: (902) 742-2311
Contact: Alain Meuse, editor
Published biweekly

Truck Logger Magazine
744 West Hastings Street, Suite 510, Vancouver, B.C. V6C 1A5
Phone: (604) 682-4080   Fax: (604) 682-3775
Contact: John Doyle, editor/publisher
Published bimonthly

The Westcoast Mariner
1496 West 72nd Avenue, Vancouver, B.C. V6P 3C8
Phone: (604) 266-7433   Fax: (604) 263-8620
Contact: David Rahn, publisher
Published monthly

Environmental Science & Management

Canadian Environmental Protection
1625 Ingleton Avenue, Burnaby, B.C. V5C 4L8
Phone: (604) 291-9900   Fax: (604) 291-1906
Contact: Dan Kennedy, editor
Published 9 times a year

Environmental Science & Engineering
10 Petch Crescent, Aurora, Ont. L4G 5N7
Phone: (905) 727-4666   Fax: (905) 841-7271
Contact: Tom Davey, publisher/editor
Published bimonthly

Hazardous Materials Management
401 Richmond Street W., Suite 139, Toronto, Ont. M5V 1X3
Phone: (416) 348-9922   Fax: (416) 348-9744
Contact: Guy Crittenden, editor
Published bimonthly

Recycling Product News
1625 Ingleton Avenue, Burnaby, B.C. V5C 4L8
Phone: (604) 291-9900   Fax: (604) 291-1906
Contact: Dan Kennedy, editor
Published bimonthly

Water & Pollution Control
Zanny Ltd., 11966 Woodbine Avenue, Gormley, Ont. L0H 1G0
Phone: (905) 887-4813   Fax: (905) 479-4834
Contact: Amy Margaret, editor
Published bimonthly

Farming

B.C. Orchardist
P.O. Drawer 423, 7602 Hudson Road, Salmon Arm, B.C. V1E 4N6
Phone: (604) 832-7703   Fax: (604) 832-4404
Contact: Ted Noonan and Frank Roberts, editors
Published monthly

Breeder & Feeder
50 Dovercliffe Road, Unit 6, Guelph, Ont. N1G 3A6
Phone: (519) 824-0334   Fax: (519) 824-9101
Contact: Joanne Hewitson, editor
Published 6 times a year

Butter-Fat
6800 Lougheed Highway, Burnaby, B.C.
Phone: (604) 420-6611   Fax: (604) 520-1626
Contact: Carol Paulson, managing editor
Published quarterly

Canada Poultryman
9547 – 152nd Street, Suite 105B, Surrey, B.C. V3R 5Y5
Phone: (604) 585-3131   Fax: (604) 585-1504
Contact: Tony Greaves, editor and manager
Published monthly

Canadian Fruitgrower
222 Argyle Avenue, Delhi, Ont. N4B 2Y2
Phone: (519) 582-2513   Fax: (519) 582-4040
Contact: Ben Steidman, editor
Published 9 times a year

Canadian Guernsey Journal
368 Woolwich Street, Guelph, Ont. N1H 3W6
Phone: (519) 836-2141
Contact: V. Macdonald, editor
Published bimonthly

Canadian Hereford Digest
5160 Skyline Way N.E., Calgary, Alta. T2E 6V1
Phone: (403) 274-1734
Contact: Kurt Gilmore, editor
Published monthly

Canadian Jersey Breeder
350 Speedvale Avenue W., Unit 9, Guelph, Ont. N1H 7M7
Phone: (519) 821-9150   Fax: (519) 821-2723
Contact: Betty Clements, editor
Published 10 times a year

Cattlemen
Box 6600, Winnipeg, Man. R3C 3A7

Phone: (204) 944-5760   Fax: (204) 942-8463
Contact: Gren Winslow, editor
Published 11 times a year

Corn–Soy Guide
Box 6600, Winnipeg, Man. R3C 3A7
Phone: (204) 944-5760   Fax: (204) 942-8463
Contact: Dave Wreford, editor
Published 3 times a year

Country Guide
Box 6600, Winnipeg, Man. R3C 3A7
Phone: (204) 944-5760   Fax: (204) 942-8463
Contact: Dave Wreford, editor
Published 10 times a year

Country Life in B.C.
3308 King George Highway, Surrey, B.C. V4P 1A8
Phone: (604) 536-7622   Fax: (604) 536-5677
Contact: Malcolm Young, editor
Published monthly

Dairy Contact
11802 – 124th Street, Suite 210, Edmonton, Alta. T5L 0M3
Phone: (403) 455-4173   Fax: (403) 455-4174
Contact: Dr. Allen Parr, editor/publisher
Published monthly

Dairy Guide
Box 6600, Winnipeg, Man. R3C 3A7
Phone: (204) 944-5760   Fax: (204) 942-8463
Contact: D. Wilkins, editor
Published quarterly

Farm & Country
100 Broadview Avenue, Suite 402, Toronto, Ont. M4M 3H3
Phone: (416) 463-8080   Fax: (416) 463-1075
Contact: John Muggeridge, managing editor
Published 18 times a year

Farm Focus
P.O. Box 128, Yarmouth, N.S. B5A 4B1
Phone: (902) 742-7111   Fax: (902) 742-2311
Contact: Heather Jones, editor
Published biweekly

The Farm Gate
15 King Street, Elmira, Ont. N3B 2R1
Phone: (519) 669-5155
Contact: Bob Verdun, editor/publisher
Published monthly

Farm Light & Power
2330 – 15th Avenue, Regina, Sask. S4P 1A2
Phone: (306) 525-3305   Fax: (306) 757-1810
Contact: L.T. Bradley, publisher
Published 10 times a year

The Giant Farm Life
Bag 5012, Main Post Office, Red Deer, Alta. T4N 6R4
Phone: (403) 346-3356   Fax: (403) 347-6620
Contact: Keith Rideout, manager
Published biweekly

Grainews
Box 6600, Winnipeg, Man. R3C 3A7
Phone: (204) 944-5411   Fax: (204) 944-5416
Contact: John Clark, publisher
Published 17 times a year

The Grower
355 Elmira Road, Suite 103, Guelph, Ont. N1K 1S5
Phone: (519) 763-8728   Fax: (519) 763-6604
Contact: Blair Adams, editor
Published monthly

Holstein Journal
333 Lesmill Road, Don Mills, Ont. M3B 2V1
Phone: (416) 441-3030   Fax: (416) 441-3038

Contact: Bonnie Cooper, editor
Published monthly

The Manitoba Co-operator
P.O. Box 9800, Winnipeg, Man. R3C 3K7
Phone: (204) 934-0401   Fax: (204) 934-0480
Contact: John Morriss, publisher/editor
Published weekly

Niagara Farmers' Monthly
P.O. Box 52, Smithville, Ont. LOR 2AO
Phone: (905) 957-3751   Fax: (905) 957-0088
Contact: Ivan Carruthers, publisher
Published 11 times a year

Ontario Corn Producer
222 Argyle Avenue, Delhi, Ont. N4B 2Y2
Phone: (519) 582-2513   Fax: (519) 582-4040
Contact: Terry Boland, managing editor
Published 11 times a year

Ontario Farmer
P.O. Box 7400, London, Ont. N5Y 4X3
Phone: (519) 473-0010   Fax: (519) 473-2256
Contact: Paul Mahon, editor
Published weekly

Ontario Milk Producer
P.O. Box 7400, London, Ont. N5Y 4X3
Phone: (519) 473-0010   Fax: (519) 473-2256
Contact: Bill Dimmick, editor
Published monthly

Quebec Farmers' Advocate
P.O. Box 80, Ste.-Anne-de-Bellevue, Que. H9X 3L4
Phone: (514) 457-2010   Fax: (514) 398-7972
Contact: Steve Gruber, editor
Published 10 times a year

Rural Roots

30 – 10th Street E., P.O. Box 550, Prince Albert, Sask. s6v 5r9
Phone: (306) 764-4276   Fax: (306) 763-3331
Contact: Barb Gustafson, editor
Published weekly

The Rural Voice

P.O. Box 429, 136 Queen Street, Blyth, Ont. nom 1h0
Phone: (519) 523-4311   Fax: (519) 523-9140
Contact: Keith Roulston, managing editor
Published monthly

Saskatchewan Farm Life

1009 Avenue P., South Saskatoon, Sask. s7m 2x4
Phone: (306) 244-1404   Fax: (306) 244-6656
Contact: Larry Hyatt, manager
Published biweekly

Sheep Canada

237 – 8th Avenue S.E., Suite 600, Calgary, Alta. t2g 5c3
Phone: (403) 264-3270   Fax: (403) 264-3276
Contact: Patrick Ottmann, publisher
Published quarterly

Simmental Country

13, 4101 – 19th Street N.E., Calgary, Alta. t2e 7c4
Phone: (403) 250-5255   Fax: (403) 250-5279
Contact: Ted Pritchett, publisher/editor
Published monthly

Union Farmer

250C – 2nd Avenue S., Saskatoon, Sask. s7k 2m1
Phone: (306) 652-9465   Fax: (306) 664-6226
Contact: Terry Pugh, editor
Published 10 times a year

Western Hog Journal

10319 Princess Elizabeth Avenue, Edmonton, Alta. t5g 0y5

Phone: (403) 474-8288   Fax: (403) 471-8065
Contact: Ed Schultz, editor
Published quarterly

The Western Producer
P.O. Box 2500, Saskatoon, Sask. S7K 2C4
Phone: (306) 665-3500   Fax: (306) 653-8750
Contact: Gary Fairbairn, editor
Published weekly

Food, Drink, & Hostelry

Bakers Journal
106 Lakeshore Road E., Suite 209, Port Credit, Ont. L5G 1E2
Phone: (905) 271-1366   Fax: (905) 271-6373
Contact: Carol Horseman, editor
Published 10 times a year

Canadian Grocer
777 Bay Street, Toronto, Ont. M5W 1A7
Phone: (416) 596-5773   Fax: (416) 593-3162
Contact: Simone Collier, managing editor
Published monthly

Canadian Hotel & Restaurant
777 Bay Street, Toronto, Ont. M5W 1A7
Phone: (416) 596-5813   Fax: (416) 593-3189
Contact: Jerry Tutunjian, editor
Published 11 times a year

Food in Canada
777 Bay Street, Toronto, Ont. M5W 1A7
Phone: (416) 596-5477   Fax: (416) 593-3189
Contact: Catherine Wilson, editor
Published 9 times a year

Food Mart News

169 West Mall, Etobicoke, Ont. M9C 1C2
Phone: (416) 620-9900   Fax: (416) 622-6688
Contact: James Paine, managing editor
Published 10 times a year

Foodservice & Hospitality

980 Yonge Street, Suite 400, Toronto, Ont. M4W 2J8
Phone: (416) 923-8888   Fax: (416) 923-6114
Contact: Rosanna Caira, editor
Published monthly

Grocer Today

401 – 4180 Lougheed Highway, Burnaby, B.C. V5C 6A7
Phone: (604) 299-7311   Fax: (604) 299-9188
Contact: Peter Legge, publisher
Published 10 times a year

Inn Business

Zanny Ltd., 11966 Woodbine Avenue, Gormley, Ont. L0H 1G0
Phone: (905) 887-4813   Fax: (905) 479-4834
Contact: Amy Margaret, editor
Published bimonthly

InnFocus

124 West 8th Street, North Vancouver, B.C. V7M 3H2
Phone: (604) 985-8711   Fax: (604) 985-7399
Contact: Jim Hutson, executive editor
Published quarterly

Manitoba Restaurant News

945 King Edward Street, Winnipeg, Man. R3H 0P8
Phone: (204) 775-0387   Fax: (204) 775-7830
Contact: Frank Yeo, editor
Published quarterly

Modern Dairy
3269 Bloor Street W., Suite 205, Toronto, Ont. M8X 1E2
Phone: (416) 239-8423
Contact: Iain Macnab, editor/publisher
Published 5 times a year

Ontario Innkeeper
920 Yonge Street, 6th Floor, Toronto, Ont. M4W 3C7
Phone: (416) 961-1028   Fax: (416) 924-4408
Contact: Gregory Kero, editor
Published twice a year

Ontario Restaurant News
169 West Mall, Etobicoke, M9C 1C2
Phone: (416) 622-9332   Fax: (416) 622-6688
Contact: Steven Isherwood, publisher/editor
Published monthly

Western Grocer
945 King Edward Street, Winnipeg, Man. R3H 0P8
Phone: (204) 775-0387   Fax: (204) 775-7830
Contact: Kelly Gray, editor
Published bimonthly

Health, Dentistry, Medicine, Pharmacy, & Nursing

Canadian Family Physician
2630 Skymark Avenue, Mississauga, Ont. L4W 5A4
Phone: (905) 629-0900   Fax: (905) 629-2761
Contact: Dr. Reg Perkin, editor
Published monthly

Canadian Journal of Continuing Medical Education
955 boulevard St.-Jean, Suite 306, Pointe Claire, Que. H9R 5K3
Phone: (514) 695-7623   Fax: (514) 695-8554
Contact: Paul Brand, executive editor
Published 10 times a year

Canadian Journal of Hospital Pharmacy
1145 Hunt Club Road, Suite 350, Ottawa, Ont. KIV 0Y3
Phone: (613) 736-9733   Fax: (613) 736-5660
Contact: Susan Tremblay, editor
Published bimonthly

The Canadian Nurse
50 The Driveway, Ottawa, Ont. K2P 1E2
Phone: (613) 237-2133   Fax: (613) 237-3520
Contact: Heather Broughton, editor-in-chief
Published monthly

Canadian Pharmaceutical Journal
1785 Alta Vista Drive, 2nd Floor, Ottawa, Ont. KIG 3Y6
Phone: (613) 523-7877   Fax: (613)523-0445
Contact: Jane Dewar, editor
Published 10 times a year

The Care Connection
Published by the Ontario Association of Registered Nursing
    Assistants, 5025 Orbitor Drive, Building 4, Suite 200,
    Mississauga, Ont. L4W 4Y5
Phone: (905) 602-4664   Fax: (905) 602-4666
Contact: Kelly Zimmer, editor
Published quarterly

Dentist's Guide
1120 Bichmount Road, Suite 200, Scarborough, Ont. MIK 5G4
Phone: (416) 750-8900   Fax: (416) 751-8126
Contact: Frank Lederer, publisher
Published quarterly

Dental Practice Management
1450 Don Mills Road, Don Mills, Ont. M3B 2X7
Phone: (416) 445-6641   Fax: (416) 442-2214
Contact: Janet Bonellie, editor
Published quarterly

Diabetes Dialogue
15 Toronto Street, Suite 1001, Toronto, Ont. M5C 2E3
Phone: (416) 363-3373   Fax: (416) 363-3393
Contact: Robert Silver, MD, editor-in-chief
Published quarterly

Doctor's Review
400 McGill Street, 3rd Floor, Montreal, Que. H2Y 2G1
Phone: (514) 397-8833   Fax: (514) 397-0228
Contact: David Elkins, publisher
Published monthly

Family Practice
1120 Birchmount Road, Suite 200, Scarborough, Ont. M1K 5G4
Phone: (416) 750-8900   Fax: (416) 751-8126
Contact: John Shaughnessy, editor
Published 32 times a year

Healthcare Advocate
10009 – 108th Street, Edmonton, Alta. T5J 3C5
Phone: (403) 498-8400   Fax: (403) 498-8465
Contact: Gerry Warner, editor
Published 10 times a year

Hospital News
23 Apex Road, Toronto, Ont. M6A 2V6
Phone: (416) 781-5516   Fax: (416) 781-5499
Contact: Donna Kell, editor
Published monthly

Journal of the Canadian Dental Association
1815 Alta Vista Drive, Ottawa, Ont. K1G 3Y6
Phone: (613) 523-1770   Fax: (613) 523-7736
Contact: Terence Davis, managing editor
Published monthly

The Medical Post
777 Bay Street, Toronto, Ont. M5W 1A7
Phone: (416) 596-5770   Fax: (416) 593-3177

Contact: Derek Cassels, editor
Published 44 times a year

Medicine North America
400 McGill Street, 3rd Floor, Montreal, Que. H2Y 2G1
Phone: (514) 397-9393   Fax: (514) 397-0228
Contact: Dr. Ian R. Hart, editor
Published monthly

Nursing BC
2855 Arbutus Street, Vancouver, B.C. V6J 3Y8
Phone: (604) 736-7331   Fax: (604) 738-2272
Contact: Bruce Wells, editor
Published 5 times a year

Ontario Dentist
4 New Street, Toronto, Ont. M5R 1P6
Phone: (416) 922-3900   Fax: (416) 922-9005
Contact: Jim Shosenberg, editor
Published 10 times a year

Ontario Medical Review
525 University Avenue, Suite 300, Toronto, Ont. M5G 2K7
Phone: (416) 599-2580   Fax: (416) 599-9309
Contact: David Fletcher, editor
Published monthly

Ontario Medicine
777 Bay Street, Toronto, Ont. M5W 1A7
Phone: (416) 596-5750   Fax: (416) 593-3162
Contact: Elizabeth Watson, editor
Published 20 times a year

Oral Health
1450 Don Mills Road, Don Mills, Ont. M3B 2X7
Phone: (416) 445-6641   Fax: (416) 442-2201
Contact: Erla Kay, publisher (442-2046)
Published monthly

Patient Care
1120 Birchmount Road, Suite 200, Scarborough, Ont. M1K 5G4
Phone: (416) 750-8900 Fax: (416) 751-8126
Contact: Vil Meere, editor
Published 10 times a year

Pharmacist's News
777 Bay Street, Toronto, Ont. M5W 1A7
Phone: (416) 596-5950 Fax: (416) 593-3162
Contact: Polly Thompson, editor
Published monthly

Pharmacy Practice
1120 Birchmount Road, Suite 200, Scarborough, Ont. M1K 5G4
Phone: (416) 750-8900 Fax: (416) 751-8126
Contact: Anne Bokma, editor
Published 10 times a year

Physician's Guide
1120 Birchmount Road, Suite 200, Scarborough, Ont. M1K 5G4
Phone: (416) 750-8900 Fax: (416) 751-8126
Contact: Heather Howie, editor
Published bimonthly

Rehab and Community Care Management
101 Thorncliffe Park Drive, Toronto, Ont. M4H 1M2
Phone: (416) 421-7944 Fax: (416) 421-0966
Contact: Helmut Dostal, managing editor
Published quarterly

Wellness MD
22 Keele Street S., King City, Ont. L0G 1K0
Phone: (905) 833-2777 Fax: (905) 833-3763
Contact: Gordon Bagley, editor
Published bimonthly

Industrial

Canadian Facility Management & Design
62 Olsen Drive, Don Mills, Ont. M3A 3J3
Phone: (416) 447-3417   Fax: (416) 447-4410
Contact: Victor von Buchstab, editor
Published bimonthly

Canadian Industrial Equipment News
1450 Don Mills Road, Don Mills, Ont. M3B 2X7
Phone: (416) 445-6641   Fax: (416) 442-2214
Contact: Olga Markovich, editor
Published monthly

Canadian Machinery & Metalworking
777 Bay Street, Toronto, Ont. M5W 1A7
Phone: (416) 596-5714   Fax: (416) 596-5881
Contact: Mike Overment, editor
Published 10 times a year

Canadian Occupational Safety
Royal Life Building, Suite 209, 277 Lakeshore Road E., Oakville,
   Ont. L6J 6J3
Phone: (905) 842-2884   Fax: (905) 842-8226
Contact: Jackie Roth, editor
Published bimonthly

Canadian Packaging
777 Bay Street, Toronto, Ont. M5W 1A7
Phone: (416) 596-5746   Fax: (416) 596-5810
Contact: Douglas Faulkner, editor
Published 11 times a year

Canadian Plastics
1450 Don Mills Road, Don Mills, Ont. M3B 2X7
Phone: (416) 445-6641   Fax: (416) 442-2213
Contact: Michael Shelley, editor
Published 8 times a year

Canadian Textile Journal
1, rue Pacifique, Ste.-Anne-de-Bellevue, Que. H9X 1C5
Phone: (514) 457-2347　Fax: (514) 457-2147
Contact: Kathryn Hanley, editor
Published 10 times a year

Equipment Journal
150 Lakeshore Road W., Suite 36, Mississauga, Ont. L5H 3R2
Phone: (905) 274-8686
Contact: E.E. Abel, publisher/editor
Published 17 times a year

Heating–Plumbing–Air Conditioning
1450 Don Mills Road, Don Mills, Ont. M3B 2X7
Phone: (416) 445-6641　Fax: (416) 442-2214
Contact: Bruce Cole, editor
Published monthly

Industrial Products & Services
277 Lakeshore Road E., Suite 209, Oakville, Ont. L6J 6J3
Phone: (905) 842-2884　Fax: (905) 842-8226
Contact: George Clifford, publisher
Published 5 times a year

Laboratory Product News
1450 Don Mills Road, Don Mills, Ont. M3B 2X7
Phone: (416) 442-2052　Fax: (416) 442-2201
Contact: Rita Tate, publisher/editor
Published bimonthly

Machinery & Equipment MRO
1450 Don Mills Road, Don Mills, Ont. M3B 2X7
Phone: (416) 442-2089　Fax: (416) 442-2214
Contact: William Roebuck, editor
Published bimonthly

Metalworking Production & Purchasing
135 Spy Court, Markham, Ont. L3R 5H6
Phone: (905) 477-3222　Fax: (905) 477-4320

Contact: Maurice Holtham, editor
Published bimonthly

New Equipment News
148 King Road E., King City, Ont. LOG IKO
Phone: (905) 833-6200   Fax: (905) 833-4200
Contact: Barrie Lehman, editor
Published monthly

Occupational Health & Safety
1450 Don Mills Road, Don Mills, Ont. M3B 2X7
Phone: (416) 445-6641   Fax: (416) 442-2200
Contact: Margaret Nearing, editor
Published 7 times a year

Ontario Industrial Magazine
801 York Mills Road, Suite 201, Don Mills, Ont. M3B IX7
Phone: (416) 446-1404   Fax: (416) 446-0502
Contact: Ralph Bryson, editor/publisher
Published monthly

Optical Prism
31 Hastings Drive, Unionville, Ont. L3R 4Y5
Phone: (905) 475-9343   Fax: (905) 477-2821
Contact: Allan Vezina, editor/publisher
Published 9 times a year

Plant
777 Bay Street, Toronto, Ont. M5W IA7
Phone: (416) 596-5776   Fax: (416) 596-5552
Contact: Ron Richardson, editor
Published 18 times a year

Plant Engineering & Maintenance
277 Lakeshore Road E., Suite 209, Oakville, Ont. L6J 6J3
Phone: (905) 842-2884   Fax: (905) 842-8226
Contact: Rae Robb, editor
Published bimonthly

Plastics Business
1450 Don Mills Road, Don Mills, Ont. M3B 2X7
Phone: (416) 445-6641   Fax: (416) 442-2213
Contact: Michael Shelley, editor
Published quarterly

Landscaping & Horticulture

Canadian Florist, Greenhouse & Nursery
1090 Aerowood Drive, Unit 1, Mississauga, Ont. L4W 1Y5
Phone: (905) 625-2730   Fax: (905) 625-1355
Contact: Peter Heywood, editor/publisher
Published monthly

Greenhouse Canada
222 Argyle Avenue, Delhi, Ont. N4B 2Y2
Phone: (519) 582-2513   Fax: (519) 582-4040
Contact: Ben Steidman, editor
Published monthly

GreenMaster
80 West Beaver Creek, Suite 18, Richmond Hill, Ont. L4B 1H3
Phone: (905) 771-7333   Fax: (905) 771-7336
Contact: Dennis Mellersh, editor
Published bimonthly

Hortwest
5830 – 176A Street, Suite 101, Surrey, B.C. V3S 4E3
Phone: (604) 574-7772   Fax: (604) 574-7773
Contact: Phil Pearsall, managing editor
Published bimonthly

Landmark
807 Manning Road N.E., Suite 200, Calgary, Alta. T2E 7M8
Phone: (403) 569-9520   Fax: (403) 569-9590
Contact: Karen Riva, editor
Published bimonthly

Landscape Trades
1293 Matheson Boulevard, Mississauga, Ont. L4W 1R1
Phone: (905) 629-1184   Fax: (905) 629-4438
Contact: Linda Erskine, editor
Published 9 times a year

The Ontario Land Surveyor
1043 McNicoll Avenue, Scarborough, Ont. M1W 3W6
Phone: (416) 491-9020   Fax: (416) 491-2576
Contact: Brian Munday, publications manager
Published quarterly

Prairie Landscape Magazine
807 Manning Road N.E., Suite 200, Calgary, Alta. T2E 7M8
Phone: (403) 569-9520   Fax: (403) 569-9590
Contact: Karen Riva, editor
Published bimonthly

Turf & Recreation
19469 – 92nd Avenue, Surrey, B.C. V4N 4G5
Phone: (604) 888-8843   Fax: (604) 888-8734
Contact: Rud Kendall, editor
Published bimonthly

Media, Music, & Communications

Broadcaster
1450 Don Mills Road, Don Mills, Ont. M3B 2X7
Phone: (416) 445-6641   Fax: (416) 442-2213
Contact: Ted Davis, editor
Published 10 times a year

Broadcast Technology
P.O. Box 420, Bolton, Ont. L7E 5T3
Phone: (905) 857-6076   Fax: (905) 857-6045
Contact: Doug Loney, publisher/editor
Published 10 times a year

Cable Communications Magazine
1421 Victoria Street N., Kitchener, Ont. N2B 3E4
Phone: (519) 744-4111   Fax: (519) 744-1261
Contact: Udo Salewsky, publisher/editor
Published bimonthly

Cablecaster
1450 Don Mills Road, Don Mills, Ont. M3B 2X7
Phone: (416) 445-6641   Fax: (416) 442-2213
Contact: Steve Pawlett, editor
Published 8 times a year

Canada on Location
366 Adelaide Street W., Suite 500, Toronto, Ont. M5V 1R9
Phone: (416) 408-2300   Fax: (416) 408-0870
Contact: Mark Smyka, executive editor
Published twice a year

Canadian Music Trade
23 Hannover Drive, Unit 7, St. Catharines, Ont. L2W 1A3
Phone: (905) 641-3471   Fax: (905) 641-1648
Contact: Jim Norris, publisher
Published bimonthly

Masthead: The Magazine about Magazines
1606 Sedlescomb Drive, Unit 8, Mississauga, Ont. L4X 1M6
Phone: (905) 625-7070   Fax: (905) 625-4856
Contact: Doug Bennet, editor
Published 10 times a year

Media West
1497 Marine Drive, Suite 300, West Vancouver, B.C. V7T 1B8
Phone: (604) 926-8765   Fax: (604) 926-7326
Contact: Paul Andrews, publisher/editor
Published bimonthly

Playback
366 Adelaide Street W., Suite 500, Toronto, Ont. M5V 1R9
Phone: (416) 408-2300   Fax: (416) 408-0870

Contact: Susan Tolusso, editor
Published biweekly

Press Review
P.O. Box 368, Station A, Toronto, Ont. M5W 1C2
Phone: (416) 368-0512   Fax: (416) 366-0104
Contact: Sheila Johnston, managing editor
Published quarterly

Professional Sound
23 Hannover Drive, Unit 7, St. Catharines, Ont. L2W 1A3
Phone: (905) 641-3471   Fax: (905) 641-1648
Contact: Jim Norris, publisher
Published quarterly

The Publisher
90 Eglinton Avenue E., Suite 206, Toronto, Ont. M4P 2Y3
Phone: (416) 332-8374   Fax: (416) 482-1908
Contact: Maureen de Yong, editor
Published 10 times a year

RPM Weekly
6 Brentcliffe Road, Toronto, Ont. M4G 3Y2
Phone: (416) 425-0257   Fax: (416) 425-8629
Contact: Walter Grealis, publisher

Miscellaneous Trade & Professional

Canadian Ceramics Quarterly
2175 Sheppard Avenue E., Suite 110, Willowdale, Ont. M2J 1W8
Phone: (416) 491-2886   Fax: (416) 491-1670
Contact: M. Sayer, editor
Published quarterly

The Canadian Firefighter
P.O. Box 95, Station D, Etobicoke, Ont. M9A 4X1
Phone: (416) 233-2516   Fax: (416) 233-2051

Contact: Lorne Campbell, editor/publisher
Published bimonthly

Canadian Funeral Director

174 Harwood Avenue S., Suite 206, Ajax, Ont. LIS 2H7
Phone: (905) 427-6121   Fax: (905) 427-6121
Contact: Scott Hillier, editor
Published monthly

Canadian Funeral News

237 – 8th Avenue S.E., Suite 600, Calgary, Alta. T2G 5C3
Phone: (403) 264-3270   Fax: (403) 264-3276
Contact: Jacqueline Bitz, editor
Published monthly

Canadian Home Economics Journal

151 Slater Street, Suite 901, Ottawa, Ont. KIP 5H3
Phone: (613) 238-8817   Fax: (613) 238-1677
Contact: Glenda Everett, editor (phone [403] 320-3343)
Published quarterly

Canadian Homestyle Magazine

598 Stillwater Court, Burlington, Ont. L7T 4G7
Phone: (905) 681-7932   Fax: (905) 681-2141
Contact: Laurie O'Halloran, publisher/editorial director
Published bimonthly

Canadian Interiors

113 Davenport Road, Toronto, Ont. M5R 1H8
Phone: (416) 966-9944   Fax: (416) 966-9946
Contact: Sheri Craig, publisher/editor
Published bimonthly

Canadian Property Management

33 Fraser Avenue, Suite 208, Toronto, Ont. M6K 3J9
Phone: (416) 588-6220
Contact: Pamela Snow, editor
Published 7 times a year

Canadian Realtor News
320 Queen Street, Suite 2100, Ottawa, Ont. KIR 5A3
Phone: (613) 234-3372   Fax: (613) 234-2567
Contact: Jim McCarthy, editor
Published monthly

Canadian Rental Service
145 Thames Road W., Exeter, Ont. NOM IS3
Phone: (519) 235-2400   Fax: (519) 235-0798
Contact: Peter Darbishire, managing editor
Published 8 times a year

Canadian Security
46 Crockford Boulevard, Scarborough, Ont. MIR 3C3
Phone: (416) 755-4343   Fax: (416) 755-7487
Contact: Robert Robinson, editor
Published 7 times a year

Canadian Vending
106 Lakeshore Road E., Suite 209, Port Credit, Ont. L5G IE3
Phone: (905) 271-1366   Fax: (905) 271-6373
Contact: Sandra Anderson, editor
Published bimonthly

The Canadian Veterinary Journal
339 Booth Street, Ottawa, Ont. KIR 7KI
Phone: (613) 236-1162   Fax: (613) 236-9681
Contact: Dr. Doug Hare, editor
Published monthly

Condominium Magazine
366 Adelaide Street W., Suite 501, Toronto, Ont. M5V IR9
Phone: (416) 585-2552   Fax: (416) 585-9741
Contact: Kevin Brown, publisher
Published monthly

Cosmetics
227 Front Street E., Suite 100, Toronto, Ont. M5A IE8

Phone: (416) 865-9362   Fax: (416) 865-1933
Contact: Ron Wood, editor
Published bimonthly

Decorating Centre

7895 Tranmere Drive, Unit 5, Mississauga, Ont. L5S 1V9
Phone: (905) 678-0331   Fax: (905) 678-0335
Contact: Tamela Adamson-McMullen, editor
Published bimonthly

Fire Fighting in Canada

222 Argyle Avenue, Delhi, Ont. N4B 2Y2
Phone: (519) 582-2513   Fax: (519) 582-4040
Contact: James Haley, editor
Published 10 times a year

Gifts & Tablewares

1450 Don Mills Road, Don Mills, Ont. M3B 2X7
Phone: (416) 445-6641   Fax: (416) 442-2213
Contact: Dawn Dickinson, editor
Published 7 times a year

Home Builder Magazine

P.O. Box 400, Victoria Station, Westmount, Que. H3Z 2V8
Phone: (514) 489-4941   Fax: (514) 489-5505
Contact: Nachmi Artzy, publisher/editor
Published bimonthly

Interior Design Outlook

717 Church Street, Toronto, Ont. M4W 2M5
Phone: (416) 921-2127   Fax: (416) 921-3660
Contact: Phillip Moody, executive editor
Published 9 times a year

Lighting Magazine

395 Matheson Boulevard E., Mississauga, Ont. L4Z 2H2
Phone: (905) 890-1846   Fax: (905) 890-5769
Contact: Bryan Rogers, editor
Published bimonthly

Materials Management & Distribution
777 Bay Street, Toronto, Ont. M5W 1A7
Phone: (416) 596-5709   Fax: (416) 596-5554
Contact: Rob Robertson, editor
Published monthly

Municipal World
P.O. Box 399, St. Thomas, Ont. N5P 3V3
Phone: (519) 633-0031   Fax: (519) 633-1001
Contact: Michael Smither, editor
Published monthly

Ontario Home Builder
178 Main Street, Unionville, Ont. L3R 2G9
Phone: (905) 479-4663   Fax: (905) 479-4482
Contact: Don Procter, editor
Published bimonthly

The Ontario Technologist
10 Four Seasons Place, Suite 404, Etobicoke, Ont. M9B 6H7
Phone: (416) 621-9621   Fax: (416) 621-8694
Contact: Ruth Klein, editor
Published bimonthly

Physics in Canada
151 Slater Street, Suite 903, Ottawa, Ont. K1P 5H3
Phone: (613) 237-3392   Fax: (613) 238-1677
Contact: J.S.C. McKee, editor
Published bimonthly

Toys & Games
501 Oakdale Road, Downsview, Ont. M3N 1W7
Phone: (416) 746-7360   Fax: (416) 746-1421
Contact: Lynn Winston, editor
Published bimonthly

Veterinarian Magazine
248 Mary Street, Rockwood, Ont. N0B 2K0
Phone: (519) 856-4050   Fax: (519) 856-4146

Contact: Maggie Clark, editor
Published bimonthly

Woodworking
135 Spy Court, Markham, Ont. L3R 5H6
Phone: (905) 477-3222   Fax: (905) 477-4320
Contact: Maurice Holtham, editor
Published 7 times a year

Printing & Photography

Canadian Printer
777 Bay Street, Toronto, Ont. M5W 1A7
Phone: (416) 596-5781   Fax: (416) 596-5965
Contact: Nick Hancock, editor
Published 10 times a year

The Graphic Monthly
1606 Sedlescomb Drive, Unit 8, Mississauga, Ont. L4X 1M6
Phone: (905) 625-7070   Fax: (905) 625-4856
Contact: Alexander Donald, editor/publisher
Published bimonthly

Photo Dealer News
130 Spy Court, Markham, Ont. L3R 5H6
Phone: (905) 475-8440   Fax: (905) 475-9246
Contact: Steven Curson, editor
Published bimonthly

Photo Retailer
440 – 850 Pierre Bertrand Boulevard, Vanier, Que. G1M 3K8
Phone: (418) 687-3550   Fax: (418) 687-1679
Contact: Don Long, editor
Published 10 times a year

PrintAction
2240 Midland Avenue, Suite 201, Scarborough, Ont. M1P 4R8
Phone: (416) 299-6007   Fax: (416) 299-6674

Contact: Scott Olson, editor
Published monthly

Professional Photographers of Canada
2020 Portage Avenue, Suite 3C, Winnipeg, Man. R3J 0K4
Phone: (204) 885-7798   Fax: (204) 889-3576
Contact: Jim Watson, editor
Published bimonthly

Transportation & Cargo

Canadian Shipper
777 Bay Street, Toronto, Ont. M5W 1A7
Phone: (416) 596-5709   Fax: (416) 596-5881
Contact: Robert Robertson, editor
Published bimonthly

Canadian Transportation Logistics
1450 Don Mills Road, Don Mills, Ont. M3B 2X7
Phone: (416) 442-2228   Fax: (416) 442-2214
Contact: Bonnie Toews, editor
Published monthly

Cargo Express
310 Dupont Street, Toronto, Ont. M5R 1V9
Phone: (416) 968-7252   Fax: (416) 968-2377
Contact: Pat Cancilla, editor
Published 10 times a year

Harbour & Shipping
1765 Bellevue Avenue, West Vancouver, B.C. V7V 1A8
Phone: (604) 922-6717   Fax: (604) 922-1739
Contact: Liz Bennett, editor
Published monthly

Manitoba Highway News
2020 Portage Avenue, Suite 3C, Winnipeg, Man. R3J 0K4
Phone: (204) 885-7798   Fax: (204) 889-3576

Contact: Al Harris, editor
Published quarterly

Marine Trades

P.O. Box 149, Rockwood Mall, 4141 Dixie Road, Mississauga,
    Ont. L4W 1V5
Phone: (905) 625-9660   Fax: (905) 625-9604
Contact: Gary Arthurs, editor
Published quarterly

Motor Truck

1450 Don Mills Road, Don Mills, Ont. M3B 2X7
Phone: (416) 445-6641   Fax: (416) 442-2213
Contact: Barry Holmes, executive editor
Published monthly

Today's Trucking

452 Attwell Drive, Suite 100, Etobicoke, Ont. M9W 5C3
Phone: (416) 798-2977   Fax: (416) 798-3017
Contact: Rolf Lockwood, editor
Published 10 times a year

Truck News

1450 Don Mills Road, Don Mills, Ont. M3B 2X7
Phone: (416) 442-2062   Fax: (416) 442-2092
Contact: Brenda Yarrow, editor
Published monthly

Truck West

1555 Dublin Avenue, Unit 9, Winnipeg, Man. R3E 3M8
Phone: (204) 831-8814   Fax: (204) 888-3853
Contact: Patrick Munro, publisher
Published monthly

Truck World

11 – 106 East 14th Street, North Vancouver, B.C. V7L 2N3
Phone: (604) 984-2002   Fax: (604) 984-2820
Contact: Kim Prinz, managing editor
Published bimonthly

Travel

Agent Canada Travel Magazine
1534 West 2nd Avenue, Suite 300, Vancouver, B.C. v6J 1H2
Phone: (604) 731-0481   Fax: (604) 731-2589
Contact: Douglas Keough, editor/publisher
Published weekly

Canadian Travel Press Weekly
310 Dupont Street, Toronto, Ont. M5R 1V9
Phone: (416) 968-7252   Fax: (416) 968-2377
Contact: Edith Baxter, editor
Published weekly

Canadian Traveller
409 Granville Street, Suite 902, Vancouver, B.C. v6C 2X4
Phone: (604) 669-7737   Fax: (604) 684-2562
Contact: Gerry Wingenbach, publisher/editor
Published monthly

Meetings & Incentive Travel
777 Bay Street, 5th Floor, Toronto, Ont. M5W 1A7
Phone: (416) 596-2697   Fax: (416) 596-5810
Contact: Lori Bak, editor
Published 8 times a year

Tours on Motorcoach
1055 Beaver Hall, Suite 400, C.P. 365, Montreal, Que. H2Y 3H1
Phone: (514) 274-0004   Fax: (514) 274-5884
Contact: Guy Jonkman, publisher/editor
Published monthly

Travel Courier
310 Dupont Street, Toronto, Ont. M5R 1V9
Phone: (416) 968-7252   Fax: (416) 968-2377
Contact: Bruce Parkinson, editor
Published weekly

Travelweek Bulletin
553 Church Street, Toronto, Ont. M4Y 2E2
Phone: (416) 924-0963   Fax: (416) 924-5721
Contact: Patrick Dineen, editor
Published twice a week

4

DAILY NEWSPAPERS

Many a successful writing career began in the pages of a small community newspaper. High-profile, high-circulation magazines are alluring, but top-quality magazine pieces are among the most difficult of literary forms, and many of these publications are disinclined to try out inexperienced writers. Discouragement mounts with each rejection slip, often to the point where a promising writing career is abandoned. A planned approach to becoming a published writer is the surest road to success.

Weekly community newspapers are a good starting point. With small staffs and budgets, their editors are often pleased to accept outside contributions, particularly feature articles that cover the local scene. And since payment is modest, there is little competition from more experienced writers. Many established writers began by writing for no pay for their local paper.

Always remember that news loses its value as quickly as it changes, and it is therefore usually gathered hurriedly – on large papers and small – by staff reporters. Therefore, it is to your advantage to concentrate on background stories about ongoing issues, or to write profiles of prominent, interesting, or unusual local citizens and institutions. Stories about travel, hobbies, lifestyles, personal finance, and business are particularly welcome. So are strong human-interest pieces – always among the best-read articles in any newspaper. Most editors like to build a stash of timely articles that do not have to be used immediately.

Writers do not propose ideas to newspapers in the same way as they do for magazines. On newspapers, time is a much more crucial factor. So rather than craft a written proposal, it is perfectly acceptable to solicit a go-ahead decision from the editor of one of the paper's sections with a quick telephone call. Initially, however, they will probably want to see tearsheets of published work. If they have published your letters, it may be worth including clippings of these, too.

If you are considering this market, your best preparation is to read critically several issues of the paper. Note the style, the story lengths preferred, the use of photographs, the paper's editorial policy, and the difference in content, construction, and tone of news stories and feature articles. If you have never studied journalism, you might need a reference book, such as *News Reporting and Writing*, by Melvin Mencher, a professor at Columbia University's School of Journalism (see Chapter 10, Resources).

Naturally, it will take more experience to sell to large, well-staffed metropolitan dailies like *The Toronto Star* or *The Winnipeg Free Press*. But even here, the outside contributor has a chance, provided he or she has some specialized knowledge, can handle human-interest material deftly, and can write full-bodied issue stories with conviction and authority. For a well-written, well-researched article on an important or intriguing subject, many of the bigger city dailies pay as much or more than the average consumer magazine. And they settle faster: most pay at the end of the month, some even on acceptance.

Freelance writers submit their manuscripts to newspapers in much the same way as they do for magazines, and many write successfully for both. They meet deadlines even when it means losing sleep. They are always aware that for the daily press, accuracy and reliability are two virtues worth cultivating, even under pressure. While the news story is essentially factual and must have a strong sense of immediacy, the feature article needs body and strength as well as originality and freshness. Timing is a key element. Keep a calendar of dates for seasonal stories – Hallowe'en, Thanksgiving, Chinese New Year, Canada Day, and so on – and read behind the news for feature ideas.

Besides writing for your city paper, look for opportunities to act as a correspondent, or stringer, for one published elsewhere. The full listing of English-language Canadian daily newspapers that follows will prove useful. For suburban weeklies, check the *CARD* directory.

Canadian newspapers are also listed in *Matthews Media Directory* (see Chapter 10, Resources).

Alberta

Advocate
2950 Bremner Avenue, Bag 5200, P.O. Box 250, Red Deer,
   Alta. T4N 5G3
Phone: (403) 343-2400   Fax: (403) 342-4051

Calgary Herald
215 – 16th Street S.E., Calgary, Alta. T2P 0W8
Phone: (403) 235-7388   Fax: (403) 235-8668

Calgary Sun
2615 – 12th Street N.E., Calgary, Alta. T2E 7W9
Phone: (403) 250-4200   Fax: (403) 291-4242

Daily Herald Tribune
10604 – 100th Street, Grande Prairie, Alta. T8V 2M5
Phone: (403) 532-1110   Fax: (403) 532-2120

Edmonton Journal
10006 – 101st Street, Edmonton, Alta. T5J 2S6
Phone: (403) 429-5400

Edmonton Sun
4990 – 92nd Avenue, Suite 250, Edmonton, Alta. T6B 3A1
Phone: (403) 468-0227   Fax: (403) 468-0128

Fort McMurray Today
8550 Franklin Avenue, Bag 4008, Fort McMurray, Alta. T9H 3G1
Phone: (403) 743-8186   Fax: (403) 790-1006

Lethbridge Herald
504 – 7th Street S., Lethbridge, Alta. T1J 3Z7
Phone: (403) 328-4411   Fax: (403) 328-4536

Medicine Hat News
3257 Dunmore Road S.E., P.O. Box 10, Medicine Hat,
   Alta. T1A 7E6
Phone: (403) 527-1101   Fax: (403) 527-0737

British Columbia

Alaska Highway News
9916 – 98th Street, Fort St. John, B.C. V1J 3T8
Phone: (604) 785-5631   Fax: (604) 785-3522

Alberni Valley Times
4918 Napier Street, P.O. Box 400, Port Alberni, B.C. V9Y 7N1
Phone: (604) 723-8171   Fax: (604) 723-0586

Chinese Times
1 East Pender Street, Vancouver, B.C. V6A 1S9
Phone: (604) 685-8575   Fax: (604) 685-1196

Cranbrook Daily Townsman
822 Cranbrook Street N., Cranbrook, B.C. V1C 3R9
Phone: (604) 426-5201   Fax: (604) 426-5003

Daily Bulletin
335 Spokane Street, Kimberley, B.C. V1A 1Y9
Phone: (604) 427-5333

Daily Courier
550 Doyle Avenue, Kelowna, B.C. V1Y 7V1
Phone: (604) 762-4445   Fax: (604) 762-3866

Daily Free Press
223 Commercial Street, P.O. Box 69, Nanaimo, B.C. V9R 5K5
Phone: (604) 753-3451   Fax: (604) 753-8730

Daily News
266 Baker Street, Nelson, B.C. V1L 4H3
Phone: (604) 352-3552   Fax: (604) 352-2418

Kamloops Daily News
63 West Victoria Street, Suite 106, Kamloops, B.C. V2C 6J6
Phone: (604) 372-2331   Fax: (604) 374-3884

Peace River Block News
901 – 100th Avenue, P.O. Box 180, Dawson Creek, B.C. V1G 4G6
Phone: (604) 782-4888   Fax: (604) 782-6770

Penticton Herald
186 Nanaimo Avenue W., Penticton, B.C. V2A 1N4
Phone: (604) 492-4002   Fax: (604) 492-2403

Prince George Citizen
150 Brunswick Street, P.O. Box 5700, Prince George,
    B.C. V2L 5K9
Phone: (604) 562-2441   Fax: (604) 562-9201

Price Rupert Daily News
P.O. Box 580, Prince Rupert, B.C. V8J 3R9
Phone: (604) 624-6781   Fax: (604) 624-2851

Trail Times
1163 Cedar Avenue, Trail, B.C. V1R 4B8
Phone: (604) 368-8551   Fax: (604) 368-3818

Vancouver Sun Province
2250 Granville Street, Vancouver, B.C. V6H 3G2
Phone: (604) 732-2515   Fax: (604) 732-2704

Vernon Daily News
3309 – 31st Avenue, Vernon, B.C. V1T 6N8
Phone: (604) 545-0671   Fax: (604) 545-7193

Victoria Times–Colonist
2621 Douglas Street, P.O. Box 300, Victoria, B.C. V8W 2N4
Phone: (604) 380-5211   Fax: (604) 380-5255

Manitoba

Brandon Sun
501 Rosser Avenue, Brandon, Man. R7A 5Z6
Phone: (204) 727-2451   Fax: (204) 725-0976

Daily Graphic
1941 Saskatchewan Avenue W., P.O. Box 130, Portage La Prairie,
    Man. R1N 3B4
Phone: (204) 857-3427   Fax: (204) 239-1270

Flin Flon Reminder
P.O. Box 727, 10 North Avenue, Flin Flon, Man. R8A 1N5
Phone: (204) 687-7339   Fax: (204) 687-4473

Winnipeg Free Press
1355 Mountain Avenue, Winnipeg, Man. R2X 3B6
Phone: (204) 697-7000   Fax: (204) 697-7370

Winnipeg Sun
1700 Church Avenue, Winnipeg, Man. R2X 3A2
Phone: (204) 694-2022   Fax: (204) 632-8709

New Brunswick

Fredericton Daily Gleaner
Prospect Street at Smythe, P.O. Box 3370, Fredericton,
    N.B., E3B 5A2
Phone: (506) 452-6671   Fax: (506) 452-7405

Telegraph–Journal & Evening Times–Globe
210 Crown Street, P.O. Box 2350, Saint John, N.B. E2L 3V8
Phone: (506) 632-8888   Fax: (506) 648-2661

Times–Transcript
939 Main Street, P.O. Box 1001, Moncton, N.B. E1C 8P3
Phone: (506) 859-4900   Fax: 859-4899

Newfoundland

Telegram
P.O. Box 5970, St. John's, Nfld. A1C 5X7
Phone: (709) 364-6300   Fax: (709) 364-9333

Western Star
West Street, P.O. Box 460, Corner Brook, Nfld. A2H 6E7
Phone: (709) 634-4348   Fax: (709) 634-9824

Nova Scotia

Amherst Daily News
P.O. Box 280, Amherst, N.S. B4H 3Z2
Phone: (902) 667-5102   Fax: (902) 667-0419

Cape Breton Post
255 George Street, P.O. Box 1500, Sydney, N.S. B1P 6K6
Phone: (902) 564-5451   Fax: (902) 562-7077

Chronicle–Herald
1650 Argyle Street, Halifax, N.S. B3J 2T2
Phone: (902) 426-2898   Fax: (902) 426-3382

Daily News
6 Louise Street, P.O. Box 220, Truro, N.S. B2N 5C3
Phone: (902) 893-9405   Fax: (902) 893-0518

Evening News
352 East River Road, New Glasgow, N.S. B2H 5E2
Phone: (902) 752-3000   Fax: (902) 752-1945

Mail–Star
1650 Argyle Street, Halifax, N.S. B3J 2T2
Phone: (902) 426-2898   Fax: (902) 426-3382

Ontario

Barrie Examiner
16 Bayfield Street, Barrie, Ont. L4M 4T6
Phone: (705) 726-6537   Fax: (705) 726-7245

Beacon Herald
108 Ontario Street, P.O. Box 430, Stratford, Ont. N5A 6T6
Phone: (519) 271-2220   Fax: (519) 271-1026

Brantford Expositor
53 Dalhousie Street, Brantford, Ont. N3T 5S8
Phone: (519) 756-2020   Fax: (519) 756-4911

Brockville Recorder & Times
23 King Street W., P.O. Box 10, Brockville, Ont. K6V 5T8
Phone: (613) 342-4441   Fax: (613) 342-4456

Cambridge Reporter
26 Ainslie Street S., Cambridge, Ont. N1R 3K1
Phone: (519) 621-3810   Fax: (519) 621-8239

Chatham Daily News
45 – 4th Street, P.O. Box 2007, Chatham, Ont. N7M 2G4
Phone: (519) 354-2000   Fax: (519) 436-0949

Cobourg Daily Star
415 King Street W., P.O. Box 400, Cobourg, Ont. K9A 4L1
Phone: (416) 372-0131   Fax: (416) 372-4966

Daily Bulletin
P.O. Box 339, Fort Frances, Ont. P9A 3M7
Phone: (807) 274-5373   Fax: (807) 274-7286

Daily Miner & News
33 Main Street S., P.O. Box 1620, Kenora, Ont. P9N 3X7
Phone: (807) 468-5555   Fax: (807) 468-4315

Globe and Mail
444 Front Street W., Toronto, Ont. M5V 2S9
Phone: (416) 585-5411   Fax: (416) 585-5275

Guelph Daily Mercury
14 Macdonnell Street, Suite 8, Guelph, Ont. N1H 6P7
Phone: (519) 822-4310   Fax: (519) 767-1681

Hamilton Spectator
44 Frid Street, Hamilton, Ont. L8N 3G3
Phone: (416) 526-3333   Fax: (416) 522-1696

Intelligencer
45 Bridge Street E., Belleville, Ont. K8N 1L5
Phone: (613) 962-9171   Fax: (613) 962-9652

Kitchener–Waterloo Record
225 Fairway Road, Kitchener, Ont. N2G 4E5
Phone: (519) 894-2231   Fax: (519) 894-3912

Lindsay Daily Post
15 William Street N., Lindsay, Ont. K9V 3Z8
Phone: (705) 324-2114   Fax: (705) 324-0174

London Free Press
369 York Street, P.O. Box 2280, London, Ont. N6A 4G1
Phone: (519) 679-1111   Fax: (519) 667-4523

Niagara Falls Review
4801 Valley Way, Niagara Falls, Ont. L2E 6T6
Phone: (416) 358-5711   Fax: (416) 356-0785

North Bay Nugget
259 Worthington Street W., P.O. Box 570, North Bay,
   Ont. P1B 8J6
Phone: (705) 472-3200   Fax: (705) 472-1438

Observer
186 Alexander Street, Pembroke, Ont. K8A 4L9
Phone: (613) 732-3691   Fax: (613) 732-2645

Orillia Packet & Times
31 Colborne Street E., Orillia, Ont. L3V 1T4
Phone: (705) 325-1355   Fax: (705) 325-7691

Oshawa Times
44 Richmond Street W., Oshawa, Ont. L1G 1C8
Phone: (416) 723-3474   Fax: (416) 723-4366

Ottawa Citizen
1101 Baxter Road, P.O. Box 5020, Ottawa, Ont. K2C 3M4
Phone: (613) 829-9100   Fax: (613) 829-5032

Peterborough Examiner
400 Water Street, P.O. Box 3890, Peterborough, Ont. K9J 8L4
Phone: (705) 745-4641   Fax: (705) 743-4581

Port Hope Guide
121C Toronto Road, P.O. Box 296, Port Hope, Ont. L1A 3W4
Phone: (416) 885-2471

St. Catharines Standard
17 Queen Street, St. Catharines, Ont. L2R 5G5
Phone: (416) 684-7251   Fax: (416) 684-8011

Sarnia Observer
140 South Front Street, Sarnia, Ont. N7T 7M8
Phone: (519) 344-3641   Fax: (519) 332-2951

Simcoe Reformer
105 Donly Drive, Simcoe, Ont. N3Y 4L2
Phone: (519) 426-5710   Fax: (519) 426-9255

Standard–Freeholder
44 Pitt Street, Cornwall, Ont. K6J 3P3
Phone: (613) 933-3160   Fax: (613) 933-7521

Star
145 Old Garden River Road, Sault Ste. Marie, Ont. P6A 5M5
Phone: (705) 759-3030   Fax: (705) 942-8690

Sudbury Star
33 Mackenzie Street, Sudbury, Ont. P3C 4Y1
Phone: (705) 674-5271   Fax: (705) 674-0624

Sun–Times
290 – 9th Street E., Owen Sound, Ont. N4K 5P2
Phone: (519) 376-2250   Fax: (519) 376-7190

Times–Journal
16 Hincks Street, St. Thomas, Ont. N5P 3W6
Phone: (519) 631-2790   Fax: (519) 631-5653

Times–News/Chronicle–Journal
75 South Cumberland Street, Thunder Bay, Ont. P7B 1A3
Phone: (807) 344-6200   Fax: (807) 345-5991

Timmins Daily Press
187 Cedar Street S., Timmins, Ont. P4N 2G9
Phone: (705) 268-5050   Fax: (705) 268-7373

Toronto Star
1 Yonge Street, Toronto, Ont. M5E 1E6
Phone: (416) 869-4321   Fax: (416) 869-4416

Toronto Sun
333 King Street E., Toronto, Ont. M5A 3X5
Phone: (416) 947-2333   Fax: (416) 947-2441

Welland–Port Colborne Tribune
228 East Main Street, Welland, Ont. L3B 3W8
Phone: (416) 732-2411   Fax: (416) 732-4883

Whig–Standard
306 King Street E., Kingston, Ont. K7L 4Z7
Phone: (613) 544-5000   Fax: (613) 544-6994

Windsor Star
167 Ferry Street, Windsor, Ont. N9A 4M5
Phone: (519) 255-5711   Fax: (519) 255-5778

Woodstock–Ingersoll Daily Sentinel Review
16 Brock Street, Woodstock, Ont. N4S 8A5
Phone: (519) 537-2341   Fax: (519) 537-3049

Prince Edward Island

Guardian & Patriot
165 Prince Street., Charlottetown, P.E.I. C1A 4R7
Phone: (902) 894-8506   Fax: (902) 566-3808

Journal–Pioneer
4 Queen Street, Summerside, P.E.I. C1N 4K5
Phone: (902) 436-2121   Fax: (902) 436-3027

Quebec

The Gazette
250 St. Antoine Street, Montreal, Que. H2Y 3R7
Phone: (514) 987-2399   Fax: (514) 987-2323

Sherbrooke Record
2850 Delorme Street, Sherbrooke, Que. J1K 1A1
Phone: (819) 569-9525   Fax: (819) 569-3945

Saskatchewan

Leader–Post
1964 Park Street, Regina, Sask. S4P 3G4
Phone: (306) 565-8211   Fax: (306) 565-8350

Prince Albert Herald
30 – 10th Street E., Prince Albert, Sask. S6V 5R9
Phone: (306) 764-4276   Fax: (306) 763-3331

StarPhoenix
204 – 5th Avenue N., Saskatoon, Sask. S7K 2P1
Phone: (306) 664-8340   Fax: (306) 664-8208

Times–Herald
44 Fairford Street W., Moose Jaw, Sask. S6H 6E4
Phone: (306) 692-6441   Fax: (306) 692-2101

5

BOOK PUBLISHERS

Unless they are crafting novels or writing on subjects deeply personal to them, professionals rarely produce books on speculation. The hard work involved – research and revisions stretched over months or years – is better invested in a firm commitment from a publisher. This follows a full proposal on how the book will be shaped, what each chapter will include, and how it will be written. Where an unpublished writer is concerned, however, most publishers will not make a final commitment until they have read the finished manuscript.

The first-time author should be under no illusions about the difficulties of breaking into the book publishing market – still less, unless you are phenomenally talented or hit on that rare winning formula, of making a living from the slender proceeds. Nonetheless, every year brings a new success story – another brilliant unknown author takes the publishing world by storm. Every writer must be a realist, *and* an optimist.

Professional writers will attest that writing books is a little easier after having consistently fed well-tailored articles to top magazines. As opposed to a long newspaper story, the magazine piece, in design, content, tone, and colour, conforms more closely to a short book, and can be a logical stepping-stone to longer, more substantial works. On the other hand, some publishers put greater trust in the newcomer than the journalist-turned-author. Certainly the disciplines are very different, though there are plenty of professional writers who have worked successfully across these boundaries. Many experienced Canadian authors supplement their royalty cheques with earnings from their magazine contributions.

Canada has all kinds of book publishers – from small presses producing two or three titles a year to large houses that turn out as many as sixty to a hundred. Most larger houses can offer authors an advance against royalties on acceptance of their proposal, though this is seldom the case with small and scholarly presses. Depending on the author and the book's potential in the marketplace, an advance can range from $500 to tens of thousands – not many of these! After publication, and once the advance has been earned, the author receives a royalty cheque every six or twelve months for the life of his or her book. An average royalty on a hardcover book is 10 per cent of the selling price. At this rate, a 3,000-copy sale of a twenty-five-dollar book would eventually yield the writer $7,500. Usually, authors can expect an 8 per cent royalty on the paperback version, but because it is cheaper than a hardcover, the paperback is likely to sell through in larger quantities so may be a bigger money-spinner. Some small presses offer royalties in copies, usually 10 per cent of the print run for adult books.

Small presses are more likely to take an interest in an unpublished writer, and are generally more receptive to unsolicited manuscripts. They also may be more accessible, offer more personal attention to their authors, and be more willing to take a risk. Nino Ricci's prize-winning first novel, *Lives of the Saints*, was published by Cormorant Press, having been rejected by a raft of the larger players. He had no difficulty placing his eagerly awaited second novel with a major house. Small presses almost always work with unagented writers. On the down side, small publishers can rarely offer an advance, their print runs tend to be low, and their distribution systems cannot match those of the big houses.

While editors are always on the lookout for high-quality fiction, non-fiction books are far easier to market. Books are normally bought well in advance of publication. Fall books, for example, are usually required to be on an editor's desk by the previous January or February. The contract for each book will have been signed a year or eighteen months prior to publication. Occasionally a title rejected by a publisher one year will be bought a couple of years later, when it fits better with the publisher's current needs. A book may be turned down because the publisher has a similar one underway. If you study a big publisher's list for one season, you'll notice that it does not publish a random selection of books so much as an editorial program of releases likely to satisfy a range of tastes.

You can save yourself much wasted time and dashed hopes by undertaking a little research into the Canadian publishing scene *before* you submit your proposal or manuscript. Use this chapter to draw up a shortlist of publishers whose programs seem most compatible with your own work, then check out some of their books at a good bookstore. If this is not practical, write to their publicity departments to request recent catalogues. Familiarity with the programs of several houses can help you develop an attractive proposal as well as target the most appropriate potential publishers.

Given how difficult it is to place a manuscript, it's worth re-emphasizing the importance of an attractive, interesting, well-presented proposal. Editors simply do not have the time to unravel an ill-prepared proposal or to sift through unwieldy, indifferently written manuscripts that arrive unannounced. It's always best to know the name of the editor or publisher to whom you are submitting. Manuscripts addressed to "The Editor" often end up in the slush pile, where they can languish for years. The sad truth is that most of the unsolicited material that crosses the editors' desks is unpublishable. Your aim must be to present a submission that will stand out dramatically from the rest. Generally, a detailed outline together with a sample chapter and a covering letter will be received best. *Always* include an SASE if you want your material returned, and prepare for a wait of up to two or three months for the editor's response. What the editor will be looking for is originality, a strong central idea, intelligent organization, clarity, an engaging writing style, and, of course, "saleability." Marketing information can be useful. Enclose a list of recent books on similar subjects with your submission (check *Books in Print* at the library). Think about your audience and how the publisher might reach it.

It is a truism that would-be authors must learn to cope with rejection. First-timers might draw comfort from the knowledge of how many great writers could paper their walls with publishers' rejection letters received early in their careers. (Coincidentally, both Faulkner's great work *The Sound and the Fury* and William Kennedy's Pulitzer Prize-winning *Ironweed* were rejected thirteen times before finding publishers. On an altogether different scale, big-selling English crime writer John Creasey, who has published more than five hundred novels, is said to have received no less than 744 rejections. And much-loved short-story writer William Saroyan claims to have begun his career with a stack of rejection slips thirty inches high!) Since editors usually don't have time to issue more than a standard rejection note, take heart if the rejection is sugared with qualified praise or, better still, specific constructive criticism. Chances are the editor is not simply letting you down gently, but genuinely sees redeeming value in your work. Be open to suggestions, and consider reworking your manuscript if the advice seems sensible. You may even be able to resubmit to the same editor.

Writing is an isolating occupation, and it is good for morale as well as immensely practical to tap into one of the many writers' groups that exist in the community – a list of provincial associations is provided in Chapter 9. For professional writers with at least one published book behind them, valuable support is available from the Writers' Union of Canada, which offers members an impressive array of services and resources, from assistance with contracts and grievances with publishers to a range of practical publications, a custom-designed insurance plan, and other benefits. Some of the union's professional guides that may be ordered by non-members for a small cost are *Help Yourself to a Better Contract*; *Tradebook Contract*; *Anthology Rates and Contracts*; *Writer's Income Tax Guide*; *Writers' Guide to Canadian Publishers*; and *Libel: A Handbook for Canadian Publishers, Editors and Writers*. Above all, the Writers' Union of Canada gives its members the opportunity to share their concerns and experiences with fellow writers, providing a forum for collective action to support their interests.

Many of these services are also available to members of the Canadian Authors Association, which has branches across the country. Founded in Montreal in 1921, the CAA has represented the interests of Canadian writers on many fronts, from championing improved copyright protection and the Public Lending Right to helping individual writers improve their contracts with publishers. (The Public Lending Right provides published writers with income from books held in libraries by compensating them according to how often their books are borrowed. In 1993, according to *Masthead* magazine, 8,393 authors received an average of $821 each – it may come as no surprise that federal cuts are expected to reduce this benefit.) They publish the quarterly magazine *Canadian Author* and *The Canadian Writer's Guide*, a handbook for freelance writers. They also administer several major literary awards. Local branches hold writing classes, workshops, and literary competitions, and organize author tours.

Specialist writers' organizations, too, offer resources and support to writers in their field. The Canadian Society of Chidren's Authors, Illustrators and Performers (CANSCAIP), through its newsletter, regular meetings, and other organized activities, offers practical advice, moral support, and useful contacts to writers of children's books. The Canadian Children's Book Centre in Toronto also offers writers and illustrators of books for children a range of resources and services. The centre has a comprehensive reference library of children's books and promotes children's writers and titles through author tours and book readings. Their publication *Get Published: The Writing for Children Kit* is particularly useful for aspiring children's authors.

Before outlining what we do cover in this chapter, perhaps it's worth clarifying what we don't. Educational publishers are not listed unless they have a significant trade publishing arm. Today more than ever, educational publishers are commissioning their books in close collaboration with schools and colleges to meet specific curricular needs. These texts are nearly always written by specialists in the field. Very few educational publishers consider unsolicited manuscripts or proposals, and fewer still are likely to look favourably upon them, unless their author has a proven track record in the area.

Neither, with a couple of exceptions, have we included publishers that specialize entirely in poetry. For a comprehensive listing, consult *Poetry Markets for Canadians* (5th edition), published by the League of Canadian Poets. Finally, as mentioned in the introduction, we have again focused on English-language publishing houses only.

The inventory that follows, then, includes all the major and many of the smaller English-language trade publishers currently operating in Canada. Some have large, general interest lists; others are more specialized, either in their subject areas or in their regional concerns; all offer market opportunities for your work.

Altitude Publishing Ltd.

P.O. Box 340, Banff, Alta. TOL 0C0

Phone: (403) 762-4548   Fax: (403) 762-2061

Contact: Stephen Hutchings, editor

Established 1979. Publishes photographic and historical books about British Columbia and the Rockies. Releases 3 or 4 new titles a year. No unsolicited manuscripts.

The Anglican Book Centre

600 Jarvis Street, Toronto, Ont. M4Y 2J6

Phone: (416) 924-9192   Fax: (416) 968-7983

Contact: The Rev. Michael Lloyd, publisher

Publishes manuscripts by Canadians on religious and contemporary issues, such as theology, spirituality, peace, justice, and feminism. Produced 12 new titles in 1993. No unsolicited manuscripts. Accepts written inquiries in the stated areas of interest.

Notable 1993 title: *No Longer Strangers: Ministry in a Multicultural Society*, Romney Moseley.

Annick Press Ltd.

15 Patricia Avenue, Willowdale, Ont. M2M 1H9

Phone: (416) 221-4802   Fax: (416) 221-8400

Contact: Rick Wilks or Anne Millyard, co-directors

Established 1975. Publishes children's literature, mainly picture books with some pre-teen novels and non-fiction – books to "project supportive and positive messages to young readers while also entertaining and enthralling them." Released 28 new titles in 1993. Accepts unsolicited manuscripts, but first send sample chapters, and "be sure your submission is appropriate to our list." No faxed submissions accepted. Guidelines available.

Notable 1993 title: *Out on the Ice in the Middle of the Bay*, Peter Cumming.

Arsenal Pulp Press

100 – 1062 Homer Street, Vancouver, B.C. V6B 2W9

Phone: (604) 687-4233   Fax: (604) 669-8250

Contact: Brian Lam, managing editor

Established 1971. Publishes fiction, culture, politics, regional,

Native subjects, and humour. "Our mandate is to publish provocative books that challenge the status quo, regardless of the subject matter." Accepts unsolicited manuscripts, but first send inquiry with outline and sample chapters. Guidelines available.

Notable 1993 title: *Whispered Art History,* Keith Wallace.

Aurora Editions

2489 Clover Street, Ottawa, Ont. KIV 8G6
Phone: (613) 526-2866   Fax: (613) 526-2866
Contact: Roma Quapp, editor/publisher

Established 1993. A new small publisher seeking original fiction and non-fiction representing a women's perspective on the world, including literary fiction, biography, and social critique by, for, and/or about women. "We are looking for writing that is literary in style, daring in its use of language, challenging in its view of the world, and yet accessible to a broad spectrum of society." Send entire manuscript for fiction, outline with sample chapter for non-fiction. Guidelines available.

Notable 1994 title: *Tale of the Ex-Fire-Eater,* Sheila Dalton.

Bantam Books Canada Inc.

105 Bond Street, 4th Floor, Toronto, Ont. M5B 1Y3
Phone: (416) 340-0777   Fax: (416) 340-1069
Contact: editorial department

Publishes fiction and non-fiction aimed at a mass market. Will not accept unsolicited manuscripts.

Beach Holme Publishers Ltd.

4252 Commerce Circle, Victoria, B.C. V8Z 4M2
Phone: (604) 727-6514   Fax: (604) 727-6418
Contact: Antonia Banyard, senior editor

Formerly Porcépic Books, established 1971. Specializes in speculative science fiction, poetry, young adult novels, Western regional history, and biography. Published 12 new titles in 1993. Accepts unsolicited manuscripts, but first send an inquiry. "After acceptance for publication, we require that all manuscripts be made available electronically." Guidelines available.

Notable 1993 title: *White Jade Tiger,* Julie Lawson.

Between the Lines
394 Euclid Avenue, Suite 203, Toronto, Ont. M6G 2S9
Phone: (416) 925-8260   Fax: (416) 324-8268
Contact: Marg Anne Morrison, managing editor

Established 1977. Publishes non-fiction books on Canadian social and political issues, culture, Third World development, gender politics, gay and lesbian politics, and the media. Produced 8 new titles in 1993. Send full proposal before submitting manuscript. Author guidelines available.

Notable 1993 title: *Rituals of Failure: What Schools Really Teach,* Sandro Contenta.

Black Moss Press
P.O. Box 143, Station A, Windsor, Ont. N9A 6L7
Phone: (519) 252-2551
Contact: Kristina Russelo, editor

Established 1969. Publishes novellas (40,000 words maximum), poetry, and children's picture books. Produced 10 new titles in 1993. No unsolicited manuscripts.

Notable 1993 title: *The Debris of Planets,* Clive Doucet.

Blizzard Publishing
301 – 89 Princess Street, Winnipeg, Man. R3B 1K6
Phone: (204) 949-0511   Fax: (204) 949-0013
Contact: Peter Atwood, managing editor

Established 1985. A literary publisher specializing in contemporary drama and theatre-related books. Publishes 8 to 10 new titles a year. Now expanding its markets beyond drama. Accepts unsolicited manuscripts, but first send an outline and sample chapters. Author guidelines available.

Notable 1993 title: *The Stillborn Lover,* Timothy Findley.

Borealis/Tecumseh Presses
9 Ashburn Drive, Ottawa, Ont. K2E 6N4
Phone: (613) 224-6837   Fax: (613) 829-7783
Contact: Glenn Clever, editor

Established 1972. Publishes poetry, fiction, and general trade with Canadian authorship or interest. Releases about 10 new books each year. Unsolicited manuscripts not accepted. Send a query together with an outline and sample chapters. Guidelines available.

Notable 1993 title: *New Canadian Drama 6: Feminist Plays,* ed. Rita Much.

The Boston Mills Press

132 Main Street, Erin, Ont. NOB 1TO
Phone: (519) 833-2407   Fax: (519) 833-2195
Contact: John Denison, publisher

Established 1974. Specializes in historical works. Releases about 20 new titles a year. Publishes local or regional history, guidebooks, and large-format pictorials. Accepts unsolicited manuscripts, but first send an inquiry. Author guidelines available.

Notable 1993 title: *At the Water's Edge: Muskoka's Boathouses,* John De Visser and Judy Ross.

Breakwater Books Ltd.

100 Water Street, P.O. Box 2188, St. John's, Nfld. A1C 6E6
Phone: (709) 722-6680   Fax: (709) 753-0708
Contact: Laura Woodford, editor

Established 1973. Publishes educational materials and a wide selection of manuscripts about Atlantic Canada, including plays, poetry, satire, biography, songbooks, cookbooks, and fiction. Main areas of interest include environmental science, enterprise education, and language arts. Released 10 new titles in 1993. "We are especially interested in Canadian writers with experience in writing for the school market." No unsolicited manuscripts. Send outline and writing sample.

Notable 1993 title: *In Hardy Country,* Tom Dawe.

Brick Books

P.O. Box 38, Station B, London, Ont. N6A 4V3
Phone: (519) 657-8579   Fax: (519) 657-8579
Contact: Kitty Lewis, general manager

Established 1975. Publishes Canadian poetry only. Released 7 new titles during 1993. Accepts unsolicited manuscripts. Guidelines available.

Notable 1993 title: *Riffs,* Dennis Lee.

Broadview Press Ltd.

P.O. Box 1243, Peterborough, Ont. K9J 7H5
Phone: (705) 743-8990   Fax: (705) 743-8353
624 – 604 1st Street S.W., Calgary, Alta. T2P 1M7
Phone: (403) 232-6863   Fax: (403) 232-6863
Contact: Don LePan, president; Michael Harrison, vice-president

Established 1985. Publishes university and college texts, specializing in the arts and social sciences, and some general trade non-fiction. Subject areas include Canadian politics, history, philosophy, English literature, ethics, and medieval studies. Covers a broad range of political and philosophical viewpoints. About 20 new titles a year. Query first, preferably with outline and sample chapters. Catalogues available on request.

Butterworths Canada Ltd.

75 Clegg Road, Markham, Ont. L6G 1A1
Phone: (905) 479-2665   Fax: (905) 479-2826
Contact: Ruth Epstein, manager, product development

Established 1912. Specializes in legal, business, and accounting materials for the professional market. Welcomes inquiries within these designated areas. Send an outline and sample chapters. No unsolicited manuscripts. Guidelines available.

Notable 1993 title: *The Conduct of an Appeal,* John Sopinka and Mark Gelowitz.

Cacanadadada Press

3350 West 21st Avenue, Vancouver, B.C. V6S 1G7
Phone: (604) 738-1195   Fax: (604) 733-5961
Contact: R.B. Hatch, director

Established 1988. Publishes general trade books, specializing in fiction, poetry, and local history, with a good mix of first-time and established authors. Interested in quality and experimental literature. Averages 5 new titles a year. Accepts unsolicited manuscripts. "First-book authors should ensure that they have some prior publication in magazines. Please send the entire manuscript, or at least the first half – odd pages are of little value – and include a short bio."

Notable 1993 title: *The East Wind Blows West,* George Jonas.

The Caitlin Press
P.O. Box 2387, Station B, Prince George, B.C. v2n 2s6
Phone: (604) 964-4953   Fax: (604) 964-4953
Contact: Cynthia Wilson, managing editor
   Established 1977. A small regional publisher specializing in trade books by B.C. Interior authors. Some literary titles by B.C. authors. Publishes about 4 or 5 titles a year. "We are interested primarily in Canada's North, particularly northern British Columbia." Accepts unsolicited manuscripts that meet these criteria. Guidelines available.
   Notable 1993 title: *Ginter,* Jan Udo Wenzel.

Camden House Publishing
7 Queen Victoria Road, Camden East, Ont. kok 1j0
Phone: (613) 378-6661   Fax: (613) 378-6123
Contact: Tracy Read, editor
   Established 1976. Publishes anthologies from *Harrowsmith* magazine and books on gardening, cooking, the natural sciences, astronomy, wildlife, and natural history. Produced 8 new titles in 1993. Accepts unsolicited manuscripts.
   Notable 1993 title: *Stencil It! Kids' Projects,* Sandra Buckingham.

Canadian Arctic Resources Committee
1 Nicholas Street, Suite 401, Ottawa, Ont. kip 7b7
Phone: (613) 236-7379   Fax: (613) 232-4665
Contact: Terry Fenge, executive director
   Established 1971. Publishes mostly scholarly non-fiction, usually related to Canada's North: its people, environment, and resource development. Particularly concerned with environmental issues. Also aboriginal rights, self-government, and international matters pertaining to northern Canada and the circumpolar world. Produces 4 to 6 new titles a year. Accepts unsolicited manuscripts, but first send an inquiry. Guidelines available.

Canadian Stage and Arts Publications Ltd.
263 Adelaide Street W., 5th Floor, Toronto, Ont. m5h 1y2
Phone: (416) 785-4300   Fax: (416) 785-4329
Contact: George Heucz, editor

Established 1975. Publishes an average of 4 new arts, science, and children's books each year. No unsolicited manuscripts.

Notable 1993 title: *Mickey, Taggy, Puppo and Cica Celebrate Toronto Zoo,* Kati Rekai.

Carleton University Press

160 Paterson Hall, Carleton University, Ottawa, Ont. K1S 5B6
Phone: (613) 788-3740   Fax: (613) 788-2893
Contact: Michael Gnarowski, director

Established 1982. Publishes scholarly and trade books focusing on Canadian studies. Subject areas include women's studies, geography, history, sociology, anthropology and aboriginal peoples, media studies, political science, law, economics, public administration, literature, art, philosophy, and the classics. Released 17 new books in 1993. Accepts full manuscripts in declared areas of interest. Guidelines available.

Notable 1993 title: *Seize the Day: Lester B. Pearson and Crisis Diplomacy,* Geoffrey A.H. Pearson.

Coach House Press

50 Prince Arthur Avenue, Suite 107, Toronto, Ont. M5R 1B5
Phone: (416) 921-3910   Fax: (416) 921-4403
Contact: Diane Martin (submissions), Laura Macdonald (general inquiries)

Established 1965. Publishes fiction, visual arts, drama, poetry, and essays. Released 18 new titles in 1993. Inquire before sending manuscripts.

Notable 1993 title: *Good Bones* (p'back), Margaret Atwood.

Cormorant Books Inc.

R.R. 1, Dunvegan, Ont. K0C 1J0
Phone: (613) 527-3348   Fax: (613) 527-2262
Contact: Jan Geddes, publisher

Established 1986. Publishes adult fiction, short and long, featuring work from the literary mainstream and from ethnic minorities. Released 9 new titles in 1993. Accepts unsolicited manuscripts. There's a 4- to 6-month response delay for submissions.

Notable 1993 title: *Drowning in Darkness,* Peter Oliva.

Coteau Books

2206 Dewdney Avenue, Suite 401, Regina, Sask. S4R 1H3
Phone: (306) 777-0170   Fax: (306) 522-5152
Contact: Shelley Sopher, managing editor

Established 1975. Publishes poetry, short stories, novels, books on writers and writing, anthologies, children's stories, women's issues, and drama. Averages 12 new titles a year. Reviews unsolicited manuscripts by Canadian writers. "We will not accept multiple/simultaneous submissions. We consider children's manuscripts only by Prairie authors."

Notable 1993 title: *The Crew*, Don Dickinson.

Crabtree Publishing Co. Ltd.

360 York Road, R.R. 4, Niagara-on-the-Lake, Ont. L0S 1J0
Phone: (905) 468-4947   Fax: (905) 468-5680
Contact: Bobbie Kalman, publisher

Established 1978. Publishes children's illustrated non-fiction written at a specific reading level to meet educational demands. Subjects include ecology, animals, and historic communities. Released 24 new titles in 1993. Accepts unsolicited manuscripts, but first send inquiry and outline.

Notable 1993 title: *Endangered Ocean Animals*, David Taylor.

Creative Publishers Ltd.

P.O. Box 8660, St. John's, Nfld. A1B 3T7
Phone: (709) 722-8500   Fax: (709) 722-2228
Contact: Donald Morgan, manager

Established 1983. Publishes mainly local history and biography by Newfoundland writers. The Killick Press imprint specializes in literary books: novels, short stories, poetry, creative non-fiction, and drama. Released 12 titles in 1993. Query first. Guidelines available.

Notable 1993 title: *Waking Up in the City of Dreams*, Bryan Hennessey.

Harry Cuff Publications Ltd.

94 LeMarchant Road, St. John's, Nfld. A1C 2H2
Phone: (709) 726-6590   Fax: (709) 726-0902
Contact: Dr. Harry Cuff, director

Established 1981. Publishes an average of 7 books a year on

Newfoundland and/or by Newfoundlanders. Accepts unsolicited manuscripts but prefers initial inquiry.

Detselig Enterprises Ltd.

1220 Kensington Road N.W., Suite 210, Calgary, Alta. T2N 3P5
Phone: (403) 283-0900   Fax: (403) 283-6947
Contact: S. McEwan, editor

Established 1975. Publishes academic, professional, and trade books. Half the list is academic/scholarly, the other half general interest non-fiction. Averages 20 new books each year. Accepts unsolicited manuscripts, but first send inquiry letter with outline and sample chapters. Guidelines available.

Notable 1993 title: *On Foreign Assignment*, Ab Douglas.

Doubleday Canada Ltd.

105 Bond Street, Toronto, Ont. M5B 1Y3
Phone: (416) 340-0777   Fax: (416) 977-8488
Contact: John Pearce, editor-in-chief

Established 1944. Interested in Canadiana, children's books, and a wide range of adult fiction and non-fiction. Published 25 new titles in 1993. No unsolicited manuscripts or book proposals.

Notable 1993 title: *Savage Messiah*, Ross Laver and Paul Kaihla.

Douglas & McIntyre Ltd.

1615 Venables Street, Vancouver, B.C. V5L 2H1
Phone: (604) 254-7191   Fax: (604) 254-9099
Contact: Saeko Usukawa, editor
Toronto office: 585 Bloor Street W., 2nd Floor, Toronto,
    Ont. M6G 1K5
Phone: (416) 537-2501   Fax: (416) 537-4647
Contact: Lucy Fraser, editor

Established 1964. Publishes general trade books but specializes in history, biography, art, outdoors and recreation, and Native subjects. Produces 50 new titles annually. Toronto office handles all children's books. A submission including an outline with two or three sample chapters preferred.

Dundurn Press Ltd.

2181 Queen Street E., Suite 301, Toronto, Ont. M4E 1E5

Phone: (416) 698-0454   Fax: (416) 698-1102
Contact: Judith Turnbull, senior editor
Established 1973. Publishes Canadian history, biography, art, and literary criticism. Averages 50 new titles annually. Accepts unsolicited manuscripts, but first send outline and sample chapters. Guidelines available.

Notable 1993 title: *More Toronto Sketches*, Mike Filey.

ECW Press

1980 Queen Street E., 2nd Floor, Toronto, Ont. M4L 1J2
Phone: (416) 694-3348   Fax: (416) 698-9906
Contact: Jack David, president
Established 1974. Publishes reference books, literary criticism on Canadian writers and their works, and biography. Released 30 titles in 1993. Accepts unsolicited manuscripts, but send a query first. Guidelines available.

Notable 1993 title: *Jerry Seinfeld: Much Ado About Nothing*, Josh Levine.

Ekstasis Editions

P.O. Box 8474, Main Post Office, Victoria, B.C. V8W 3S1
Phone: (604) 385-3378
Contact: Carol Ann Sokoloff, editor
Established 1982. A literary press publishing elegant editions of poetry, novels, short story collections, children's stories (under the Cherubim imprint), and criticism, along with general environmental and New Age trade books. Averages 6 new books each year. Accepts written inquiries with outlines or sample chapters. Guidelines available.

Notable 1993 title: *Islands: Poems in the Traditional Forms of Japan*, Robin Skelton.

Exile Editions Ltd.

P.O. Box 67, Station B, Toronto, Ont. M5T 2C0
Phone: (416) 922-8221
Contact: Barry Callaghan, president
Established 1976. Publishes fiction, drama, poetry, and fiction and poetry in translation. Produced 12 new titles in 1993. Rarely

accepts unsolicited manuscripts. Be sure to study both *Exile* quarterly and the Exile Editions list before deciding to submit.

Notable 1993 title: *There Are No Elders,* Austin Clarke.

Fifth House Publishers

620 Duchess Street, Saskatoon, Sask. S7K 0R1
Phone: (306) 242-4936   Fax: (306) 242-7667
Contact: Charlene Dobmeier, managing editor

Established 1982. Publishes general trade books: serious and popular non-fiction, with some children's books, and a strong Native list. Releases 16 to 18 books a year. Accepts unsolicited manuscripts, but first send an inquiry. Guidelines available.

Notable 1993 title: *Firing the Heather: The Life and Times of Nellie McClung,* Mary Hallett and Marilyn Davis.

Fitzhenry & Whiteside Ltd.

195 Allstate Parkway, Markham, Ont. L3R 4T8
Phone: (905) 477-9700   Fax: (905) 477-9179
Contact: Robert Read, senior vice-president

Established 1966. Publishes a wide selection of general trade and education books, especially Canadian adult non-fiction and children's books. Releases about 30 titles a year. Reviews unsolicited manuscripts, but first send an outline or sample chapters.

Notable 1993 title: *Art for Enlightenment,* Rebecca Sisler.

Formac Publishing Co. Ltd.

5502 Atlantic Street, Halifax, N.S. B3H 1G4
Phone: (902) 421-7022   Fax: (902) 425-0166
Contact: Carolyn MacGregor, publisher

Established 1977. Publishes regional titles, including history, folklore, cookbooks, and guidebooks, Canadian biography, and children's books. Released 9 new titles in 1993. Accepts unsolicited manuscripts, but first send an outline or sample chapter.

Notable 1993 title: *A Victorian Lady's Album: Kate Shannon's Halifax and Boston Diary of 1892,* Della Stanley.

Garamond Press

77 Mowat Avenue, Suite 403, Toronto, Ont. M6K 3E3

Phone: (416) 516-2709   Fax: (416) 513-5652
Contact: Peter Saunders, director

Established 1981. Publishes academic and university texts. Subject areas include women's studies, cultural and labour studies, education, Third World topics, and ethnicity. Releases 6 to 8 new titles a year. No unsolicited manuscripts. Please note that this is a very specialized house. Written inquiries only. Guidelines available.

Notable 1993 title: *Hockey Night in Canada: Sport, Identities and Cultural Politics*, Richard Gruneau and David Whitson.

General Store Publishing House

1 Main Street, Burnstown, Ont. KOJ 1GO
Phone: (613) 432-7697   Fax: (613) 432-7184
Contact: Tim Gordon, publisher

Established 1980. Publishes history, military, cookbooks, regional titles on the Ottawa Valley, sports, and some children's books. Released 14 titles in 1993. Accepts unsolicited manuscripts.

Notable 1993 title: *The Canadian Beaver Book*, Jim Cameron.

Goose Lane Editions/Fiddlehead Poetry Books

469 King Street, Fredericton, N.B. E3B 1E5
Phone: (506) 450-4251   Fax: (506) 459-4991
Contact: Laurel Boone, acquisitions editor

Established 1958. Publishes Canadian adult literary fiction, non-fiction, and poetry. Produces about 12 new titles a year. Accepts unsolicited manuscripts, but send an inquiry first for non-fiction. Guidelines available.

Greey de Pencier Books

56 The Esplanade, Suite 302, Toronto, Ont. M5E 1A7
Phone: (416) 868-6001   Fax: (416) 868-6009
Contact: Sheba Meland, editor-in-chief

Established 1968. Publishes children's books, with an emphasis on non-fiction: nature, science, the environment, and children's activities; also general interest picture books and chapter books. Publishes books from *OWL*, with the *OWL* magazine imprint. Averages 10 new titles a year. Accepts unsolicited manuscripts, but first send outline and sample chapters.

Notable 1993 title: *On the Shuttle: Eight Days in Space,* Barbara Bondar with Dr. Roberta Bondar.

Grosvenor House Press Inc.

King West Centre, 2 Pardee Avenue, Suite 203, Toronto,
  Ont. M6K 3H5
Phone: (416) 532-3211   Fax: (416) 532-9277
Montreal office: 1456 Sherbrooke Street W., Suite 301, Montreal,
  Que. H3G 1K4
Phone: (514) 284-1138   Fax: (514) 284-0415
Contact: Anne Behrens, publishing manager
    Established 1982. Publishes in the medical field. Averages 8 titles a year. No unsolicited manuscripts. Written inquiries only.

Groundwood Books

585 Bloor Street W., 2nd Floor, Toronto, Ont. M6G 1K5
Phone: (416) 537-2501   Fax: (416) 537-4647
Contact: Lucy Fraser, editor
    A division of Douglas and McIntyre. Publishes children's books, especially picture books and novels for children of all ages. Averages 15 to 20 new titles a year. Prefers full unsolicited manuscripts rather than query letters. Send SASE; no cheques or money orders. Guidelines available.

Guernica Editions Inc.

P.O. Box 633, Station N.D.G., Montreal, Que. H4A 3R1
Phone: (514) 256-5599   Fax: (514) 254-1999
Contact: Antonio D'Alfonso, editor
    Established 1978. Specializes in prose and poetry addressing the Italian/North American experience. Also translates Québécois authors. Publishes 16 to 20 titles a year. No unsolicited manuscripts. Inquiries welcome. "We want writers interested in ethnicity and a new world vision."
    Notable 1993 title: *Benedetta in Guysterland,* Giose Rimanelli.

Gutter Press

1600 Bathurst Street, Suite 405, Toronto, Ont. M5P 3H9
Phone: (416) 787-8274 (evenings)

Contact: Sam Hiyate, editor/publisher

A gutsy new imprint of Steel Rail Publishing, specializing in "hip, contemporary, dangerous urban fiction." Produces 4 to 8 titles a year. Welcomes work by new writers, but check out the Gutter Press list before submitting sample chapters.

Notable 1993 title: *Stalking the Gilded Boneyard,* Christine Slater.

HMS Press

P.O. Box 340, Station B, London, Ont. N6A 4W1

Phone: (519) 434-4740

Contact: Wayne Ray, president

Specializes in books on disk. Averages 6 new titles a year. Interested in any well-written manuscript, any genre, any style: poetry, essays, history, biography, etc. Sold on computer diskette. Payment in kind plus royalties. "Do not send hard copy. Submit on disk in ASCII or WordPerfect."

Notable 1993 title: *Tailhook: What Really Happened,* Michael Dominic.

Hancock House Publishers Ltd.

19313 Zero Avenue, Surrey, B.C. V4P 1M7

Phone: (604) 538-1114   Fax: (604) 538-2262

Contact: Myron Shutty, editor

Established 1970. Specializes in Pacific Northwest history and biography, nature guides, Native culture, and natural history. Publishes about a dozen titles a year. No unsolicited manuscripts. Send a one- or two-page synopsis, a sample chapter, and biographical/marketing support material. Guidelines available.

Notable 1993 title: *Descent into Madness: Diary of a Killer,* Vernon Frolick.

Harbour Publishing

P.O. Box 219, Madeira Park, B.C. VON 2HO

Phone: (604) 883-2730   Fax: (604) 883-9451

Contact: Howard White, president

Established 1974. Publishes books on West Coast regional history and culture, both literary and non-fiction, as well as poetry and guides. Specializes in B.C. authors and women's issues. Published

20 titles in 1993. Accepts unsolicited manuscripts, but send letter of inquiry first. Guidelines available.

Notable 1993 title: *Reaching for the Beaufort Sea,* Al Purdy.

Harlequin Enterprises Ltd.

225 Duncan Mill Road, Don Mills, Ont. M3B 3K9
Phone: (416) 445-5860   Fax: (416) 445-8655
Contact: Candy Lee, vice-president, retail marketing and editorial

Established 1949. Each year publishes more than 700 mass-market paperback romances (Harlequin and Silhouette imprints) and mystery and action adventures (Golden Eagle and Worldwide Library imprints). Interested in receiving manuscript outlines, particularly those with series potential, in either fiction or non-fiction. Accepts unsolicited manuscripts, but initial inquiry preferred. Tip sheets available. New authors contracted only on full manuscript.

HarperCollins Canada Ltd.

55 Avenue Road, Suite 2900, West Tower at Hazelton Lanes,
    Toronto, Ont. M5R 3L2
Phone: (416) 975-9334   Fax: (416) 975-9884
Contact: Harold Hill, acquisitions editor

Publishes a wide range of fiction, non-fiction, business, young adult fiction, children's books, and collections. Produces over 100 titles each year. No unsolicited manuscripts. Agented writers only.

Notable 1993 title: *Headhunter,* Timothy Findley.

The Frederick Harris Music Co. Ltd.

529 Speers Road, Oakville, Ont. L6K 2G4
Phone: (905) 845-3487   Fax: (905) 845-1208
Contact: Trish Sauerbrei, managing editor

Established 1904. A not-for-profit publisher of music education materials, particularly curriculum material for the Royal Conservatory of Music. Released 15 new titles in 1993. Accepts unsolicited manuscripts. Guidelines available.

Notable 1993 title: *Ride with Me: A Journey from Unison to Part-Singing,* John Barron.

Hartley & Marks Ltd.

3661 West Broadway, Vancouver, B.C. V6R 2B8

Phone: (604) 739-1771   Fax: (604) 738-1913
Contact: Sue Tauber, editorial director
   Established 1973. Publishes practical non-fiction. Subject areas include innovative health, meditation, personal self-help, architecture, building, country living, practical crafts and technical books, and practical Asian traditions. Produced 9 new titles in 1993.

Harvest House Ltd.

1200 Atwater Avenue, Suite 1, Montreal, Que. H3Z 1X4
Phone: (514) 932-0666   Fax: (514) 933-1702
Contact: Maynard Gertler, editor
   Established 1959. Publishes general trade books, with special interest in history, biography, science, the social sciences, the environment, and public affairs. Also some scholarly books. Accepts unsolicited manuscripts.
   Notable 1993 title: *Canadian Medical Schools: Two Centuries of Medical History 1822-1992*, N. Tait McPhedran, MD.

Herald Press

490 Dutton Drive, Waterloo, Ont. N2L 6H7
Phone: (519) 887-8500   Fax: (519) 887-3111
Contact: David Garber, book editor
   Established in 1908 in the U.S., and in 1974 in Canada. Owned by the Mennonite Church. Publishes works on family life, Christian community, peace, a disciplined Church, and programs of evangelistic and mission outreach. Specializes in books for children aged 9 to 14, and Christian or religious fiction. Produced 32 new titles in 1993. Writer's guidelines available.
   Notable 1993 title: *No Permanent City*, Harry Loewen.

Heritage House Publishing Co. Ltd.

5543 – 129th Street, Surrey, B.C. V3X 3G5
Phone: (604) 596-5245   Fax: (604) 574-9942
Contact: Art Downs, president
   Established 1969. Specializes in original works on genealogy, history, travel, fishing, and general outdoors in British Columbia. Averages 4 new books a year. Accepts unsolicited manuscripts.

Highway Book Shop
R.R.1, Cobalt, Ont. POJ 1CO
Phone: (705) 679-8375   Fax: (705) 679-8511
Contact: Paul Bogart, production manager
 Began its serious publishing program in 1970. Publishes adult trade, fiction, non-fiction, and children's books – mainly by Canadian authors and with Northern themes. Priority given to local, northeastern Ontario history. Also interested in Native Canadian works. Adult and young adult fiction accepted on Northern and Native themes. Averages 10 new titles each year. Accepts unsolicited manuscripts as outlined above. First send outline with sample chapters. Guidelines available.
 Notable 1993 title: *The Age of Steam on Lake Temiskaming,* Bruce W. Taylor.

Horsdal & Schubart Publishers Ltd.
425 Simcoe Street, Suite 623, Victoria, B.C. V8V 4T3
Phone: (604) 360-2031   Fax: (604) 360-0829
Contact: Marlyn Horsdal, president/editor
 Established 1985. Specializes in Canadian non-fiction, with an emphasis on Western history and biography, politics, and sport; also the occasional work of fiction. Published 8 titles in 1993. Accepts unsolicited manuscripts, but phone or send letter of inquiry first.
 Notable 1993 title: *Forgive Me My Press Passes,* Jim Taylor.

Hounslow Press
2181 Queen Street E., Suite 301, Toronto, Ont. M4E 1E5
Phone: (416) 698-0454   Fax: (416) 698-1102
Contact: Tony Hawke, general manager
 Established 1972. (A subsidiary of Dundurn Press.) Publishes popular non-fiction, illustrated books, and a distinguished line of Canadian fiction and poetry. Produced 7 new titles in 1993. Send initial query letter.
 Notable 1993 title: *The $50,000 Stove Handle,* Gordon Pape.

Hyperion Press Ltd.
300 Wales Avenue, Winnipeg, Man. R2M 2S9
Phone: (204) 256-9204   Fax: (204) 255-7845

Contact: Dr. Marvis Tutiah, president

Established 1978. Specializes in craft and how-to books for all ages, and children's picture books (for under-12s). Averages 8 to 10 new titles a year. Accepts unsolicited manuscripts.

Notable 1993 title: *The Singing Snake,* Stefan Czernecki and Timothy Rhodes.

Irwin Publishing

1800 Steeles Avenue W., Concord, Ont. L4K 2P3
Phone: (905) 660-0611   Fax: (905) 660-0676
Contact: Norma Pettit, managing editor

Established 1945. Specializes in texts and teacher-support materials for elementary and high schools, some college, and professional books. Also, with sister company Stoddart Publishing, young adult novels. Releases 15 to 20 titles a year. Query with outline.

Jesperson Press

39 James Lane, St. John's, Nfld. A1E 3H3
Phone: (709) 753-5700   Fax: (709) 753-5507
Contact: Albert Johnson, publishing assistant

Established 1977. Publishes trade and educational books. Accepts unsolicited manuscripts.

Juniper Books Ltd.

R.R. 2, Renfrew, Ont. K7V 3Z5
Phone: (613) 432-8992
Contact: Carol McCuaig, editor

Established 1980. A small publisher specializing in regional history, particularly the history of the Ottawa Valley. Produced 3 titles in 1993. No unsolicited manuscripts, but inquiries welcome.

Notable 1993 title: *Centennial Echoes,* Betty O'Brien.

Key Porter Books

70 The Esplanade, 3rd Floor, Toronto, Ont. M5E 1R2
Phone: (416) 862-7777   Fax: (416) 862-2304
Contact: Susan Renouf, vice-president and editor-in-chief

Established 1980. Publishes mostly non-fiction in areas including politics, the environment, business, health, and natural history. Beginning mainstream adult and young children's fiction list.

Produced 63 titles in 1993. Prefers to see inquiry with outline and sample chapter before full manuscript. Guidelines available.

Notable 1993 title: *Born Naked*, Farley Mowat.

Kids Can Press Ltd.

29 Birch Avenue, Toronto, Ont. M4V 1E2
Phone: (416) 925-5437   Fax: (416) 960-5437
Contact: Valerie Hussey, publisher

Established 1973. Publishes quality books for children of all ages, including picture books, fiction, and junior and senior level information books. Averages 25 new titles each year. Accepts unsolicited manuscripts, but send outline and sample chapters for longer manuscripts. "Please familiarize yourself with our list before sending a manuscript. Request a catalogue if you're having trouble getting a good sense of the entire publishing program."

Alfred A. Knopf Canada

33 Yonge Street, Suite 210, Toronto, Ont. M5E 1G4
Phone: (416) 777-9477   Fax: (416) 777-9470
Contact: Catherine Yolles, editor

Established 1991. Publishes literary fiction and non-fiction. Committed to good Canadian literature and to bringing the best in international literature to Canadians. About 20 new titles a year. Accepts unsolicited manuscripts, but first send an inquiry.

Notable 1993 title: *The Wives of Bath*, Susan Swan.

Lancelot Press

P.O. Box 425, Hantsport, N.S. B0P 1P0
Phone: (902) 684-9129   Fax: (902) 684-3685
Contact: William Pope, editor

Established 1966. Publishes mostly non-fiction of particular interest to Atlantic Canada, but also interested in work of high quality and general interest, though very few novels and poetry collections. Released 17 titles in 1993. Accepts unsolicited manuscripts, but first send outline and sample chapters.

Notable 1993 title: *Collision at Sea*, Gregory P. Pritchard.

Lester Publishing Ltd.

56 The Esplanade, Suite 507A, Toronto, Ont. M5E 1A7

Phone: (416) 362-1032   Fax: (416) 362-1647
Contact: Janice Weaver, assistant editor

Established 1991. Publishes trade non-fiction and children's books. Adult list focuses on social issues and current affairs, along with some literary fiction. Children's list includes high-quality picture books and young adult fiction. Averages 15 new titles a year. Accepts unsolicited manuscripts, but first send query letter with outline or sample chapters. Guidelines available.

Notable 1993 title: *Mario*, Lawrence Martin.

Little, Brown & Co. (Canada) Ltd.

148 Yorkville Avenue, Toronto, Ont. M8Y 2L4
Phone: (416) 967-3888   Fax: (416) 967-4591
Contact: Ann Ledden, vice-president

Incorporated in 1954. A substantial international distributor of fiction/non-fiction adult and chidren's books with a small local publishing program (7 titles in 1993). No unsolicited manuscripts. Outlines and sample chapters considered.

Notable 1993 title: *A Suitable Boy*, Vikram Seth.

Lone Pine Publishing

10426 – 81st Avenue, Suite 206, Edmonton, Alta. T6E 1X5
Phone: (403) 433-9333   Fax: (403) 433-9646
Contact: Glenn Rollans, editor-in-chief

Established 1980. Specializes in natural history, popular history, outdoor recreation, and travel. Most books have a regional focus. Now has offices in Vancouver, Edmonton, and Washington State. Publishes about 30 new titles each year. Accepts unsolicited manuscripts, but first send an inquiry.

James Lorimer & Co. Ltd.

35 Britain Street, Toronto, Ont. M5A 1R7
Phone: (416) 362-4762   Fax: (416) 362-3939
Contact: publishing assistant

Established 1971. Specializes in books on Canadian politics, economics, and urban and social issues for the university and trade markets. Also children's/young adult (age 7 to 15) fiction addressing Canadian social issues. No picture books, fantasy, horror, or science fiction. Averages 15 new titles each year. Please send for guidelines before submitting.

Notable 1993 title: *The Politics of Kim Campbell,* Murray Dobbin.

Macfarlane, Walter & Ross

37A Hazelton Avenue, Toronto, Ont. M5R 2E3
Phone: (416) 924-7595   Fax: (416) 924-4254
Contact: Jan Walter, president

Established 1988. Publishes high-quality, popular non-fiction aimed at Canadian and international audiences, primarily in the fields of politics, business, history, biography, and popular culture. Produced 8 new titles in 1993. Send query first.

Macmillan Canada

29 Birch Avenue, Toronto, Ont. M4V 1E2
Phone: (416) 963-8830   Fax: (416) 923-4821
Contact: Denise Schon, vice-president and publisher

Publishes a variety of general trade books, primarily for and by Canadians. Specializes in cookbooks, sports, business, health, nutrition, and popular literary fiction. Averages 35 new books each year. Accepts inquiries with outline and sample chapters.

Maxwell Macmillan Canada

1200 Eglinton Avenue E., Suite 200, Don Mills, Ont. M3C 3N1
Phone: (416) 449-6030   Fax: (416) 449-0068
Contact: Patrick Gallagher, editorial director

Specializes in school and college publishing. Also young adult and non-fiction trade books in such areas as social psychology, politics, and religion. Accepts manuscript outlines and sample chapters.

McClelland & Stewart Inc.

481 University Avenue, Suite 900, Toronto, Ont. M5G 2E9
Phone: (416) 598-1114   Fax: (416) 598-7764
Contact: editorial department

Established 1906. Publishes a wide selection of fiction, and non-fiction on history, natural history, politics, religion, biography, and sports. Also publishes poetry, reference books, and textbooks at the college level. Releases about 80 titles a year. "We are 'The Canadian Publisher' and take our role to publish the best in Canadian fiction, non-fiction, and poetry very seriously. With a stable of authors ranging from Margaret Atwood through Pierre Berton on to Leonard Cohen and then to Alice Munro and Pierre Trudeau, this house is not a good point of entry for the beginning author." No unsolicited manuscripts. Send an inquiry for fiction, an outline for non-fiction.

Notable 1993 title: *Memoirs,* Pierre E. Trudeau.

McGill–Queen's University Press

McGill University, 3430 McTavish Street, Montreal,
    Que. H3A 1X9
Phone: (514) 398-3750   Fax: (514) 398-4333
Contact: Philip Cercone, editor
Queen's University office: Queen's University, Kingston,
    Ont. K7L 2P6
Phone: (613) 545-2155   Fax: (613) 545-6822
Contact: Professor Donald Akenson, editor

Established 1969. Publishes scholarly books on Arctic and Northern studies and history; political science with special emphasis on Canadian urban life; Commonwealth and Canadian literature; and books on architecture, philosophy and religion, North American Native peoples, anthropology, and sociology. Averages 60 new titles a year.

McGraw-Hill Ryerson Ltd.

300 Water Street, Whitby, Ont. L1N 9B6
Phone: (905) 430-5143   Fax: (905) 430-5020
Contact: Don Broad, publisher, consumer and prof. division

Established 1944. Publishes adult non-fiction consumer and reference books, notably in the areas of business, finance, real estate, military history, aviation, sports, and food and drink. Averages 40 titles a year. No fiction or children's manuscripts. Query letter and outline must be submitted first.

Notable 1993 title: *Eagleson: The Fall of a Hockey Czar,* Dave Houston and Bill Shoalts.

The Mercury Press

137 Birmingham Street, Stratford, Ont. N5A 2T1

Contact: Beverley Daurio, editor

Established 1978. Publishes Canadian adult fiction, non-fiction, and poetry. New short story writers should pursue journal publication widely before submitting work. Unsolicited manuscripts considered but rarely contracted. About 10 new titles each year. For an overview of list, send 9 in. x 12 in. SASE for catalogue.

Notable 1993 title: *Saints and Runners: Stories and a Novella,* Libby Scheier.

Micromedia Ltd.

20 Victoria Street, Toronto, Ont. M5C 2N8
Phone: (416) 362-5211   Fax: (416) 362-6161
Contact: Louise Fast, vice-president and general manager

Established 1972. Publishes microform, electronic, and print. Produces indexes, abstract databases, and printed directories. Frequently offers employment to business and legal writers. No unsolicited manuscripts.

Mika Publishing Company

200 Stanley Street, Belleville, Ont. K8N 5B2
Phone: (613) 962-4022
Contact: Helma Mika, editor

Established 1962. Specializes in local Canadian histories: county, township, and city. Publishes an average of 5 or 6 titles a year. Accepts written inquiry with outline for manuscripts that fall within stated area of interest.

Moonstone Press

175 Brock Street, Goderich, Ont. N7A 1R4
Phone: (519) 524-5645   Fax: (519) 524-6185
Contact: Peter Baltensperger, publisher

Established 1984. Publishes adult and children's fiction, and poetry. List emphasizes southwestern Ontario writers and new writers and illustrators. Averages 5 new titles a year. Accepts unsolicited manuscripts, but first send outline and sample chapters. No multiple submissions. "We look for literary excellence; no social issues or moralistic topics." Guidelines available.

Notable 1993 title: *Stones to Harvest,* Henry Beissel.

NC Press Ltd.

345 Adelaide Street W., Suite 400, Toronto, Ont. M5V 1R5
Phone: (416) 593-6284   Fax: (416) 593-6204
Contact: editorial department
  Established 1970. Interested in books on art, economics, history, poetry, politics, women's issues, Native peoples, multiculturalism, the environment, agriculture, health, food, literary criticism, and theatre. Canadian non-fiction for the intelligent layperson. Released 14 titles in 1993. Send query first.
  Notable 1993 title: *Food, Sex and Salmonella: The Risks of Environmental Intimacy,* David Waltner-Toews.

New World Perspectives

3652, avenue Laval, Montreal, Que. H2X 3C9
Phone: (514) 282-9298   Fax: (514) 987-9724
Contact: Marilouise Kroker, editor
  Established 1984. Publishes university-level books on feminism, social and political theory, technology, and postmodernism. No unsolicited manuscripts. Inquiries only.
  Notable 1993 title: *Spasm: Virtual Reality, Android Music, Electric Flash* (book/CD), text Arthur Kroker, music Steve Gibson.

NeWest Publishers Ltd.

10359 – 82nd Avenue, Suite 310, Edmonton, Alta. T6E 2V9
Phone: (403) 432-9427   Fax: (403) 432-9429
Contact: Eva Radford, editorial co-ordinator
  Established 1977. Publishes literature and non-fiction pertaining to Western Canada. Averages 8 new titles a year. No poetry. Accepts unsolicited manuscripts. Guidelines available.
  Notable 1993 title: *Boundless Alberta,* ed. Aritha Van Herk

Nimbus Publishing Ltd.

P.O. Box 9301, Station A, Halifax, N.S. B3K 5N5
Phone: (902) 455-4286   Fax: (902) 455-3652
Contact: Dorothy Blythe, managing editor
  Established 1978. Publishes general trade books on all aspects of Atlantic Canada, including cultural and natural history, folklore and myth, Native customs, the environment, nautical books, cookbooks, children's, and photographic books. Most books are by first-time

authors who have in-depth knowledge of their subject. Released 26 new titles in 1993. Accepts unsolicited manuscripts.

Notable 1993 title: *Sharing a Robin's Life,* Linda Johns.

NuAge Editions

P.O. Box 8, Station E, Montreal, Que. H2T 3A5
Phone: (514) 272-5226   Fax: (514) 271-1218
Contact: the publisher

Established 1986 as a Concordia University project. Now run independently as a small press to develop new, young, and unknown English-language writers in Quebec. Publishes fiction, drama, non-fiction, and, occasionally, poetry. Released 6 titles in 1993.

Oberon Press

400 – 350 Sparks Street, Ottawa, Ont. KIR 7S8
Phone: (613) 238-3275   Fax: (613) 238-3275
Contact: Nicholas Macklem, general manager

Established 1966. Publishes Canadian fiction, poetry, history, biography, art, and children's books. Produced 18 new books in 1993. Accepts unsolicited manuscripts, but first send sample chapters. Multiple submissions not considered.

Oolichan Books

P.O. Box 10, Lantzville, B.C. VOR 2HO
Phone: (604) 390-4839   Fax: (604) 390-4839
Contact: Rhonda Bailey, managing editor

Established 1974. Publishes poetry, fiction, regional history, biographies, and special limited editions. Released 9 new titles in 1993. Considers unsolicited manuscripts, but send initial letter of inquiry and sample.

Notable 1993 title: *Visible Light,* Carol Windley.

Orca Book Publishers Ltd.

P.O. Box 5626, Station B, Victoria, B.C. V8R 6S4
Phone: (604) 380-1229   Fax: (604) 380-1892
Contact: Bob Tyrrell (young adult and adult); Ann Featherstone
    (children's and juvenile)

Established 1984. Children's/juvenile and young adult titles comprise about half the list. Adult titles include history, fiction, outdoor adventure, and guidebooks. A West Coast regional bias. Averages 15 to 20 new titles each year. Send a query with outline and two or three sample chapters. No unsolicited manuscripts. Guidelines available.

Notable 1993 title: *WHO*, Richard Thompson, illust. Martin Springett.

Outcrop, The Northern Publishers

P.O. Box 1350, Yellowknife, N.W.T. X1A 2N9
Phone: (403) 920-4652   Fax: (403) 873-2844
Contact: Ronne Heming, publisher

Established 1975. Publishes general non-fiction about Canada's North, with an emphasis on history and biography. Released 4 new titles in 1993. No unsolicited manuscripts. Inquiries welcome.

Notable 1993 title: *McDougall's Bash*, Erik Watt.

Oxford University Press

70 Wynford Drive, Don Mills, Ont. M3C 1J9
Phone: (416) 441-2941   Fax: (416) 441-0345
Contact: Susan Froud, managing director

Established in Canada in 1904. Publishes general trade, university-level textbooks and upper-level university books, junior and senior high school textbooks, and children's books. Averages 40 new titles each year. Accepts unsolicited manuscripts, but first send a query with outline and sample chapters. Author guidelines available.

Notable 1993 title: *Canadian Stories of the Sea*, Victor Suthren.

Pemmican Publications Inc.

1635 Burrows Avenue, Unit 2, Winnipeg, Man. R2X 0T1
Phone: (204) 589-6346   Fax: (204) 589-2063
Contact: Sue MacLean, manager

Established 1980. Publishes books of concern or interest to Native people, particularly the Métis. Released 8 new titles in 1993. Accepts unsolicited manuscripts, but first send sample chapters. Guidelines available.

Notable 1993 title: *Nanabosho, Soaring Eagle and the Great Sturgeon*, Joseph McLellan.

Penguin Books Canada Ltd.

10 Alcorn Avenue, Suite 300, Toronto, Ont. M4V 3B2

Phone: (416) 925-2249   Fax: (416) 925-0068
Contact: editorial department
    Established in Canada in 1974. Publishes a wide selection of trade fiction and non-fiction. Released 37 new hardcover titles and 88 books in 1993. No unsolicited manuscripts.
    Notable 1993 title: *The Night Inside*, Nancy Baker.

Penumbra Press

435 Stillmeadow Circle, Waterloo, Ont. N2L 5M1
Phone: (519) 746-8758   Fax: (519) 746-8758
Contact: John Flood, president
    Established 1979. Publishing program spans literary and visual arts, children's books, and books about the North. Released 8 new titles in 1993. Accepts unsolicited manuscripts, but prefers initial queries. No multiple submissions. Guidelines available.
    Notable 1993 title: *Montreal Movie Palaces*, Dane Lanken.

Playwrights Canada Press

54 Wolseley Street, 2nd Floor, Toronto, Ont. M5T 1A5
Phone: (416) 947-0201   Fax: (416) 947-0159
Contact: Tony Hamill, managing editor
    Established 1972. Publishes Canadian plays in single editions, anthologies, and collections. All plays must have had professional theatre production. No unsolicited manuscripts, please. Query first.

Polestar Press Ltd.

2758 Charles Street, Vancouver, B.C. V5K 3A7
Phone: (604) 251-9718   Fax: (604) 251-9718
Contact: Michelle Benjamin, publisher
    Established 1980. Publishes fiction and poetry, children's fiction and non-fiction, sports books, and general trade non-fiction. Released 12 new titles in 1991. Accepts unsolicited manuscripts, but prefers initial query with sample chapters. Guidelines available.
    Notable 1993 title: *Alaska Highway Two-Step*, Caroline Woodward.

The Porcupine's Quill Inc.

68 Main Street, Erin, Ont. N0B 1T0
Phone: (519) 833-9158

Contact: Paul Caulfield, general manager

Established 1974. Specializes in Canadian literature. Published 10 titles in 1993. Does not often accept unsolicited manuscripts.

Pottersfield Press

R.R. 2, Porters Lake, N.S. B0J 2S0
Contact: Lesley Choyce, editor

Established 1979. Publishes general non-fiction, novels, and books of interest to Atlantic Canada. Particularly interested in biography proposals. Averages 5 new titles a year. Accepts proposals and/or full manuscripts. No phone calls, please.

Notable 1993 title: *Visions of Kerouac*, Ken McGoogan.

The Prairie Publishing Company

P.O. Box 2997, Winnipeg, Man. R3C 4B5
Phone: (204) 885-6496   Fax: (204) 775-3277
Contact: Ralph Watkins, editor/owner

Established 1969. Interested in manuscripts relating to Prairie history and development. Also publishes children's books and some biography.

Prentice-Hall Canada Inc.

1870 Birchmount Road, Scarborough, Ont. M1P 2J7
Phone: (416) 293-3621   Fax: (416) 299-2540
Contact: Tanya Long, managing editor (trade)

Established 1960. Publishes trade non-fiction and education texts at all levels. Trade program specializes in business, personal finance, current affairs, and general reference. Published 15 titles in 1993. Accepts unsolicited manuscripts, but first send outline and sample chapters.

Notable 1993 title: *Building Wealth in the '90s*, Gordon Pape.

Press Gang Publishers

603 Powell Street, Vancouver, B.C. V6A 1H2
Phone: (604) 253-2537   Fax: (604) 253-7870
Contact: Barbara Kuhne, managing editor

Established 1974. "Press Gang Publishers Feminist Co-operative is committed to producing quality books with social and literary merit. We prioritize women's work and include writing by lesbians and by women from diverse cultural and class backgrounds. Our list features vital and provocative fiction, poetry, and non-fiction." Published 6 books in 1993. Send initial inquiry with sample chapter (fiction) or outline (non-fiction).

Notable 1993 title: *Ravensong*, Lee Maracle.

Quarry Press

P.O. Box 1061, 221 King Street E., Kingston, Ont. K7L 4Y5
Phone: (613) 548-8429   Fax: (613) 548-1556
Contact: Bob Hilderley, president

Established 1965. Publishes poetry, fiction, educational texts, children's books, and manuscripts about theatre and drama. Averages 15 new titles a year. No unsolicited manuscripts.

Ragweed Press Inc./gynergy books

P.O. Box 2023, Charlottetown, P.E.I. C1A 7N7
Phone: (902) 566-5750   Fax: (902) 566-4473
Contact: Lynn Henry, senior editor

Established 1974. Publishes regional literature and history, children's books, and feminist and lesbian writing. Releases an average of 12 new titles a year. Accepts unsolicited manuscripts, but send an inquiry first.

Notable 1993 title: *Next Teller: A Book of Canadian Storytelling*, Dan Yashinsky.

Random House of Canada Ltd.

33 Yonge Street, Suite 210, Ont. M5E 1G4
Phone: (416) 777-9477   Fax: (416) 777-9470
Contact: Douglas Pepper, executive editor

Publishes a wide selection of fiction and a general trade nonfiction list. Averages 40 titles each year. No unsolicited manuscripts or book proposals.

Notable 1993 title: *The Stone Diaries*, Carol Shields.

Red Deer College Press

P.O. Box 5005, 56th Avenue and 32nd Street, Red Deer,
   Alta. T4N 5H5
Phone: (403) 342-3321   Fax: (403) 340-8940
Contact: Dennis Johnson, managing editor; Tim Wynne-Jones,

children's editor, ph. (613) 267-6205, fax (613) 264-8558; Joyce Doolittle, drama editor

Established 1975. Publishes poetry, fiction and non-fiction for adults and children, illustrated children's books, young adult fiction, and drama. Produces 10 to 12 books a year. Query first with outline and sample chapters. Reports in 3 months. Manuscripts accepted for publication must be supplied on Mac disk in MS Word.

Reed Books Canada

75 Clegg Road, Markham, Ont. L6G 1A1
Phone: (905) 479-2665   Fax: (905) 479-3758
Contact: editorial department

Established in Canada in 1991. A division of Butterworths Canada, part of Reed International Books, and a major international book distributor. Publishes general trade fiction and non-fiction with a preference for adult non-fiction. No unsolicited manuscripts.

Rocky Mountain Books

4 Spruce Centre S.W., Calgary, Alta. T3C 3B3
Phone: (403) 249-9490   Fax: (403) 249-2968
Contact: Gillean Daffern, editor

Established 1976. Specializes in outdoor recreation (including skiing, hiking, climbing, biking, and whitewater), guidebooks, history pertaining to the Canadian Rockies, and the natural history of Alberta, British Columbia, and the Yukon. Published 7 titles in 1993. Accepts book proposals with outlines and writing samples. No complete unsolicited manuscripts.

Notable 1993 title: *Coyote Music*, Grant MacEwan.

Royal British Columbia Museum

Publishing and Visual Services, 675 Belleville Street, Victoria,
B.C. V8V 1X4
Phone: (604) 387-6357   Fax: (604) 387-5360
Contact: Tara Steigenberger, publications co-ordinator

Established 1912. Publishes non-fiction concerning the human and natural history of British Columbia and the museum's activities. Produces popular as well as scientific titles. Also interested in moving into children's books. Currently averages 9 titles a year. No unsolicited manuscripts. Written inquiries should include outline.

Notable 1993 title: *Our Living Legacy: Proceedings from a Symposium on Biological Diversity.*

Royal Ontario Museum

Publication and Print Services, 100 Queen's Park, Toronto, Ont. M5S 2C6

Phone: (416) 586-5581   Fax: (416) 586-5827

Contact: Glen Ellis, managing editor

Publishes manuscripts relating to the museum's collection, with some general-readership and children's books. Averages 10 new titles each year. No unsolicited manuscripts; inquiries only. Priority is given to (1) ROM authors, (2) research associates, (3) others.

Notable 1993 title: *Tales of the Anishinaubaek,* Basil Johnston.

Rubicon Publishing Inc.

116 Thomas Street, Oakville, Ont. L6J 3A8

Phone: (905) 849-8777   Fax: (905) 849-7579

Contact: Pamela Wyatt, editorial assistant

Established 1987. Publishes educational and children's literature. Concerned to reflect the multicultural nature of Canadian society and avoid stereotyping people by sex, race, age, or physical or mental abilities. Released 7 titles in 1993. Accepts unsolicited manuscripts, but first send an outline. Guidelines available.

Notable 1993 title: *Looking for a Hero,* David Boyd.

Scholastic Canada Ltd.

123 Newkirk Road, Richmond Hill, Ont. L4C 3G5

Phone: (905) 883-5300   Fax: (905) 882-1684

Contact: Laura Peetoom, editor, children's books

Established in Canada in 1957. Specializes in children's books, both fiction and non-fiction, from preschool to young adult. Averages 50 titles a year. Also publishes professional materials for teachers. No unsolicited manuscripts; inquiries only. Author guidelines available.

Notable 1993 title: *Something from Nothing,* Phoebe Gilman.

Seal Books

105 Bond Street, Toronto, Ont. M5B 1Y3

Phone: (416) 340-0777   Fax: (416) 340-7081

Contact: editorial department

Established 1977. Publishes fiction and non-fiction paperbacks for the mass market, and commercial reprints. No unsolicited manuscripts.

Second Story Press

760 Bathurst Street, Toronto, Ont. M5S 2R6
Phone: (416) 537-7850   Fax: (416) 537-7850
Contact: Lois Pike or Margie Wolfe, editorial

Publishes fiction, non-fiction, children's literature, and books on contemporary issues of particular relevance to women. Averages 9 titles a year. Accepts unsolicited manuscripts, but first send outline.

Notable 1993 title: *Frictions II: Stories by Women,* ed. Rhea Tregebov.

Self-Counsel Press

1481 Charlotte Road, North Vancouver, B.C. V7J 1H1
Phone: (604) 986-3366   Fax: (604) 986-3947
Contact: Ruth Wilson, managing editor

Established 1971. Specializes in self-help books on law and business by experts in their fields. Also publishes some reference and psychology books. Averages 20 new books a year. Accepts unsolicited manuscripts, but prefers an initial inquiry, outline, and, preferably, sample chapters. "Do your homework first! Ask for our catalogue, and be sure your idea fits into Self-Counsel's concept." Author guidelines available.

Notable 1993 title: *Start and Run a Profitable Travel Agency,* Richard Cropp and Barbara Braidwood.

Somerville House Books Ltd.

3080 Yonge Street, Suite 5000, Toronto, Ont. M4N 3N1
Phone: (416) 488-5938   Fax: (416) 488-5506
Contact: Patrick Crean, editorial director; Jane Somerville, publisher

Established 1983. Publishes general trade books, focusing on children's non-fiction/educational and literature, with a small part of the program devoted to esoteric works of adult literary fiction and metaphysics. Published 8 new titles in 1993. Contact Michelle

Bennett by phone or letter for unsolicited manuscript inquiries (send outline and one sample chapter).

Notable 1993 title: *We So Seldom Look on Love,* Barbara Gowdy.

Sono Nis Press

1745 Blanshard Street, Victoria, B.C. v8w 2j8
Phone: (604) 382-1024   Fax: (604) 382-1575
Contact: Richard Morriss, president, or Angela Addison, editor

Established 1968. Publishes history, historical biography, maritime history, transportation history, regional history, poetry, and some guidebooks. Produced 11 new titles in 1993. Accepts unsolicited manuscripts, but send inquiry first.

Notable 1993 title: *Journey Back to Peshawar,* Rono Murray.

Stoddart Publishing Co. Ltd.

34 Lesmill Road, Don Mills, Ont. M3B 2T6
Phone: (416) 445-3333   Fax: (416) 445-5967
Contact: Don Bastian, managing editor

Established 1964. Publishes timely, innovative, and original works across a broad range of non-fiction subjects, as well as fiction for adults, young adults, and children, and a few picture books. Produces 60 to 100 new titles each year. Accepts unsolicited manuscripts, but first send a synopsis and two sample chapters.

Notable 1993 title: *The Generals,* J.L. Granatstein.

Talon Books Ltd.

1019 East Cordova Street, Suite 201, Vancouver, B.C. V6A 1M8
Phone: (604) 253-5261   Fax: (604) 255-5755
Contact: Karl Siegler, editor

Established 1967. Specializes in drama, serious fiction, poetry, popular non-fiction, women's literature, social issues, and ethnography. No unsolicited poetry or children's literature. For the rest, first send an outline and sample chapter.

Notable 1993 title: *The Ends of the Earth,* Morris Panych.

Theytus Books Ltd.

P.O. Box 20040, Penticton, B.C. V2A 8K3
Phone: (604) 493-7181   Fax: (604) 493-5302

Contact: Greg Young-Ing, manager

Established 1981. Publishes First Nation literature, fiction and non-fiction, art, music, and educational books by aboriginal authors. Released 11 new titles in 1993. Accepts unsolicited manuscripts, but first send an inquiry with outline and sample chapters. Guidelines available.

Notable 1993 title: *Courageous Spirits: Aboriginal Heroes of Our Children,* Jo-ann Archibald, Val Friesen, and Jeff Smith.

Thistledown Press Ltd.
633 Main Street, Saskatoon, Sask. S7H 0J8
Phone: (306) 244-1722   Fax: (306) 244-1762
Contact: Patrick O'Rourke, editor-in-chief

Established 1975. Specializes in Canadian poetry, short fiction, and young adult fiction. Published 12 new titles 1993. The New Leaf Editions series is devoted to books of up to 64 pages by previously unpublished writers. Submit a sample with writing/publishing history rather than a full manuscript.

Notable 1993 title: *It's a Hard Cow,* Terry Jordan.

Tundra Books
345 Victoria Avenue, Suite 604, Montreal, Que. H3Z 2N2
Phone: (514) 932-5434   Fax: (514) 484-2152
Contact: Arjun Basu, assistant editor

Established 1967. Specializes in children's books as works of art. Also publishes coffee-table books on art and architecture. Produced 13 new titles in 1993. Does not accept unsolicited manuscripts, but welcomes letters of inquiry. "With a few notable exceptions, such as Carrier, Tundra works with artists as authors." Guidelines available.

Notable 1993 title: *The Longest Home Run,* Roch Carrier, illust. Sheldon Cohen.

Turnstone Press
100 Arthur Street, Suite 607, Winnipeg, Man. R3B 1H3
Phone: (204) 947-1555   Fax: (204) 942-1555
Contact: James Hutchison, managing editor

Established 1976. A literary press publishing poetry, fiction, and literary criticism. Accepts unsolicited manuscripts.

Notable 1993 title: *Sitting Opposite My Brother,* David Bergen.

UBC Press

6344 Memorial Road, Vancouver, B.C. V6T 1Z2
Phone: (604) 822-3259   Fax: (604) 822-6083
Contact: Jean Wilson, senior editor

Established 1971. Publishes non-fiction for scholarly, educational, and general audiences in the humanities, social sciences, and natural sciences. Subject areas include Native studies, Canadian political science and history, sociology, geography, Asian and Pacific studies, economics, and urban studies. No unsolicited manuscripts. Released 24 titles in 1993. Send an inquiry with outline and sample chapters. Guidelines available.

Notable 1993 title: *Land Resource Economics and Sustainable Development*, G. Cornelis van Kooten.

United Church Publishing House

85 St. Clair Avenue E., Toronto, Ont. M4T 1M8
Phone: (416) 925-5931   Fax: (416) 925-9692
Contact: Peter Gordon White, editor-in-chief

Established in 1829 as Ryerson Press. Publishing program is not limited to "religious" matters, but rather reflects the broader interests of church members. Subjects include environmental and peace issues, social justice, and ethics. Averages 12 new titles a year. No unsolicited manuscripts. Send a letter of inquiry with a brief outline of material. Guidelines available.

Notable 1993 title: *Walking the Way: Christian Ethics as a Guide*, Terence R. Anderson.

University of Alberta Press

141 Athabasca Hall, Edmonton, Alta. T6G 2E8
Phone: (403) 432-3662   Fax: (403) 492-0719
Contact: Norma Gutteridge, director

Established 1969. Specializes in scholarly non-fiction and university-level textbooks, history, politics, education, natural sciences, Native studies, literary criticism, Slavic and Eastern European studies, Middle Eastern studies, anthropology, and archaeology. Mainly publishes original research with a strong Western Canadian interest. Averages 10 new titles a year. Accepts unsolicited manuscripts, but query first. Guidelines available.

Notable 1993 title: *A Bargain for Humanity: Global Security by 2000,* Douglas Roche.

University of Calgary Press

2500 University Drive N.W., Calgary, Alta. T2N 1N4
Phone: (403) 220-7578   Fax: (403) 282-0085
Contact: Joan Barton, editorial secretary
Established 1981. Publishes scholarly and trade books in a wide variety of subject areas. Will consider any innovative scholarly manuscript. Released 17 new titles in 1993. A complete manuscript, with prospectus, will be considered if it satisfies scholarly criteria but also appeals to a larger audience. Guidelines available.
Notable 1993 title: *Maxwell Bates: A Biography of an Artist,* K.M. Snow.

University of Manitoba Press

106 Curry Place, Suite 244, Winnipeg, Man. R3T 2N2
Phone: (204) 474-9495/474-9242   Fax: (204) 275-2270
Contact: Patricia Dowdall, director
Established 1967. Publishes scholarly books in the humanities and social sciences, including history, Native studies, Icelandic studies, and women's studies, and general interest books about the Prairie region. Averages 6 new titles each year. No unsolicited manuscripts. Inquiries only. Author guidelines available.

University of Toronto Press

10 St. Mary Street, Suite 700, Toronto, Ont. M4Y 2W8
Phone: (416) 978-2239   Fax: (416) 978-4738
Contact: Ron Schoeffel, editor-in-chief
Established 1901. A large university press publishing scholarly and general works, and academic journals. Editorial program includes classical, medieval, Renaissance, and Victorian studies, modern languages, English and Canadian literature, literary theory and criticism, women's studies, social sciences, Native studies, philosophy, law, religion, music, education, modern history, geography, and political science. Averages 100 new titles each year. Accepts unsolicited manuscripts. Use *Chicago* or *MLA* for style, though internal consistency is the most important.

Notable 1993 title: *Historical Atlas of Canada, Volume II: The Land Transformed, 1800–1891*, R. Louis Gentilcore et al.

Vanwell Publishing Ltd.

1 Northrup Crescent, Box 2131, St. Catharines, Ont. L2M 6P5
Phone: (905) 937-3100   Fax: (905) 937-1760
Contact: Lynn Hunt, general editor

Established 1983. Specializes in Canadian military history and regional titles focusing on the past and present of the Niagara region. Publishes fiction and non-fiction, and an educational series on Canadian history and geography. Averages 7 titles a year. Reviews unsolicited manuscripts if relevant to this publishing program.

Véhicule Press

P.O. Box 125, Place du Parc Station, Montreal, Que. H2W 1M4
Phone: (514) 844-6073   Fax: (514) 844-7543
Contact: Simon Dardick, general editor

Established 1973. Publishes fiction and poetry within the context of social history, and occasional titles on the history of science with a feminist orientation. Released 13 titles in 1993. No unsolicited manuscripts. Inquiries only.

Notable 1993 title: *Mr. Blue*, Jacques Poulin, trans. Sheila Fischman.

Whitecap Books Ltd.

1086 West 3rd Street, North Vancouver, B.C. V7P 3J6
Phone: (604) 980-9852   Fax: (604) 980-8197
Contact: Pat Crowe, editorial director

Established 1977. Specializes in natural history and regional guidebooks. Also interested in gardening, children's non-fiction, cooking, history, and giftbooks. Published 24 books in 1993. No fiction. Welcomes proposals and inquiries. No unsolicited manuscripts.

Notable 1993 title: *The Emerald Sea*, Dale Sanders and Diane Swanson.

John Wiley & Sons Canada Ltd.

22 Worcester Road, Rexdale, Ont. M9W 1L1

Phone: (416) 236-4433   Fax: (416) 236-4446
Contact: Karen Milner, editor, trade
Established 1968. Publishes post-secondary educational books on a wide variety of topics; also professional reference and a growing number of trade books on current affairs and business. Averages 15 new titles a year. Written inquiries only.

Notable 1993 title: *Canadian Political Babble*, David Olive.

Wilfrid Laurier University Press
Wilfrid Laurier University, Waterloo, Ont. N2L 3C5
Phone: (519) 884-1970, ext. 6123   Fax: (519) 725-1399
Contact: Sandra Woolfrey, director and senior editor
Established 1974. Publishes scholarly books (and 11 academic journals) in the humanities and social sciences, along with important books of general interest on film, culture, and the environment. Subject areas include literary criticism, religious studies, Canadian studies, and history. Produces 10 to 15 books each year. Accepts unsolicited manuscripts, but first send outline. Guidelines available.

Notable 1993 title: *Antisemitism in Canada: History and Interpretation,* ed. Alan Davies.

Wolsak and Wynn Publishers Ltd.
P.O. Box 316, Don Mills P.O., Don Mills, Ont. M3C 2S7
Phone: (416) 222-4690   Fax: (416) 736-5731
Contact: Maria Jacobs, publisher/editor
Publishes poetry only – about 5 new books a year. Will consider unsolicited material after an initial written inquiry.

Women's Press
517 College Street, Suite 233, Toronto, Ont. M6G 4A2
Phone: (416) 921-2425   Fax: (416) 921-4428
Contact: Martha Ayim or Ann Decter, co–managing editors
Established 1972. A feminist publishing collective committed to anti-racist/anti-classist publishing and to the develpment of feminism in Canada and internationally. Strongly interested in access to print for lesbians and writers of colour. Publishes non-fiction, fiction, poetry, plays, and children's books. Averages 10 new titles a year. Accepts unsolicited manuscripts, but first send a letter of inquiry.

Notable 1993 title: *And Still We Rise: Feminist Political Mobilizing in Contemporary Canada,* ed. Linda Carty.

York Press Ltd.
P.O. Box 1172, Fredericton, N.B. E3B 5C8
 Fax: (506) 458-8748
Contact: Dr. Saad Elkhadem, editor
 Established 1975. Publishes dictionaries, educational texts at the college level, scholarly publications, reference books, and manuscripts on literary criticism and comparative literature. Strong emphasis on high-quality creative writing and Arabic/Egyptian literature and scholarship.

6

LITERARY AGENTS

In the United States most writers, established or not, place their books through an agent; even magazine writers often sell their work this way. Literary agents have played a lesser role in Canadian publishing. The pool of agents has always been small here, and Canadian publishers have traditionally acted as agents for their authors when it comes to selling their works to foreign markets.

Like publishers, most agents are very circumspect about taking on unpublished writers, though publication in journals or high-quality magazines can help. Plenty of published writers don't use an agent. Some seek the advice of a lawyer when it comes to contract signing. Don't use the family solicitor for this, though, and bear in mind that very few lawyers in Canada specialize in publishing law. Far better to consult your regional branch of the Canadian Authors Association or the Writers' Union of Canada, who have access to all the necessary expertise and experience to help you pick through the minefield of the contract's small print.

There are, however, many advantages to securing a good agent. Most large publishers prefer to contract agented authors. A manuscript recommended by an agent will inevitably be taken more seriously than one submitted by an unknown writer. And it will probably be read and acted on sooner because the publisher can be confident that it has merit and is in a publishable condition. Indeed, books are occasionally contracted purely on the basis of a good proposal and a convincing pitch by the agent.

Established authors tend to use agents more, and may seek their counsel long before they actually begin writing a particular book. Because fiction is considerably harder to sell than non-fiction, fiction writers depend heavily on agents. Most literary agents, however, put a higher priority on maintaining a stable of proven non-fiction authors, because non-fiction sells in greater quantities than fiction, and since most agents work on commission, they will earn more from representing these clients.

Good agents deserve every penny they earn. When the author makes money, the agent does too, so he or she will work hard to secure the best terms for their client. They develop long-term relationships with publishers and editors, with whom they can exchange ideas, learning their needs and interests, and they keep in close touch with what is sought after in the publishing marketplace. In so doing, they become expert at gauging the commercial possibilities of an author's proposal.

For new clients, it is on the strength of the agent's "first read" of the manuscript or proposal that he or she will agree to work with the writer. At contract-signing time, the agent can advise the writer on clauses that stipulate what rights the author should sell, or can negotiate every detail of a publisher's contract on the writer's behalf. The agent who fully understands the marketplace, publishing contracts, copyright law, and the broader sales possibilities of a book can negotiate a better publishing contract, often with a bigger advance against royalties.

Agents in Canada usually charge 15 or 20 per cent of the value of all rights sold. An agent today may evaluate a manuscript, suggest structural changes, sell the revised work to a publisher, negotiate the contract, secure an advance, and participate in designing a marketing program. He or she then often works closely with the author over the long term, helping the client to develop a career. Some agents are now, rather controversially, charging supplementary "handling" fees, which may cover the costs of everything from reading, evaluation, and editorial work to the agent's office expenses. But beware of agents who make more money from you, the author, than from the sale of your work. Insist on a strict accounting of fees and an upper limit to expenses.

This chapter lists most of the active literary agencies in Canada. Several others chose not to be included. Well-established agencies usually have a full slate of clients and consequently don't go out of their way to promote their services. As you will discover, agents tend to have very specific requirements and are becoming more and more selective. Finding an agent, some claim, can be harder than finding a publisher! But every writer should consider the effort, since, in most cases, the relationship between agent and author is to great mutual advantage.

Acacia House Publishing Services Ltd.

51 Acacia Road, Toronto, Ont. M4S 2K6
Phone: (416) 484-8356   Fax: (416) 484-8356
Contact: Frances Hanna

Subject interests: Fiction with international potential. No horror, occult, science fiction, or adult fantasy. For non-fiction, no self-help, fitness, true crime, or business books.

Comments: Queries only, with writing sample (up to 50 pages). For evaluation, charges $1 per double-spaced page over 50 pages. Evaluates only complete manuscripts.

The Array Agency

4141 Dixie Road, P.O. Box 46, Mississauga, Ont. L4W 1V0
Contact: Shawn Heather

Subject interests: Non-fiction by new and established writers.

Comments: A small new agency now accepting clients. Accepts unsolicited manuscripts. Agency commission is 15 per cent. No reading fees, but new clients are charged an up-front fee of $250 to cover administration costs. Send a query with an outline and sample chapters. Mail queries only.

Author Author Literary Agency

P.O. Box 34051, 1200 – 37th Street S.W., Calgary, Alta. T3C 3W2
Phone: (403) 242-0226   Fax: (403) 242-0226
Contact: Joan Rickard

Subject interests: Prefers adult fiction and non-fiction. Will also handle juvenile novels, adult and juvenile textbooks, New Age writing, and magazine stories/articles. No poetry or screenplays.

Comments: Welcomes unpublished writers. Accepts unsolicited queries and outlines. Reads unsolicited manuscripts if accompanied by reading fee. Reports within two weeks on queries, one month on manuscript outlines and up to three sample chapters, two months on complete manuscripts. Fees range from $75 for evaluating up to three sample chapters to $450 for full service (reading, editing, evaluating, and marketing) on an 85,000-word manuscript.

Authors Marketing Services Ltd.
217 Degrassi Street, Toronto, Ont. M4M 2K8
Phone: (416) 463-7200   Fax: (416) 469-4494
Contact: Larry Hoffman
   Subject interests: Adult fiction and non-fiction.
   Comments: No unsolicited manuscripts. Unpublished writers are charged evaluation/handling fees. Query only.

The Bukowski Agency
125B Dupont Street, Toronto, Ont. M5R 1V4
Phone: (416) 928-6728   Fax: (416) 963-9978
Contact: Denise Bukowski
   Subject interests: General adult trade books. Prefers upmarket fiction and non-fiction. No genre fiction (science fiction, romance, westerns); no children's or sports books; no scriptwriters or playwrights.
   Comments: No unsolicited manuscripts or unpublished writers. Does not charge evaluation or other handling fees.

Canadian Speakers' and Writers' Service Ltd.
44 Douglas Crescent, Toronto, Ont. M4W 2E7
Phone: (416) 921-4443   Fax: (416) 922-9691
Contact: Matie Molinaro, Paul Molinaro, Julius Molinaro
   Subject interests: Non-fiction, fiction, plays for the stage, television, and motion pictures. Also cartoons and subjects suited to animation adaptation.
   Comments: Reads unpublished writers. Evaluation fees are charged based on medium and length. No unsolicited manuscripts.

Great North Artists Management
350 Dupont Street, Toronto, Ont. M5R 1V9
Phone: (416) 925-2051   Fax: (416) 925-3904
Contact: Shain Jaffe
   Subject interests: Plays and film and television properties.
   Comments: No evaluation or other handling fees. Query only.

J. Kellock and Associates Ltd.

11017 – 80th Avenue, Edmonton, Alta. T6G OR2
Phone: (403) 433-0274   Fax: (403) 439-9649
Contact: Joanne Kellock

Subject interests: Adult commercial and literary fiction; non-fiction; all works for children, including picture books, first readers, middle readers, and young adult.

Comments: No unsolicited manuscripts. Written queries accepted. Reads unpublished writers. Evaluation and editorial fees charged. "There are two kinds of novels selling today: extraordinarily well-written commercial genre; and brilliantly written, stylistically innovative literature. Children's picture books are toughest to place, thus any first picture book must be unique, universal, and altogether wonderful. Do not supply illustrations with story unless the illustrator has a Fine Arts degree or has previously illustrated a published book for children."

Livingston Cooke, Inc.

200 First Avenue, Toronto, Ont. M4M 1X1
Phone: (416) 406-3390   Fax: (416) 406-3389
Contact: Dean Cooke

Subject interests: Non-fiction.

Comments: Accepts inquiries, but no unsolicited manuscripts and no unpublished writers. At present, no evaluation or other handling fees are charged.

Pamela Paul Agency Inc.

253A High Park Avenue, Toronto, Ont. M6P 2S5
Phone: (416) 769-0540   Fax: (416) 769-0540
Contact: Pamela Paul

Subject interests: Film and television (writers and directors); literary fiction and non-fiction.

Comments: No unsolicited manuscripts. Reads unpublished writers. No evaluation/handling fees. Written queries only. "A deliberately small agency with a quality list and special emphasis on selling literary properties for film and television."

Beverley Slopen Agency

131 Bloor Street W., Suite 711, Toronto, Ont. M5S 1S3

Phone: (416) 964-9598
Contact: Beverley Slopen
   Subject interests: General fiction and non-fiction. No children's books, science fiction, or fantasy.
   Comments: No unsolicited manuscripts or unpublished writers. Does not charge evaluation/handling fees.

Lucinda Vardey Agency

297 Seaton Street, Toronto, Ont. M5A 2T6
Phone: (416) 922-0250   Fax: (416) 925-4943
Contact: Lucinda Vardey
   Subject interests: General and literary fiction and non-fiction.
   Comments: No unsolicited manuscripts. No unpublished writers please.

Sterling Lord Associates (Canada) Ltd.

10 St. Mary Street, Suite 510, Toronto, Ont. M4Y 1P9
Phone: (416) 964-3302   Fax: (416) 975-9209
Contact: Doreen Potter
   Subject interests: General trade except for poetry and short stories.
   Comments: Accepts unsolicited manuscripts. Reads unpublished writers. Does not charge evaluation or other handling fees. Query first.

7

AWARDS, COMPETITIONS, & GRANTS

This chapter is divided into two sections: the first lists a broad range of the literary prizes and competitions open to Canadian writers; the second outlines the main sources of provincial and federal funding available.

Most of the prizes and competitions may be applied for directly. Among several exceptions are premier awards such as the Harbourfront Festival Prize, conferred each year on a celebrated writer in mid-career, and McClelland & Stewart's prestigious Journey Prize, for the best short fiction from Canada's literary journals. In some cases, the judges prefer to receive submissions from publishers, but usually, so long as the application criteria are met, individual applications are also accepted.

Please note that application deadlines are subject to change, and that the following short entries do not include full eligibility criteria or entry conditions. Some contests, for instance, require a small entry fee, or the provision of several copies of the work so that they can be circulated among the nominating jury. Applicants should always write for full guidelines before making a submission.

Canadian writers are also eligible for a number of overseas-sourced awards, and you'll find these in standard international reference books such as *Literary Market Place*. New Canadian awards are usually advertised in such industry publications as *Books in Canada*, *Canadian Author*, and *Quill & Quire* – available in good bookstores and libraries – and in some literary journals. Journalism, magazine, and other writing awards are listed in the *Sources* directory (see Chapter 10, Resources).

Arts council and other government grants are designed to buy the writer time to devote to his or her work for a specified period in order to support a work-in-progress or the completion of a specific creative project through meeting a varying combination of living, research, travel, or professional development costs. Such financial support is most often targeted towards the successful published author, but gifted new writers are sometimes also eligible. The Canada Council's Explorations Program, for instance, and several provincial initiatives are open to new as well as established writers. All these programs require applicants to develop detailed project proposals and budgets and to provide writing samples and other support materials.

Awards & Competitions

Alberta New Fiction Competition
Alberta Community Development, Arts & Cultural Industries
    Branch, 3rd Floor, Beaver House, 10158 – 103rd Street,
    Edmonton, Alta. T5J 0X6
Phone: (403) 427-6315
Deadline: December 1, 1995
A biennial competition open to all adult Alberta writers, from emerging to established authors. A cash prize of $5,000 goes to the best publishable full-length adult novel manuscript (minimum of 60,000 words).

Alberta Playwriting Competition
Alberta Playwrights' Network, 125 – 9th Avenue S.E., Suite 320,
    Calgary, Alta. T2G 0P6
Phone: (403) 269-8564 or 1-800-269-8564   Fax: (403) 269-8564
Deadline: October 15
A winning play script is selected in each of the following categories: an open category for a full-length play script on any subject (prize, $2,000 plus workshop); a "discovery" category for new

writers (prize, $1,500 plus workshop); an open category for a one-act play (prize, $1,000 plus workshop). Annual.

Alberta Write for Radio Competition
Alberta Community Development, Arts & Cultural Industries
    Branch, 3rd Floor, Beaver House, 10158 – 103rd Street,
    Edmonton, Alta. T5J 0X6
Phone: (403) 427-6315
Deadline: September 29
    For half-hour radio drama scripts. A jury selects up to three winners, each of whom is awarded a $500 honorarium to offset the costs of the workshop as preparation for a possible contract with CBC national radio. Annual.

Alberta Writing for Youth Competition
Alberta Community Development, Arts & Cultural Industries
    Branch, 3rd Floor, Beaver House, 10158 – 103rd Street,
    Edmonton, Alta. T5J 0X6
Phone: (403) 427-6315
Deadline: December 1994
    A biennial competition offering Alberta writers a cash prize of $5,000. Guidelines unavailable at time of writing.

Authors' Awards
Ray Argyle, Periodical Marketers of Canada, 2 Berkeley Street,
    Suite 503, Toronto, Ont. M5A 2W3
Phone: (416) 363-4549   Fax: (416) 363-6691
Deadline: July 31
    Prizes of $1,000 are awarded to the best paperback work of fiction and the best paperback work of non-fiction, chosen on literary merit by an expert panel. Non-monetary recognition, based on sales, is also given to the book of the year and to the author of the year. Annual.

The B.C. Book Prizes
Alan Twigg, B.C. Bookworld, 3516 West 13th Avenue (rear),
    Vancouver, B.C. V6R 2S3
Phone: (604) 736-4011   Fax: (604) 736-4011
Deadline: December

A $1,500 prize is awarded in each category for the year's most outstanding achievement in fiction, non-fiction, children's literature, and poetry by a British Columbia writer. An equivalent prize is also conferred on the local book that "contributes most to an understanding of British Columbia." Governed by the West Coast Book Prize Society but now administered by B.C. Bookworld. Sponsored by the British Columbia Booksellers Association. Annual.

CBC/Saturday Night Literary Competition

Robert Weaver, CBC Radio Performance, P.O. Box 500,
   Station A, Toronto, Ont. M5W 1E6
Phone: (416) 205-6001
Deadline: December 31

One prize of $10,000 is awarded in each category to the writers of the year's most outstanding short stories, poetry, and personal essays (which may be memoirs, autobiographical sketches, or travel sketches). Required length: 2,000 to 3,500 words. Annual.

Canadian Authors Association Awards

Jeffrey Holmes, 275 Slater Street, Suite 500, Ottawa,
   Ont. KIP 5H9
Phone: (613) 233-2846   Fax: (613) 235-8237

Air Canada Award

Deadline: April

A prize comprising two return tickets to any destination served by Air Canada is awarded to the most promising young writer under 30. Contenders are nominated by the Canadian Authors Association (to whom recommendations should be sent) and other writers' associations. Annual.

The Vicky Metcalf Body of Work Award

Deadline: December 31

A prize of $10,000 is awarded to the author of the year's best body of work by a Canadian. Annual.

The Vicky Metcalf Short Story Awards

Deadline: December 31

A prize of $3,000 is conferred on the writer of the best short story published in a Canadian magazine or anthology during the previous year; the editor of this work receives a further $1,000. Annual.

CAA Literary Awards

Deadline: December

A prize of $5,000 and a sterling-silver medal is awarded in recognition of the year's outstanding books in the categories of fiction, non-fiction, poetry, and drama by Canadian writers. Entries should manifest "literary excellence without sacrifice of popular appeal." Annual.

Canadian Historical Association Awards

395 Wellington Street, Ottawa, Ont. K1A 0N3
Phone: (613) 233-7885

John Bullen Prize

Deadline: November 30 (1994: non-Canadian)

A prize of $500 is awarded, in alternate years, for the best doctoral dissertation in Canadian history and the best doctoral dissertation in history other than Canadian.

Albert B. Corey Award

Deadline: February 1995

A prize of $2,000 is awarded in recognition of the best work addressing the history of Canadian–American relations or of the two countries. This award, which is co-sponsored by the American Historical Association, is conferred biennially.

The Wallace K. Ferguson Award

Deadline: December 15

A $1,000 prize is awarded for the best work of history by a Canadian writer on a non-Canadian subject. Annual.

Sir John A. Macdonald Prize

Deadline: December 15

A prize of $1,000 is awarded in recognition of a non-fiction work of history that has made a significant contribution to an understanding of Canada's past. Annual.

Mr. Christie's Book Awards

Marlene Yustin, c/o Christie Brown and Co., 2150 Lakeshore
  Boulevard W., Toronto, Ont. M8V 1A3
Phone: (416) 503-6000
Deadline: January 31

Awards of $7,500 each are presented in three categories, in
English and in French: the best children's book (7 years and under),
the best children's book (8 to 11 years), and the best children's book
(12 to 16 years). The winners are chosen by an expert panel, which
judges entries on their ability to inspire the imagination of the reader,
to recognize the importance of play, to bring delight and edification,
and to help children understand the world, both intellectually and
emotionally. Open to Canadian citizens or landed immigrants at the
time of the book's publication. Annual.

City of Dartmouth Book Award

Sharon MacDonald, c/o Dartmouth Regional Library, 60 Alderney
  Drive, Dartmouth, N.S. B2Y 4P8
Phone: (902) 464-2312
Deadline: December

A $1,000 prize is awarded for a work of fiction or non-fiction that
best reflects the spirit of Nova Scotia or its people. Open to any Canadian writer. Annual.

City of Toronto Book Awards

Linda Ott, c/o City Clerk's Department, 22nd Floor, East Tower,
  City Hall, Toronto, Ont. M5H 2N2
Phone: (416) 392-7797   Fax: (416) 392-7799
Deadline: January 30

Prize money totalling $15,000 is apportioned in recognition of
works of literary merit, in all genres, that are evocative of Toronto.
Each shortlisted writer receives $1,000, the balance going to the
winner. Annual.

City of Vancouver Book Award

Russell Kelly, B.C. Bookworld, 3516 West 13th Avenue (rear),
  Vancouver, B.C. V6R 2S3
Phone: (604) 736-4011   Fax: (604) 736-4011
Deadline: June

A $2,000 cash prize is awarded in October at the opening of the Vancouver International Writers' Festival. Entered books must be primarily set in or about Vancouver, though the author's place of residence is not restricted, and the book may be written/published anywhere in the world. Books may be fiction, non-fiction, poetry, or drama, written for children or adults, and may deal with any aspects of the city, including its history, geography, current affairs, or the arts. Apply for guidelines. Annual.

Dafoe Prize

J.E. Rae, Department of History, University of Manitoba, 500
    Dysart Road, Winnipeg, Man. R3T 2M8
A cash prize of $5,000 is awarded for a distinguished work of non-fiction by a Canadian, or an author resident in Canada, that "contributes to the understanding of Canada and/or its place in the world." Annual.

Distance Writing Prize

Geist, 1062 Homer Street, Suite 100, Vancouver, B.C. V6B 2W9
Phone: (604) 681-9161   Fax: (604) 669-8250
Deadline: November 1
A $500 cash prize goes to the best unpublished fiction or non-fiction prose composition containing references to at least two Canadian towns separated by at least two time zones. Preferred length 2,500 words. Maximum length 4,000 words. Apply for full entry conditions. Annual.

Arthur Ellis Awards

David Skene-Melvin, Crime Writers of Canada, 225 Carlton
    Street, Toronto, Ont. M5A 2L2
Phone: (416) 962-7947
Deadline: December 31
Prizes are awarded in the following categories in the genre: the best novel, the best first novel, the best short story, and the best true crime story, and the best genre criticism/reference. A shortage of sponsors currently rule out the cash prizes offered in the past, though we hope this situation will be remedied. Open to any writer resident in Canada or any Canadian living abroad. Setting and imprint immaterial. Annual.

The Marian Engel Award

c/o The Writers' Development Trust, 24 Ryerson Avenue, Suite
  201, Toronto, Ont. M5T 2P3
Phone: (416) 861-8222   Fax: (416) 861-0090

An award of $10,000 is conferred on a Canadian woman writer in
mid-career, recognizing her collective works and the promise of her
future contribution to Canadian literature. Canada's premier literary award for women. Annual.

The Lionel Gelber Prize

Greg Gatenby, Harbourfront, 410 Queen's Quay W., Toronto,
  Ont. M5V 2Z3
Phone: (416) 973-4760
Deadline: July 1

Presented at the International Authors Festival at Harbourfront,
Toronto, in October, an award of $50,000 goes to the year's best-
written book on international relations appealing both to the scholarly and the general reader. The winner is selected by a panel of five
people knowledgeable in the field of international relations. Applicants may be of any nationality, but the book must be available in
Canada, either in the original or in a new translation. Copyright
must be of the year of entry or after November 1 of the previous year.
Bound manuscripts are also accepted. Annual.

**Government of Newfoundland and Labrador Arts and
  Letters Competition**

Arts and Culture Centre, P.O. Box 1854, St. John's, Nfld. A1C 5P7
Phone: (709) 576-5253
Deadline: April

Three prizes are awarded in each category in recognition of outstanding short stories, poetry, and drama by residents of Newfoundland. First prize, $600; second prize, $300; third prize, $150.
Annual.

Governor General's Literary Awards

Josiane Polidori, Canada Council, P.O. Box 1047, 99 Metcalfe
  Street, Ottawa, Ont. K1P 5V8
Phone: (613) 598-4376   Fax: (613) 598-4410
Deadline: August 31

Seven awards of $10,000 are conferred in recognition of the best books of the year in French and English in the following categories: fiction, non-fiction, poetry, drama, children's books, translation, and illustration. Books must be submitted by publishers. Administered by the Canada Council. Annual.

Harbourfront Festival Prize

Greg Gatenby, Harbourfront, 410 Queen's Quay W., Toronto,
   Ont. M5V 2Z3
Phone: (416) 973-4760

This prestigious prize is awarded to a Canadian writer in mid-career who has made a substantial contribution to Canadian letters through his or her writing *and* his or her efforts on behalf of other Canadian writers or writing. A cash prize of $7,000 is supplemented by $4,000 in office equipment to enhance the writer's working environment. The winner is chosen by a jury of three. No submissions.

IODE National Book Award

Helen Dick, 40 Orchard View Boulevard, Suite 254, Toronto,
   Ont. M4I 1B9
Phone: (416) 889-6823
Deadline: January 31

A $3,000 prize is awarded in recognition of the year's best children's book of at least 1,000 words. Work previously published or produced is ineligible. Annual.

IODE Toronto Book Award

Grace Scott, 40 St. Clair Avenue W., Toronto, Ont. M4T 1M9
Phone: (416) 925-5078
Deadline: December 1

A $1,000 prize is conferred on the author or illustrator of the best children's book of the year written by a Toronto area resident. Annual.

The Journey Prize

Trish Lyon, McClelland & Stewart Inc., 481 University Avenue,
   Suite 900, Toronto, Ont. M5G 2E9
Phone: (416) 598-1114, ext. 333   Fax: (416) 598-7764
Deadline: December 31

The $10,000 Journey Prize is awarded to a new and developing writer of distinction. A selection of the best short fiction or novel excerpts to be published during the year in Canada's literary journals is collected in *The Journey Prize Anthology*, published by McClelland & Stewart. The prizewinner is drawn from this collection. McClelland & Stewart makes its own donation of $2,000 to the journal that published the winning entry. Submissions accepted from journal editors only. Annual.

Stephen Leacock Memorial Medal for Humour

Jean Bradley Dickson, P.O. Box 854, Orillia, Ont. L3V 6K8
Phone: (705) 325-6546
Deadline: December 31

A $5,000 cash award and a sterling-silver medal is awarded for the year's best humorous book written by a Canadian in prose, verse, or as drama. Send 10 copies of book, $25 entry fee, plus author bio and photo. Annual.

League of Canadian Poets Awards

Emanuel Goncalves, 24 Ryerson Avenue, Toronto, Ont. M5T 2P3
Phone: (416) 363-5047   Fax: (416) 860-0826

Gerald Lampert Memorial Award

Deadline: January 31

A $1,000 cash award is given in recognition of the best first book of poetry by a Canadian. Annual.

National Poetry Contest

Deadline: January 31

Three prizes – of $1,000, $750, and $500 – are awarded for the best unpublished poems not exceeding 75 written lines. Fifty of the submitted poems, including the three winners, will be published in an anthology. Annual.

Pat Lowther Memorial Award

Deadline: January 31

A $1,000 prize recognizes the best book of poetry written by a Canadian woman and published in Canada. Annual.

McNally Robinson Award for the Manitoba Book of the Year
Andrea Philp, Manitoba Writers' Guild, 100 Arthur Street,
 Suite 206, Winnipeg, Man. R3B 1H3
Phone: (204) 942-6134
Deadline: December 31
 Sponsored by McNally Robinson Booksellers, a $2,500 prize is awarded for an outstanding book in any genre written by a Manitoba resident. Annual.

The Gordon Montador Award
c/o The Writers' Development Trust, 24 Ryerson Avenue,
 Suite 201, Toronto, Ont. M5T 2P3
Phone: (416) 861-8222   Fax: (416) 861-0090
 A $2,000 joint prize goes to the author and publisher of the year's best Canadian book of non-fiction on contemporary social issues. Annual.

National Business Book Awards
Sylvie Mackay, 1231 Yonge Street, Suite 300, Toronto,
 Ont. M4T 2Z1
Phone: (416) 585-5310
Deadline: mid-December
 Two annual awards are made to recognize excellence in Canadian business writing. The winner receives $10,000; second place-winner gets $5,000. Sponsored by Coopers and Lybrand and the *Financial Times of Canada*. Annual.

The bpNichol Chapbook Award
The Phoenix Community Works Foundation, 316 Dupont Street,
 Toronto, Ont. M5R 1V9
Phone: (416) 964-7919
Deadline: March 30
 A prize of $1,000 is offered for the best poetry chapbook published in English in Canada. The chap-book should be between 10 and 48 pages long. Annual.

The Alden Nowlan Award
New Brunswick Department of Municipalities, Culture &

Housing, Arts Branch, P.O. Box 6000, Fredericton,
   N.B. E3B 5H1
Phone: (506) 453-2555   Fax: (506) 453-2416

A cash prize of $5,000 (offered biennially), recognizes the outstanding achievements and contribution to literature of a New Brunswick writer. This award is next offered in 1995. Deadline and conditions unavailable at time of writing.

QSPELL Book Awards

Jeanne Randle, c/o Fraser Hickson Library, 4855 Kensington
   Avenue, Montreal, Que. H3X 3S6
Phone: (514) 489-5301
Deadline: May

Prizes, each worth $2,000, are awarded for the finest work of fiction, non-fiction, and poetry written in English by a writer who has lived in Quebec for at least three of the past five years. Annual.

Saskatchewan Writers' Guild Awards

Paul Wilson, P.O. Box 3986, Regina, Alta. S4P 3R9
Phone: (306) 757-6310
Deadline: not set

A $1,000 prize is conferred to recognize excellent unpublished manuscripts by Saskatchewan writers. Awards rotate between fiction, non-fiction, poetry, and drama. Annual.

J.I. Segal Award

Louise Roskies, Jewish Public Library of Montreal, Edifice
   Cummings, 5151 chemin de la Côte Sainte-Catherine,
   Montreal, Que. H3W 1M6
Phone: (514) 345-2629
Deadline: May

A $1,000 prize is awarded to honour the best work of fiction, non-fiction, or poetry on a Jewish theme published in Canada in either French or English. Annual.

W.H. Smith/Books in Canada First Novel Award

Anita Miecznikowski, Publisher, *Books in Canada,* 130 Spadina
   Avenue, Suite 603, Toronto, Ont. M5V 2L4

Phone: (416) 601-9880
Deadline: December 31

A $5,000 prize is awarded for the best first novel published in English by a Canadian. Annual.

Edna Staebler Award for Creative Non-Fiction

Lynne Hanna, Office of Institutional Relations,
  Wilfrid Laurier University, 75 University Avenue W., Waterloo,
  Ont. N2L 3C5
Phone: (519) 884-1970, ext. 3067   Fax: (519) 884-8848
Deadline: April 30

A $3,000 prize is awarded for an outstanding work of creative non-fiction, which must be written by a Canadian and have a Canadian location and significance. A first and second prize may be awarded at the discretion of the jury. To be eligible, an entry must be the writer's first or second published book. Established to give recognition and encouragement to new writers. Administered by Wilfrid Laurier University. Annual.

Student Writing Awards

Books in Canada, 130 Spadina Avenue, Suite 603, Toronto,
  Ont. M5V 2L4
Deadline: July 15

Three prizes are awarded in each of two categories: poetry (up to two poems with a total maximum of 2,500 words) and short fiction (maximum 2,500 words). First prize is $1,000, second prize $500, third prize $250. Entrants must be full-time undergraduate students. Co-sponsored by Book City and *Books in Canada*. Annual.

Trillium Book Award

Gartly Wagner, Ministry of Culture, Tourism and Recreation,
  Libraries and Community Information Branch, 77 Bloor Street
  W., 3rd Floor, Toronto, Ont. M7A 2R9
Phone: (416) 314-7611   Fax: (416) 314-7635
Deadline: November 15/December 17

To honour outstanding achievement in writing by an Ontario author, a $12,000 prize is presented to the author. A further $2,500 goes to the publisher. The work, which may be in English or French and in any genre – fiction, non-fiction, children's, poetry, drama –

should contribute to a better understanding of Ontario and Ontario society. Textbooks and chap-books not eligible. Submission deadline depends on publication date. Annual.

The Bronwen Wallace Award

c/o The Writers' Development Trust, 24 Ryerson Avenue, Suite 201, Toronto, Ont. M5T 2P3
Phone: (416) 861-8222   Fax: (416) 861-0090
Deadline: January 15

An award of $1,000 is presented, in alternate years, to a Canadian poet or a Canadian short fiction writer under the age of 35 who is unpublished in book form but whose work has appeared in at least one independently edited magazine or anthology. Applicants should submit up to 2,500 words of unpublished prose fiction in English (1995) or 5 to 10 pages of unpublished poetry in English (1996).

Jon Whyte Memorial Essay Prize

Writers Guild of Alberta, 10523 – 100th Avenue, Edmonton, Alta. T5J 0A8
Deadline: August 31

Alberta writers are invited to submit essays of up to 3,500 words addressing the theme "The Changing Face of Alberta – A Personal Contemplation." The winning essay will earn a $2,000 prize from the Alberta Foundation for the Arts, will be published by the *Edmonton Journal* and the *Calgary Herald*, and produced for radio by CKUA (Access) Radio. Annual.

Writers' Federation of Nova Scotia Awards

Jane Buss, 1809 Barrington Street, Suite 901, Halifax, N.S. B3J 3K8
Phone: (902) 423-8116   Fax: (416) 422-0881

Atlantic Writing Competition

Deadline: August 27

Seven categories for unpublished manuscripts – novel, non-fiction book, short story, personal essay, poetry, writing for children, and play – receive small cash prizes of between $50 to $200 for first, second, and third placegetters.

Thomas Raddall Atlantic Fiction Award

Deadline: April 15

A $2,000 prize is awarded for an outstanding novel or collection of short stories, in English or French, by a native or resident of Atlantic Canada. Co-sponsored by the Writers' Development Trust. Annual.

Evelyn Richardson Memorial Literary Trust Award

Deadline: April 15

An $1,000 prize is awarded for an outstanding work of non-fiction by a native or resident of Nova Scotia. Annual.

Writers Guild of Alberta Annual Awards

Writers Guild of Alberta, 10523 – 100th Avenue, Edmonton, Alta.
   T5J 0A8

Phone: (403) 426-5892   Fax: (403) 424-7943

Deadline: December 31

A $500 prize is awarded for excellent achievement by an Alberta writer in each of the following categories: children's literature, drama, non-fiction, novel, poetry, and short fiction. Annual.

The Writers' Union of Canada Short Prose Competition for New Writers

The Writers' Union of Canada, 24 Ryerson Avenue, Toronto,
   Ont. M5T 2P3

Deadline: November 3

An award to discover new writers of fiction and non-fiction. A $2,000 cash prize ($500 to first runner-up) goes to the best piece of unpublished prose (fiction or non-fiction) of between 2,000 and 2,500 words by a Canadian citizen or landed immigrant who has not published a book and has produced no more than two paid articles or stories. The author agrees to permit publication of the winning entry in *Books in Canada*. The runner-up receives $500. Apply for full entry conditions. Annual.

Grants

Alberta Foundation for the Arts

Scot Morison, Alberta Community Development, Arts Branch,
3rd Floor, Beaver House, 10158 – 103rd Street, Edmonton,
Alta. T5J 0X6

Phone: (403) 427-6315   Fax: (403) 422-9132

Four categories of writing grants are available to the professional, published writer: The Senior Writer Grant, to a maximum of $25,000, is available to veterans with at least four published books (or equivalent) behind them. The Intermediate Writer Grant, worth a maximum of $11,000, is designed for the professional who has published at least one book (or equivalent). The Junior Writer Grant, of up to $4,000, is open to those who have published two stories or articles in different periodicals (or equivalent). In addition, the Special Project Grant of up to $5,000 may be applied for. Competition deadlines are May 1 for the senior category, May 1 and October 1 for the others.

British Columbia Ministry of Small Business, Tourism & Culture

Cultural Services Branch, 800 Johnson Street, 5th Floor, Victoria,
B.C. V8V 1X4

Phone: (604) 356-1728   Fax: (604) 387-4099

Contact: Walter K. Quan, Co-ordinator, Arts Awards Programs

Assistance to a maximum of $5,000 for specific creative projects is available for professional writers of B.C. with at least two published books behind them. One juried competition is held annually.

The Canada Council

99 Metcalfe Street, P.O. Box 1047, Ottawa, Ont. K1P 5V8

Phone: 1-800-263-5588, (613) 598-4319 locally or a.h.

Fax: (613) 598-4390

The Canada Council has developed several support programs for individual writers. The Grants to Artists Program offers grants to published writers to research and write new literary works including fiction, poetry, drama, children's literature, biographies, essays, or criticism. The aim of this program is to give writers time to pursue their creative work. Arts Grant A, for nationally or internationally recognized writers, encompasses "subsistence" and "project and travel costs" allowances to a maximum of $31,000. Arts Grant B, for recognized professional writers offers similar support to a maximum of $17,000. Non-fiction writers may be eligible for a Regular Grant (to a maximum of $18,000) or a Small Grant (maximum $5,000). Professionals may also be eligible for a Short-Term Grant (to a maximum $4,000) or a Travel Grant for an approved project or purpose. The Explorations Program offers project grants to emerging writers (phone [613] 598-4336). For details of eligibility conditions and length of tenure, request a copy of the Grants to Artists brochure.

Manitoba Arts Council

525 – 93 Lombard Avenue, Winnipeg, Man. R3B 3B1
Phone: (204) 945-0422   Fax: (204) 945-5925
Contact: Pat Sanders, Writing and Publishing Officer

Several potential sources of funding for writers: The Writers A Grant, worth up to $10,000, is designed to support concentrated work on a major writing project by professional Manitoba writers who show a high standard of work and exceptional promise. The Writers B Grant, with similar designation and eligibility, is worth up to $5,000. The Writers C Grant, worth up to $2,000, for which unpublished writers who show exceptional promise are eligible, is available to support a variety of developmental writing projects. The Major Arts Grant supports personal creative projects of 6 to 10 months' duration by writers of exceptional accomplishment. Covering living and travel expenses, and project costs, this grant is worth up to $25,000. Finally, published Manitoba writers can apply for a Short-Term Project Grant, to a maximum of $1,000, to support work in progress or significant career opportunities. Write for guidelines, eligibility criteria, and application procedures.

New Brunswick Department of Municipalities, Culture & Housing

Arts Branch, P.O. Box 6000, Fredericton, N.B. E3B 5H1
Phone: (506) 453-2555   Fax: (506) 453-2416

Several potential sources of funding support exist for the professional writer in New Brunswick. Funds up to a maximum $6,000 in any two-year period may be applied for in the form of a Creation Grant to support the research, development, and execution of an approved original project. The Arts Awards Program offers study grants worth $1,000 to $2,500 to student and professional writers.

Newfoundland & Labrador Arts Council
P.O. Box 98, Station C, St John's, Nfld. A1C 5H5
Phone: (709) 726-2212   Fax: (709) 726-0619

Newfoundland writers can apply to the NLAC for funding support under the Project Grant Program. Project grants are intended to help individuals carry out work in their field and may be used for living expenses and materials, study, and travel costs. Grants generally range from $500 to $2,000 or slightly higher. The amount of grant money available is based on the number of applications.

Newfoundland & Labrador Arts & Letters Competition
Newfoundland & Labrador Department of Tourism & Culture,
    Cultural Affairs Division, P.O. Box 1854, St. John's,
     Nfld. A1C 5P9
Phone: (709) 729-3650   Fax: (709) 729-5952

This competition aims to stimulate original creative work in literature and other arts by both amateurs and professionals in the province. First prize in poetry, fiction, and non-fiction categories in the senior division is $600, for poetry and fiction or non-fiction in the junior division, $300. Annual.

Northwest Territories Arts Council
Department of Education, Culture and Employment, Government
    of the N.W.T., P.O. Box 1320, Yellowknife, N.W.T. X1A 2L9
Phone: (403) 920-3103   Fax: (403) 873-0107
Contact: Peter Cullen, Arts Liaison Co-ordinator

The mandate of the N.W.T. Arts Council is to nurture and promote the visual, literary, and performing arts in the territories. Contributions of up to $21,400 (10 percent of the total funding budget) may be applied for. In 1993/4 the council funded a total of 37 projects, granting applicants between $500 and $12,000. Deadlines are January 31 and April 30. For applications and guidelines, call or write to the Arts Liaison Co-ordinator.

Nova Scotia Department of Tourism, Culture & Recreation
Cultural Affairs Division, P.O. Box 456, Halifax, N.S. B3J 2R5
Phone: (902) 424-6389   Fax: (902) 424-2668

The professional writer may apply for a project grant to a maximum of $2,000 to assist with the cost of completing research or manuscript preparation for a project in which a trade publisher has expressed serious interest.

Ontario Arts Council

The Literature Office, 151 Bloor Street W., Suite 500, Toronto,
Ont. M5S 1T6

Phone: (416) 961-1660   Fax: (416) 961-7796

The Ontario Arts Council offers three main grant programs for Ontario-based writers. The Writers' Reserve program assists talented emerging and established writers in the creation of new work in fiction, poetry, writing for children, literary criticism, arts commentary, history, biography, or politics/social issues. Writers' Reserve grants are awarded through designated book and periodical publishers, who recommend authors for funding support up to a maximum of $5,000. The Works-in-Progress program offers support (up to a maximum of $20,000) in the completion of major book-length works of literary merit in poetry or prose by published writers. Finally, the Arts Writing program supports (up to $5,000 per project) the creation by published Ontario writers of new works of criticism, commentary, and essays on literature, the arts, and the media intended for periodical publication or inclusion in an anthology or catalogue, or documentary scripts for radio broadcast. Write to the Literature Office, Ontario Arts Council, for detailed guidelines and application forms for all these programs.

Prince Edward Island Council of the Arts

P.O. Box 2234, Charlottetown, P.E.I. C1A 8B9

Phone: (902) 368-4410   Fax: (902) 368-4417

Arts assistance grants to the value of $2,000 are available to support Island writers. The annual Island Literary Awards (deadline February 15), sponsored by the PEI Council of the Arts, include the following: the Milton Acorn Poetry Award (first prize, trip for two to New York); the Carl Sentner Short Story Award (first prize, $500); the Feature Article Award (first prize, $500); and the Lucy Maud Montgomery P.E.I. Children's Literature Award (first prize, $500).

Ministère des Affaires culturelles

225, Grande Allée Est, 3 étage, bloc B, Québec City, Que. G1R 5G5

Phone: (418) 644-2581   Fax: (418) 644-0380

The Support Program for Professional Artists offers several types of grant to creative writers who have published at least one book or who have been published in a journal. Most grants are directed towards Québécois. Inquire about funding for English-language writers. At the time of writing, a proposed new arts council is expected to deliver support to anglophones.

Saskatchewan Arts Board

3475 Albert Street, T.C. Douglas Building, 3rd Floor, Regina,
   Sask. s4s 6x6

Phone: (306) 787-4056 or 1-800-667-7526 (Sask.)
   Fax: (306) 787-4199

Under the Individual Assistance Program: A Grants, for professional, provincially or nationally recognized artists, offer up to $20,000 in Creative Grants and up to $15,000 in Study and Research Grants. Deadline: March 1. B Grants, for professionals who have completed basic training or education in their discipline, offer up to $12,000 in Creative Grants, up to $7,500 in Study and Research Grants. Deadlines: March 1, July 1, November 1. C Grants, for emerging professionals, offer up to $2,000 for Creative and Study and Research Grants. Deadlines: March 1, July 1, November 1. The Literary Arts Program supports writers as well as book and periodical publishers and literary organizations. Literary Arts Project Grants aim to meet the needs of professional or emerging Saskatchewan writers. The Literary Playscript Commissioning Grant Program supports the creation, performance, and appreciation of new literary works by Saskatchewan playwrights. The Literary Script Reading Program provides, at a subsidized rate, professional evaluation of manuscripts by other Saskatchewan writers, who receive a fee for their services.

Yukon Department of Tourism

Arts Branch, P.O. Box 2703, Whitehorse, Yukon Y1A 2C6
Phone: (403) 667-8592   Fax: (403) 667-4656

Yukon writers may be eligible for an Advanced Artist Award of up to $5,000 for a specific project. Funding for the program is obtained from lotteries revenues and administered by the Arts Branch.

8

PROFESSIONAL DEVELOPMENT

Writers at every level of experience can extend their skills and find fresh ideas through all manner of writing courses and workshops. Some believe creative writing is best fostered in the university or college environment, by working with a good teacher who understands literary devices and structures and the power of language. Many skills peculiar to non-fiction writing, generally considered more a craft than an art, can be learned through courses or workshops led by experienced writers who have discovered not only how to refine ideas, but how to research them, transform them into workable structures, and, finally, market them. Some creative writers swear by the hothouse atmosphere, creative exchange of ideas, and collective reinforcement to be derived from workshops led by expert facilitators.

Local branches of the Canadian Authors Association, libraries, and the adult education classes offered by boards of education are some sources of writing courses and workshops. Regional writers' associations sometimes organize them, too, and are always a good source of information about what's currently available in your area.

This chapter is divided into two parts: first, a review of the country's most interesting writing schools, workshops, and retreats; second, a survey of the best opportunities for the development of writing skills currently offered by Canadian colleges and universities.

This larger section includes most significant writing and journalism programs – in the mainstream and in extension departments – as well as a number of university-based workshops. The list is far from exhaustive. Many universities, colleges of applied arts, and community colleges offer writing courses at some level, depending on staff availability and demand. Not all courses are taught every year, and programs can change at short notice. Continuing education courses are open to all, but entry to credit courses is generally limited to those with specific academic prerequisites – though experienced writers can sometimes win special permission from the course convenor. Find out where you stand before developing your plans.

The summer courses, generally about a week long and built around daily small-group workshop sessions, offer participants the chance to increase their technical skills, to submit their work to group scrutiny and critical feedback, and to enjoy, and learn from, the company of fellow writers as well as editors, agents, and other publishing people. Courses are sometimes streamed in order to cater to different levels of experience. Workshop facilitators are often nationally or internationally acclaimed authors, and some course participants enrol simply for the chance to work with them, but the best facilitators aren't necessarily the top literary names.

The workshop experience can be intense and demanding, and the rewards illusive. To get the most from them, bring at least one well developed piece of writing with you, be prepared to work hard during and outside the main sessions, but also use the opportunity to rub shoulders with other seekers, to network, and to bask in that all-too-rare sense of a community of writers.

Finally, for those writers harried by family and job obligations, frustrated by the distractions of city living, and with a manuscript they simply must finish, writers' retreats and colonies offer peaceful seclusion, a beautiful rural setting, and a "room of one's own" in which to work without interruption, with meals and accommodation taken care of. Note that these are not teaching situations.

The writer's opportunities for professional development are extraordinarily diverse in Canada. Before you commit yourself, define your needs and carefully evaluate each program to see how it might meet these needs.

Creative Writing Schools, Workshops, & Retreats

The Banff Centre for the Arts
P.O. Box 1020, Station 28, Banff, Alta. TOL OCO
Phone: (403) 762-6180   Fax: (403) 762-6345
Contact: Lorraine Schindel, Assistant Registrar
Offers a wide range of non-credit journalism and creative writing courses. One of Canada's foremost writing schools, founded in 1933, Banff offers promising writers a five-week summer course on full scholarship (10 fiction writers and 10 poets are chosen each year, having submitted a full-length, unedited manuscript or work in progress). Participants in these writing studios work independently, with a resource available for consultation and editorial assistance. The school also offers programs in radio drama and dramatic writing for T.V., a film and theatre workshop, and a playwright's colony. The arts journalism program provides established journalists with an opportunity to develop a major essay or article on a subject in the arts.

The Crowsnest Pass Writers' Workshop & Retreat
c/o *absinthe*, P.O. Box 61113, Kensington Postal Outlet, Calgary,
   Alta. T2N 4S6
Phone: (403) 283-6802   Fax: (403) 283-6802
An intensive six days of workshops in June, with evening discussion groups, readings, and excursions, organized and operated by the Calgary-based *absinthe* literary society. Workshops focus on individual participants' writing and on a variety of writerly concerns. Creative writers of all levels and backgrounds work with experienced facilitators, including internationally acclaimed writers-in-residence, and resource personnel. For those wanting extra writing time, the retreat offers an additional week in the Crowsnest's rugged mountain setting. Workshop fees, including meals and accommodation, are $380 (double occupancy) or $490 (private room). Retreat fees, depending on availability, are $40 less in each case. Applicants must submit a 10- to 20-page writing sample. First Nations writers and writers of colour are encouraged to apply.

En'owkin International School of Writing

En'owkin Centre, 257 Brunswick Street, Penticton, B.C. V2A 5P9

Phone: (604) 493-7181   Fax: (604) 493-5302

Contact: Office of the Registrar

Offers Native students a two-year credit program leading to a certificate in First Nations Creative Writing awarded jointly with the University of Victoria. Established First Nations writers, dramatists, and visual artists work directly with students to assist them to find their voice as writers through an appreciation of First Nations cultural and literary traditions. Graduates receive a two-year credit towards a Bachelor of Fine Arts degree at the University of Victoria.

The Humber School for Writers

Humber College, Room K107, 205 Humber College Boulevard,
  Etobicoke, Ont. M9W 5L7

Phone: (416) 675-5094

Contact: Nancy Abell

One of Canada's best although youngest schools for writers has now established a unique 30-week certificate program in creative writing. This extraordinary program offers promising writers the opportunity to send their work-in-progress (novel, short stories, or poetry) directly to their instructor, who provides editorial feedback by mail on a continuing basis throughout the academic year. Current instructors are the distinguished writers Timothy Findley, Carole Corbeil, Paul Quarrington, and D.M. Thomas. Admission is decided on the basis of a 15-page writing sample along with a detailed proposal of the work to be completed during the course. Enrolment, which must be made by November, is limited. At the time of writing, the course fee for Canadians and permanent residents is $792.

Kingston School of Writing

P.O. Box 1061, Kingston, Ont. K7L 4Y5

Phone: (613) 548-1556

A division of Quarry Press, the Kingston School of Writing stages creative writing workshops in fiction, poetry, children's writing, and creative non-fiction throughout the year. The week-long summer workshop in July offers writers at all levels the opportunity to work intensively with a faculty of professional authors and editors. Admission is open to writers at all levels. A 5- to 10-page writing sample will be used to place participants in the appropriate class and to prepare for one-on-one tutorials. Tuition fees are $325 for the week. Private room, breakfast, and lunch on Queen's University campus costs $45 per day.

Kootenay School of Writing

152 West Hastings Street, Suite 306, Vancouver, B.C. v6b 1g8
Phone: (604) 688-6001

Developed on the model of the artist-run centre, this is the only writer-run centre in Canada. Offers writing workshops, run by practising writers, in poetry, fiction, and theoretical concerns (e.g., modernism and gender, Foucauldian theory) in the fall and spring. Hosts a visiting foreign writer-in-residence and regular readings and talks by visiting writers. All events are open to the public, most for a small admission charge.

Maritime Writers' Workshop

Department of Extension and Summer Session, University of New
   Brunswick, P.O. Box 4400, Fredericton, N.B. e3b 5a3
Phone: (506) 454-9153
Contact: Glenda Turner

An annual, week-long summer program designed to help writers at all levels of experience. Offers instruction in fiction, poetry, feature writing, and writing for children. As well as workshops and individual tuition, the program includes lecture/discussions, public readings by instructors (all successful published writers), and guest speakers. All participants are required to submit manuscript samples of their work by May. Tuition fees in 1993 were $250 (room and meal charges extra). Scholarships of varying amounts up to the full cost of tuition and board are awarded on the basis of need and talent.

Sage Hill Writing Experience

P.O. Box 1731, Saskatoon, Sask. s7k 3s1
Phone: (306) 652-7395

Sage Hill's 10-day summer writing workshops are held every August at the Sage Hill Conference Centre in rural Saskatchewan,

75 kilometres northeast of Saskatoon. The centre has private rooms with writing areas, meeting rooms, recreational facilities, and home-style cooking. The program offers workshops at introductory, inter-mediate, and advanced levels in fiction, poetry, and playwriting (though not all these courses are available each year). The low instructor-to-writer ratio (usually 6 to 1) and high quality faculty (all established writers) helps make these workshops among the most highly valued in Canada. Substantial individual tuition time is also considered important. Fees per course of $475 include accommoda-tion and meals. Scholarships are available. Enrolment is limited. Applicants should send for guidelines. Registration deadline May 1.

An annual Youth Writing Camp, for Saskatchewan writers aged 13 to 18, has also been organized. For this free, four-day creative writing day camp held in Saskatoon, out-of-towners need to arrange their own accommodation and travel.

Saskatchewan Writers/Artists Colonies & Retreats
c/o P.O. Box 3986, Regina, Sask. S4P 3R9
Phone: (306) 757-6310   Fax: (306) 565-8554
The Saskatchewan Colonies were established in 1979 to provide an environment where writers and artists (especially but not exclu-sively from Saskatchewan) could work free from distractions in serene and beautiful locations. They are not teaching situations but retreats, providing uninterrupted work time and opportunities for a stimulating exchange of ideas with fellow writers and artists after hours. Costs are subsidized by the Saskatchewan Lotteries Trust. St. Peter's Abbey is a Benedictine Abbey near the town of Humboldt. Emma Lake is in forest country north of Prince Albert.

An eight-week summer colony (July–August) and a two-week winter colony (February) are held at St. Peter's Abbey. Applicants may request as much time as they need, but accommodation, in pri-vate rooms, is limited to eight people per week. Emma Lake hosts a two-week summer colony in August. Participants are housed in cabins or single rooms. Individual retreats of up to a month are offered year round at St. Peter's, with no more than three individuals being accommodated at a time. Fees, including meals, are $100 per week. Applicants are required to submit a 10-page writing sample, a résumé, description of work to be done at the colony, and two refer-ences. It's best to book two to three months ahead in each case.

Sechelt Writer-in-Residence Programs

Festival of the Written Arts, P.O. Box 2299, Sechelt, B.C. VON 3A0
Phone: (604) 885-9631   Fax: (604) 885-3967

Five-day writer-in-residence workshops are held three times a year – in November, in the spring, and in August. Past workshops, which are all led by celebrated established writers, have focused on the writing of fiction in many genres, and of poetry, history, travel, cookbooks, as well as scriptwriting and writing for magazines. Participants range from beginners to published authors. Classes are limited to 10 to 12 students to allow adequate time for individual tuition. Fees, inclusive of tuition, accommodation, and meals, in 1993 were $265 to $295. Write or phone for further information.

University of Toronto Writers' Workshop

158 St. George Street, Toronto, Ont. M5S 2V8
Phone: (416) 978-2400   Fax: (416) 978-6666

A week-long summer course (held in July) pivoting around daily intensive three-hour workshops, with up to 12 participants per instructor. The course also includes individual consultations, skill-building sessions, visiting writers, editors, and other experts, and readings. Admission is based on writing samples: a 20-page (maximum) work-in-progress is worked on during the week; each workshop requires a sample of 3 to 10 pages. The fee is $450, with an extra charge for residence accommodation. Limited financial assistance may be available.

West Word Summer School/Writing Retreat for Women

210 – 640 West Broadway, Vancouver, B.C. V5Z 1G4
Phone: (604) 872-8014

Canada's only writing school for women, sponsored by the West Coast Women and Word Society, offers a two-week live-in program in August for women writers at all levels of experience from across the country. The program covers three genres: fiction, poetry, and creative documentary. All facilitators are experienced professional writers, and classes are limited to eight. Class time is 9 a.m. to noon, and each participant has the opportunity of at least one hour of individual critique each day. Guest readers attend, and students are encouraged to organize their own readings. Each participant has a private room containing a work desk. Applicants must submit a

15-page writing sample and a brief bio, noting in particular their cultural background/heritage. The fee of $600 covers room, board, and tuition. Partial scholarship help is available. Deadline for applications is May. Send early for brochure.

Creative Writing & Journalism at Colleges & Universities

University of Alberta
Edmonton, Alta. T6G 2M7
Phone: (403) 492-3111   Fax: (403) 492-7219
Contact: Office of the Registrar
Phone: (403) 492-3116   Fax: (403) 492-0627
The English Department offers courses in creative writing of fiction, poetry, and non-fiction.
Faculty of Extension, 4 – 14A Extension Centre, University of
Alberta, Edmonton, Alta. T6G 2T4
Phone: (403) 492-3033   Fax: (403) 492-1857
Contact: M. Hertwig-Jaksch, program co-ordinator
A full range of creative writing courses is offered on a semester basis. These include fiction workshops, poetry writing, writing for children, writing for film and television, and non-fiction freelance writing. Courses are presented twice each academic year. Several journalism courses, including Magazine Article Writing and Words into Print, are also offered.

Algonquin College of Applied Arts and Technology
1385 Woodroffe Avenue, Nepean, Ont. K2G 1V8
Phone: (613) 727-4723   Fax: (613) 727-7684
Contact: Bob Louks, Co-ordinator, Journalism Program
A two-year print journalism diploma program, which includes practical experience on the college newspaper, *The Algonquin Times*. Also offers courses in journalism, editing, photo journalism, and desktop publishing, and a two-year creative advertising diploma program, which teaches a wide range of practical media and communication skills.

University of British Columbia
204 – 2075 Wesbrook Mall, Vancouver, B.C. V6T 1Z1

Phone: (604) 822-2712   Fax: (604) 822-3599
Contact: Department of Creative Writing
   The Creative Writing Department offers programs of study leading to BFA and MFA degrees. A wide range of creative writing courses is available, including writing for screen and television, fiction, theatre, and poetry. Students may choose to take a double major in creative writing and another subject. A diploma in applied creative non-fiction is open to graduates and those with professional experience.
   The literary journal *PRISM international* (see Literary & Scholarly) is edited by department graduate students.

Cambrian College of Applied Arts and Technology

1400 Barrydowne Road, Sudbury, Ont. P3A 3V8
Phone: (705) 566-8101 or 1-800-461-7145   Fax: (705) 524-7334
Contact: Office of the Registrar
   Offers diploma courses leading to a journalism major.
   Continuing Education holds evening creative writing classes.
   Publishes *The Shield,* a biweekly journalism lab paper.

Camosun College

3100 Foul Bay Road, Victoria, B.C. V8P 5J2
Contact: Office of the Registrar
   Courses in prose fiction, drama, and poetry are taught. Courses in writing for the print and electronic media are offered as components of the two-year Applied Communications program. Students write and produce *Camas,* a college news magazine, and some radio and cable television programs.
   Continuing Education offers occasional journalism courses.
   Students are encouraged to submit material to *Camas* and two other campus journals, *The Camosun Review* and *The Bound With Glue Review.*

Canadore College of Applied Arts and Technology

P.O. Box 5001, 100 College Drive, North Bay, Ont. P1B 8K9
Phone: (705) 474-7600, ext. 5123   Fax: (705) 474-2384
Contact: Mark Sherry, Diector of Admissions & Liaison
   The two-year print journalism diploma program includes courses in research and interviewing, newswriting, feature writing, keyboard

skills, photo journalism, communications, and Canadian politics and economics. Journalism students produce a weekly newspaper, *The Quest*.

Continuing Education offers a course in creative writing and courses in business writing. Canadore's Summer School of the Arts holds week-long creative writing workshops.

Carleton University

Student Liaison and Publication Services, 315 Administration
  Building, 1125 Colonel By Drive, Ottawa, Ont. KIS 5B6
Phone: (613) 788-3663 or 1-800-267-7366 (Ontario and Quebec)
  Fax: (613) 788-3517
Contact: Jean Mullan, Assistant Director of Admissions (Liaison)

The School of Journalism offers a four-year program leading to an honours Bachelor of Journalism for students who have completed a first degree. A one-year master's degree program is available for students with a BJ and journalists with substantial working experience. Students may be eligible for the two-year master's program. Some creative writing courses are also given through the Department of English Language and Literature, including restricted-entry seminars in poetry and fiction.

The Carleton Professional Development Centre offers an introductory course in creative writing and several courses in technical and business writing.

Publishes the student newspaper *The Charlatan*.

Centennial College of Applied Arts and Technology

P.O. Box 631, Station A, Scarborough, Ont. MIK 5E9
Phone: (416) 694-3241, ext. 3420
Contact: Ron Dodge, Chair, Communication Arts

Three-year diploma programs in print journalism, broadcasting, and creative advertising are offered. So are two-year diploma programs in book and magazine publishing and in corporate communication. Programs include courses in reporting, editing, scriptwriting, broadcast journalism, production for radio and television, documentary film writing, cinematography, magazine writing, public relations, newspaper feature writing, computer graphics, and more. All programs emphasize practical skills.

Concordia University (Loyola Campus)

7141 Sherbrooke Street W., Montreal, Que. H4B 1R6

Phone: (514) 848-2624

Contact: Bruce Smart, Registrar

The English Department's Creative Writing program offers workshops in playwriting, poetry, and fiction, and gives courses in advanced composition and non-fiction, leading to bachelor's and master's degrees. The Department of Fine Arts offers courses in playwriting through its theatre program. The Journalism Department has degree programs offering courses in writing and reporting, feature and magazine writing, editing, and writing for radio and television news and public affairs. Undergraduate and graduate programs have quotas, so students are screened for admission.

Conestoga College of Applied Arts and Technology

299 Doon Valley Drive, Kitchener, Ont. N2G 4M4

Phone: (519) 748-3516   Fax: (519) 895-1097

Contact: Betty Martin, Registrar

An 80-week journalism diploma program prepares graduates to work as reporter–photographers in newspapers or magazines, or as story editors and reporters for radio or television stations. Graduates are equipped with such editing skills as headline writing, design, and layout. Each student spends a minimum of two months working on a local newspaper or magazine. Public relations courses are also offered, as are research and computer skills.

Courses available through the Centre for Continuing Education include How to Sell What You Write, Writing for Children, Writing: How to Say What You Mean, Marketing Your Writing, and Creative Writing Workshop.

Douglas College

P.O. Box 2503, New Westminster, B.C. V3L 5B2

Phone: (604) 527-5400   Fax: (604) 527-5095

Contact: Maurice Hodgson, Convenor, Creative Writing

College credit and university transfer courses in creative writing and communication are available. Courses include Introductory Fiction, Drama, Poetry; second-year courses in short fiction; a multi-genre course; screen writing; and personal narrative.

The Print Futures professional writing program is a two-year diploma program preparing students for a professional writing career. Includes courses in writing, research, editorial, and design skills, public relations writing, and writing for magazines and trade publications. For more information, contact the English and Communications Department (phone [604] 527-5465).

Publishes the literary journal *Event* (see Literary & Scholarly).

Durham College of Applied Arts and Technology

2000 Simcoe Street N., P.O. Box 385, Oshawa, Ont. L1H 7L7
Phone: (905) 721-2000   Fax: (905) 721-3182
Contact: Ann Marie Stevenson, Program Officer

Offers a Communication Arts program leading to a two-year diploma in journalism or advertising, or a three-year public relations diploma. Graduates of other colleges and universities may qualify for direct entry into a special one-year program concentrating on practical subjects.

Continuous Learning offers the following credit courses for a Communication Arts certificate: Introduction to Newswriting, Mass Media Communication, Writing I, Introduction to Journalism. Also two creative writing courses: Skills for Fiction Writers and Getting Published.

Publishes *The Chronicle,* a college newspaper that provides students with experience in writing, editing, design, layout, art, photography, and production.

George Brown College of Applied Arts and Technology

P.O. Box 1015, Station B, Toronto, Ont. M5T 2T9
Phone: (416) 867-2092   Fax: (416) 867-2302
Contact: Peggy Needham, Co-ordinator, English Department

Offers a wide range of creative writing courses and seminars, with the option of qualifying for a certificate in creative writing. Included are Writing for Magazines 1 and 2, Writing a Novel, Creating Short Stories 1 and 2, Poetry and Fiction Workshops, Writing TV Scripts that Sell, Writing for Children, Writing Science Fiction and Fantasy, Romance Writers' Workshop, Writing Mysteries, and Journalism: Springboard to a Career, among others. Classes are held three times a year, one night a week. Courses in technical and business writing are also offered.

George Brown's annual Storymakers conference, held over a

weekend in August, offers a choice of workshops, guest speakers, and readings. Registration fee in 1993 was $130, including some meals.

Georgian College of Applied Arts and Technology
1 Georgian Drive, Barrie, Ont. L4M 3X9
Phone: (705) 728-1951   Fax: (705) 722-5123
Contact: School of Continuous Learning, instructors Tom Arnett and Paul Lima

The School of Continuous Learning offers a very broad range of useful part-time courses on demand, including Writing the Novel, Scriptwriting, Write Better, Creative Writing, Getting Your Writing Published, Writing for Business, Short Story Writing, Fiction Writing, Planning Your Novel, and Writing for Children.

Holland College
140 Weymouth Street, Charlottetown, P.E.I. C1A 4Z1
Phone: (902) 566-9591   Fax: (902) 566-9505
Contact: Martin Dorrell, Journalism Instructor

The Creative Arts Department offers a one-year diploma program in journalism.

Publishes *The Surveyor*.

Humber College of Applied Arts and Technology
205 Humber College Boulevard, Etobicoke, Ont. M9W 5L7
Phone: (416) 675-3111   Fax: (416) 675-2427
Contact: Inquiry Centre

Offers a three-year diploma course in print and broadcast journalism.

See separate listing earlier in this chapter for the Humber School for Writers.

University of King's College, School of Journalism
6350 Coburg Road, Halifax, N.S. B3H 2A1
Phone: (902) 422-1271   Fax: (902) 423-3357
Contact: Dr. P. Robertson, Registrar

Two journalism programs are offered: the first, a four-year program, leading to an honours BJ degree, for students entering directly from high school; the second, an intensive one-year program, leading to a BJ, for students who already have a bachelor's degree. Students in the four-year honours program take courses in arts or science at Dalhousie University. All students take courses in broadcast and print journalism, research techniques, interviewing, history of journalism, media law, and journalism ethics, and select from a wide variety of optional courses. Both programs teach journalism from a practical point of view.

Lethbridge Community College

Community Education, Lethbridge Community College,
   Lethbridge, Alta. TIK IL6
Contact: Office of the Registrar
   Diploma program for Communication Arts offers courses in journalism. A weekly newspaper certificate program available through Distance Education.
   Publishes *The Endeavour,* a semi-monthly newspaper.

Loyalist College of Applied Arts and Technology

P.O. Box 4200, Belleville, Ont. K8N 5B9
Phone: (613) 969-1913 (Post Secondary Admissions Office)
Contact: Phone the Post Secondary Admissions Office or write to
   the Registrar
   Two-year full-time journalism program includes courses in newspaper production, feature writing, and scriptwriting. There is also the option of a two-year agricultural journalism program.

McMaster University

Commons Building, Room 116 (CCE) or Gilmour Hall, Room 103
   (Degree Study), 1280 Main Street, Hamilton, Ont. L8S 4L8
Phone: (416) 525-9140   Fax: (416) 546-1690 (CCE)
Contact: Susan Porter, Registrar; Gord Raymond, Degree Study;
   Ann Howard, Continuing Education
   Offers credit courses in practical criticism and creative writing.
   Continuing Education offers a broad range of creative and practical writing courses.
   Two campus publications, *Courier* and *Silhouette,* offer freelance opportunities.

Mohawk College

P.O. Box 2034, Hamilton, Ont. L8N 3T2
Phone: (905) 575-1212   Fax: (905) 575-2378
Contact: Terry Mote, Manager, Student Liaison & Career Services

Creative Writing, Writing for Radio, Script Writing, Grammar and Composition for Media are courses within the Media Studies program.

Continuing Education offers Creative Writing as a 13-week credit course. The two-year, full-time Broadcast Journalism diploma program includes a range of broadcasting and media courses. Continuing Education has two 13-week credit courses: Report Writing – Business; and Report Writing – Technical.

Publishes the college newspaper *The Satellite*.

University of New Brunswick

P.O. Box 4400, Fredericton, N.B. E3B 5A3
Phone: (506) 453-4666   Fax: (506) 453-4599
Contact: Office of the Registrar

Two creative writing courses with a BA credit are offered. Also an MA degree with a creative writing option (i.e., one-third of course work, plus thesis).

Continuing Education provides a non-credit fundamentals of writing course.

The university has a writer-in-residence and sponsors the Maritime Writers' Workshop. Also publishes *The Brunswickan*.

Niagara College of Applied Arts and Technology

Woodlawn Road, Welland, Ont. L3B 5S2
Phone: (613) 735-2211   Fax: (613) 735-5365
Contact: Continuing Education

Offers two-year print journalism diploma course.

Continuing Education offers the following courses for credit: Writing for Publication, Writing Children's Literature, Communication and Literature, and Creative Writing. The occasional unit in journalism is also offered.

Publishes a biweekly newspaper, *Niagara News*.

University of Ottawa

Ottawa, Ont. KIN 6N5

Phone: (613) 564-3311   Fax: (613) 564-9906

Contact: Office of the Registrar

Offers undergraduate course in creative writing. Also a BA in Communication Studies.

Publishes *Fulcrum,* the student newspaper, *Gazette,* a tabloid, and a quarterly journal, *Alumni News/Revue de l'Université d'Ottawa.* Also publishes *The Canadian Short Story Series* and *Re-Appraisals of Canadian Literature,* a journal of criticism sponsored by the English Department.

Continuing Education offers creative writing courses, such as Poetry Workshop, Creative Writing (beginners), Popular Fiction Writing, Advanced Fiction Workshop, and Writing for Results, depending on staff availability and demand.

Parkland Regional College

P.O. Box 790, Prince William Drive, Melville, Sask. SOA 2PO

Phone: (306) 728-4471   Fax: (306) 728-2576

Contact: Office of the Registrar

The University of Saskatchewan runs a two-year pre-Journalism off-campus course and junior and senior degree-credit English courses.

Courses (mostly non-credit) are offered as requested by community groups in the region.

Red Deer College

P.O. Box 5005, Red Deer, Alta. T4N 5H5

Phone: (403) 342-3304   Fax: (403) 340-8940

Contact: Dr. Birk Sproxton, English Department

Diploma and degree course in creative writing. Students may major in writing with English Department courses.

Writers' workshops are sponsored. Also contact general interest co-ordinator, Continuing Education Department, phone (403) 342-3539.

Red River Community College

2055 Notre Dame Avenue, Winnipeg, Man. R3H 0J9

Phone: (204) 632-2142   Fax: (204) 697-4738

Contact: Betty Podosky, Registrar

Creative Communications is a two-year, practical-based diploma program preparing students to work in print and electronic journalism, advertising, and public relations. Also offers three credit courses in creative writing.

Continuing Education offers three sessions each of creative writing and Introduction to Journalism.

Students in the Creative Communications program write for the college newspaper, *Projector*.

University of Regina

Wascana Parkway, Regina, Sask. S4S OA2
Phone: (306) 585-4584
Contact: Office of the Registrar

A four-year Bachelor of Arts in Journalism and Communication (BAJC) is offered. Many creative writing courses are available, and although a student cannot major in creative writing, three or four courses may be applied to an English major.

Continuing Education offers journalism and creative writing courses and sponsors writers' conferences (phone [306] 779-4806).

The English Department produces the literary journal *The Wascana Review* biannually.

Ryerson Polytechnical Institute

350 Victoria Street, Toronto, Ont. M5B 2K3
Phone: (416) 979-5000
Contact: Information Centre

A highly respected school of journalism. The Faculty of Applied Arts offers a four-year degree program, which also includes courses in English literature and the humanities. Students may choose to specialize in newspaper, magazine, or broadcast streams after second year. Also offers a two-year program for postgraduate students. Students produce *The Ryersonian,* a twice-weekly newspaper, and the biannual *Ryerson Review of Journalism,* as well as news and public affairs programs for radio and television.

Continuing Education offers part-time certificate programs in magazine journalism and publishing, and a wide range of creative writing courses and workshops, as well as courses in screen writing, media writing and technical writing. Journalism courses include Feature Writing for the Freelance Market, Freelancing: The Future, and Writing for Print Media.

The Eyeopener is another student-run publication on campus.

Seneca College of Applied Arts and Technology

1750 Finch Avenue E., North York, Ont. M2J 2X5

Phone: (416) 491-5050   Fax: (416) 491-9187

Contact: Office of the Registrar

Options in television and radio scripting, playwriting, and journalism are available to day students in the Broadcasting/Radio & Television program at the School of Communication Arts. A one-year post-diploma program in Corporate Communications offers day students the opportunity to engage in an intensive learning experience designed to graduate mature, flexible communicators with good writing, technical, managerial, and human skills who can quickly become productive in a corporate communications position.

Continuing Education offers courses in various creative writing subjects. These change each semester according to demand and the availability of suitable instructors.

Sheridan College

1430 Trafalgar Road, Oakville, Ont. L6H 2L1

Phone: (905) 845-9430, ext. 2760

Contact: Jo Kleimeyer, Journalism Department

The Journalism Department offers a two-year diploma in print journalism; also a one-year postgraduate program. Students produce a weekly tabloid newspaper, *The Sheridan Sun* (5,000 copies, 28 times a year). Includes courses in magazine writing, marketing magazine articles, desktop publishing, and design.

Continuing Education offers Writing Mystery and Horror, Writing Fantasy and Science Fiction, Writing in the Romantic Mode, Creative Writing 1 and 2, and Creative Writing Workshop; also Writing for Business, Writing Lab, and Write to Publish.

Simon Fraser University at Harbour Centre

515 West Hastings Street, Vancouver, B.C. V6B 5K3

Phone: (604) 291-5077   Fax: (604) 291-5098

Contact: Gladys We, Program Assistant

The Writing and Publishing program of the School of Continuing Studies offers a very broad range of professional development courses for writers, editors, and others working in publishing. Includes non-credit certificates in Business Writing and Technical Writing.

Sir Sandford Fleming College

Brealey Drive, Peterborough, Ont. K9J 7B1
Phone: (705) 749-5542   Fax: (705) 749-5540
Contact: Office of the Registrar

Continuing Education offers regular 8-week creative writing courses to "develop the skills necessary for successful, marketable writing."

University of Toronto

Toronto, Ont. M5S 1A1
Phone: (416) 978-3190   Fax: (416) 978-2836 (Dept. of English)
Phone: (416) 978-2400   Fax: (416) 978-6666 (School of
    Continuing Studies)
Contact: Alvan Bregman, Vice-Provost, Arts and Science

Each year the English Department offers credit courses in creative writing. The School of Continuing Studies offers non-credit courses in business and creative writing on campus and via distance education.

The University of Toronto Press publishes *U of T Quarterly* and many academic journals. There are two campus newspapers, *The Varsity* and *the newspaper*; individual colleges also publish their own student newspapers. Student literary magazines include *Acta Victoriana* (Victoria College), *Salterra* (Trinity College), and *The Gargoyle* (University College). Hart House publishes a literary annual.

University of Toronto School of Continuing Studies

158 St. George Street, Toronto, Ont. M5S 2V8
Phone: (416) 978-2400   Fax: (416) 978-6666
Contact: Office of the Registrar

Liberal Studies offers a broad range of non-credit creative and practical writing courses and workshops. Fields covered include scriptwriting for film and television, the novel, short fiction, storybuilding, writing for business, and English usage.

See separate entry earlier in this chapter for Continuing Studies' annual Writers' Workshop.

Vancouver Community College

100 West 49th Street, Vancouver, B.C. V5Y 2Z6
Contact: Office of the Registrar

Offers diploma courses in journalism. Transfer courses in creative writing lead to a degree from a nearby university.

Continuing Education offers creative writing courses.

Publishes *VCC Voice,* a newspaper.

University of Victoria

P.O. Box 1700, Victoria, B.C. v8w 2Y2

Phone: (604) 721-8107   Fax: (604) 721-8653

Contact: Admissions Office

Through the Department of Creative Writing (phone [604] 721-7306), students can major in creative writing, choosing courses (lectures and workshops) in fiction, non-fiction, poetry, drama, aspects of journalism, publishing, and multimedia. The Creative Writing Co-operative Education program is open to students working towards a career in writing, publishing, or communications; work terms are designed to combine practical work experience with course study. The department does not offer a graduate program.

Continuing Education may offer a Native creative writing course.

University of Western Ontario

Graduate School of Journalism, Middlesex College, University of
    Western Ontario, London, Ont. N6A 5B7

Phone: (519) 661-3383   Fax: (519) 661-3848

Contact: Peter Desbarats, Dean

A four-year BA course in journalism is offered, as well as a 12-month master's course, and a certificate course in Native journalism. An elective course in creative writing is also available to full-time students.

Continuing Education runs several journalism courses.

University of Windsor

Windsor, Ont. N9B 3P4

Phone: (519) 973-7014   Fax: (519) 973-7050

Contact: Joseph Saso, Director, Liaison

Writing courses are available at both the general and honours level. Students may take a BA honours or an MA degree in creative writing. The BA requires completion of eight creative writing courses. There is also a BA, general and honours, degree and an MA in communication studies, with courses available in news writing, scriptwriting, broadcasting, and press studies. An honours co-op BA in English is also offered.

Contact Continuing Education at 1-800-263-1242 for further information about distance education courses, which vary each term depending on demand.

Publishes *The University of Windsor Review*, *University of Windsor Magazine*, and *The Lance*.

York University

4700 Keele Street, North York, Ont. M3J 1P3
Phone: (416) 736-5910   Fax: (416) 736-5460
Contact: Professor R. Teleky, Co-ordinator, or Sue Parsram,
  Administrative Secretary

Offers students the chance to major in creative writing, with workshop courses in poetry, prose, fiction, screenwriting, playwriting, and other related subjects.

9

WRITERS' ORGANIZATIONS & SUPPORT AGENCIES

Alberta Community Development
Arts & Cultural Industries Branch, 3rd Floor, Beaver House,
    10158 – 103rd Street, Edmonton, Alta. T5J 0X6
Phone: (403) 427-6315

Alberta Foundation for the Arts
5th Floor, Beaver House, 10158 – 103rd Street, Edmonton,
    Alta. T5J 0X6
Phone: (403) 427-9968   Fax: (403) 422-1162

Association of Canadian Publishers
2 Gloucester Street, Suite 301, Toronto, Ont. M4Y 1L5
Phone: (416) 413-4929   Fax: (416) 413-4920

**Association of English-language Publishers of Quebec
    (AEAQ)**
3720 Park Avenue, Suite 102, Montreal, Que. H2X 2J1
Phone: (514) 849-0837   Fax: (514) 849-9826

Book & Periodical Council
35 Spadina Road, Toronto, Ont. M5R 2S9
Phone: (416) 975-9366   Fax: (416) 975-1839

British Columbia Ministry of Small Business, Tourism & Culture
Cultural Services Branch, 800 Johnson Street, 5th Floor, Victoria, B.C. v8v 1x4
Phone: (604) 356-1728   Fax: (604) 387-4099

The Canada Council
99 Metcalfe Street, P.O. Box 1047, Ottawa, Ont. k1p 5v8
Phone: 1-800-263-5588; (613) 598-4319 local or a.h.
   Fax: (613) 598-4390

Canadian Authors Association
275 Slater Street, Suite 500, Ottawa, Ont. k1p 5h9
Phone: (613) 233-2846   Fax: (613) 235-8237

Canadian Book Marketing Centre
2 Gloucester Street, Toronto, Ont. m4y 1l5
Phone: (416) 413-4930   Fax: (416) 413-4920

Canadian Children's Book Centre
35 Spadina Road, Toronto, Ont. m5r 2s9
Phone: (416) 975-0010   Fax: (416) 975-1839

Canadian Copyright Institute
35 Spadina Road, Toronto, Ont. m5r 2s9
Phone: (416) 975-1756   Fax: (416) 975-1839

Canadian Magazine Publishers Association
2 Stewart Street, Toronto, Ont. m5v 1h6
Phone: (416) 362-2546   Fax: (416) 362-2547

Canadian Poetry Association
Carrot Common P.O., Box 65100, Toronto, Ont. m4k 3z2
Phone: (519) 434-4740

Canadian Reprography Collective (CANCOPY)
214 King Street W., Suite 312, Tonronto, Ont. m5h 3s6
Phone: (416) 971-5633   Fax: (416) 971-9882

Canadian Society of Children's Authors, Illustrators & Performers (CANSCAIP)
542 Mount Pleasant Road, Suite 103, Toronto, Ont. M4S 2M7
Phone: (416) 322-9666

Crime Writers of Canada
225 Carlton Street, Toronto, Ont. M5A 2L2
Phone: (416) 962-7947

Federation of British Columbia Writers
P.O. Box 2206, Main Post Office, Vancouver, B.C. V6B 3W2
Phone: (604) 683-2057   Fax: (604) 683-8269

Federation of English Writers of Quebec
c/o Scott Lawrence, 478 Red Cross, Lasalle, Que. H8R 2X9

Freelance Editors' Association of Canada (FEAC)
35 Spadina Road, Toronto, Ont. M5R 2S9
Phone: (416) 975-1379   Fax: (416) 975-1839
P.O. Box 1688, Station A, Vancouver, B.C. V6C 2P7
Phone: (604) 681-7184

Island Writers Association (P.E.I.)
P.O. Box 1204, Charlottetown, P.E.I. C1A 7M8
Phone: (902) 566-9748

Literary Press Group
2 Gloucester Street, Suite 301, Toronto, Ont. M4Y 1L5
Phone: (416) 413-4929   Fax: (416) 413-4920

Literary Translators Association of Canada
1030, rue Cherrier, Suite 510, Montreal, Que. H2L 1H9
Phone: (514) 526-6653   Fax: (514) 526-0826

Magazines Canada
50 Holly Street, Toronto, Ont. M4S 3B3
Phone: (416) 482-7307   Fax: (416) 482-9633

Manitoba Arts Council
525 – 93 Lombard Avenue, Winnipeg, Man. R3B 3B1
Phone: (204) 945-2237   Fax: (204) 945-5925

Manitoba Writers' Guild
100 Arthur Street, Suite 206, Winnipeg, Man. R3B 1H3
Phone: (204) 942-6134   Fax: (204) 942-5754

**New Brunswick Department of Municipalities, Culture &
Housing, Arts Branch**
P.O. Box 6000, Fredericton, N.B. E3B 5H1
Phone: (506) 453-2555   Fax: (506) 453-2416

**Newfoundland & Labrador Department of Tourism &
Culture, Cultural Affairs Division**
P.O. Box 1854, St. John's, Nfld. A1C 5P9
Phone: (709) 729-3650   Fax: (709) 729-5952

Northwest Territories Arts Council
Department of Education, Culture and Employment, Government
of the N.W.T., P.O. Box 1320, Yellowknife, N.W.T. X1A 2L9
Phone: (403) 920-3103   Fax: (403) 873-0107

**Nova Scotia Department of Tourism, Culture & Recreation,
Cultural Affairs Division**
P.O. Box 456, Halifax, N.S. B3J 2R5
Phone: (902) 424-6389   Fax: (902) 424-2668

Ontario Arts Council
151 Bloor Street, Suite 500, Toronto, Ont. M5S 1T6
Phone: (416) 961-1660   Fax: (416) 961-7796

Prince Edward Island Council of the Arts
P.O. Box 2234, Charlottetown, P.E.I. C1A 8B9
Phone: (902) 368-4410   Fax: (902) 368-4417

PEN (Poets, Playwrights, Essayists, Editors, & Novelists)
The Writers' Centre, 24 Ryerson Avenue, Toronto, Ont. M5T 2P3
Phone: (416) 860-1448   Fax: (416) 860-0826

Periodical Writers Association of Canada
The Writers' Centre, 24 Ryerson Avenue, Toronto, Ont. M5T 2P3
Phone: (416) 868-6913   Fax: (416) 860-0826

Playwrights Union of Canada
54 Wolseley Street, 2nd Floor, Toronto, Ont. M5T 1A5
Phone: (416) 947-0201   Fax: (416) 947-0519

QSPELL (Quebec Society for the Promotion of English Language Literature)
c/o Fraser Hickson Library, 4855 Kensington Avenue, Montreal, Que. H3X 3S6
Phone: (514) 845-5811/489-5301   Fax: (514) 845-6917

Saskatchewan Arts Board
3475 Albert Street, T.C. Douglas Building, 3rd Floor, Regina, Sask. S4S 6X6
Phone: (306) 787-4056 or 1-800-667-7526 (Sask.)
Fax: (306) 787-4199

Saskatchewan Writers' Guild
P.O. Box 3986, Regina, Sask. S4P 3R9
Phone: (306) 757-6310   Fax: (306) 565-8554

Speculative Writers Association of Canada
10523 – 100th Avenue, Edmonton, Alta. T5J 0A8
Phone: (403) 424-7943   Fax: (403) 424-7943

Writers' Alliance of Newfoundland & Labrador
P.O. Box 2681, St. John's, Nfld. A1C 5M5
Phone: (709) 739-5215   Fax: (709) 739-0630

Writers' Federation of Nova Scotia
1809 Barrington Street, Suite 901, Halifax, N.S. B3J 3K8
Phone: (902) 423-8116   Fax: (902) 422-0881

Writers Guild of Alberta
10523 – 100th Avenue, Edmonton, Alta. T5J 0A8 (main office)

Phone: (403) 426-5892   Fax: (403) 424-7943
223 – 12th Avenue S.W., Suite 104, Calgary,
  Alta. T2R 0G9 (regional office)
Phone: (403) 265-2226

Writers' Union of Canada

The Writers' Centre, 24 Ryerson Avenue, Toronto, Ont. M5T 2P3
Phone: (416) 868-6914   Fax: (416) 860-0826
3102 Main Street, 3rd Floor, Vancouver, B.C. V5T 3G7
Phone: (604) 874-1611

Yukon Department of Tourism, Arts Branch

Arts Branch, P.O. Box 2703, Whitehorse, Yukon Y1A 2C6
Phone: (403) 667-8592   Fax: (403) 667-4656

10

RESOURCES

Stylebooks, Handbooks, & Guides

The Canadian Style: A Guide to Writing and Editing, Department of the Secretary of State of Canada, Dundurn Press, Toronto, 1985.

The Canadian Writer's Guide: Official Handbook of the Canadian Authors' Association (11th ed.), Fitzhenry & Whiteside, Toronto, 1992.

The Chicago Manual of Style (14th ed. rev.), University of Chicago Press, Chicago, 1993.

Editing Canadian English, Freelance Editors' Association of Canada, Douglas & McIntyre, Vancouver, 1988.

Appelbaum, Judith. *How to Get Happily Published*, HarperPerennial, New York, 1992.

Barker-Sandbrook, Judith. *Thinking Through Your Writing Process*, McGraw-Hill Ryerson, Toronto, 1989.

Bernstein, Theodore M. *Watch Your Language*, Atheneum, New York, 1976

————. *Miss Thistlebottom's Hobgoblins: The Careful Writer's Guide to the Taboos, Bugbears and Outmoded Rules of English Usage*, Simon & Schuster, New York, 1971.

————. *The Careful Writer*, Atheneum, New York, 1965.

Blackburn, Bob. *Words Fail Us: Good English and Other Lost Causes*, McClelland & Stewart, Toronto, 1993.

Blundell, William E. *The Art and Craft of Feature Writing*, Plume, New York, 1988.

Braine, John. *Writing a Novel*, Methuen, London, 1974.

Casewit, Curtis. *Freelance Writing: Advice from the Pros*, Macmillan, New York, 1974.

Cheney, Theodore A. Rees. *Getting the Words Right: How to Rewrite, Edit & Revise*, Writer's Digest Books, Cincinnati, 1983.

Clayton, Joan. *Journalism for Beginners: How to Get into Print and Get Paid for It*, Piatkus, London, 1992.

Cook, Clair Kehrwald. *Line by Line: How to Improve Your Own Writing*, Houghton Mifflin, Boston, 1985.

Drobot, Eve, and Tennant, Hal. *Words for Sale* (3rd ed.), Periodical Writers Association of Canada, 1991.

Elbow, Peter. *Writing with Power*, Oxford University Press, New York, 1981.

Franklin, Jon. *Writing for Story*, Atheneum, New York, 1986.

Gager, Diane, and Coppess, Marcia Hibsch. *Get Published: Editors from the Nation's Top Magazines Tell You What They Want*, Henry Holt, New York, 1986.

Gardner, John. *The Art of Fiction: Notes on Craft for Young Writers*, Vintage, New York, 1983.

Gibaldi, Joseph, and Achtert, Walter S. *The MLA Handbook for Writers of Research Papers*, Modern Language Association of America, New York, 1988.

Goldberg, Natalie. *Writing Down the Bones: Freeing the Writer Within*, Shambhala, Boston and London, 1986.

———. *Wild Mind: Living the Writer's Life*, Bantam, New York, 1990.

Hodgins, Jack. *A Passion for Narrative: A Guide for Writing Fiction*, McClelland & Stewart, Toronto, 1993.

Kane, Thomas S., and Ogden, Karen C. *The Canadian Oxford Guide to Writing*, Oxford University Press, Toronto, 1993.

Kernaghan, E., Kernaghan, P, and Surridge, E. *The Upper Left-Hand Corner*, J.J. Douglas, Vancouver, 1979.

Konner, Linda. *How to Be Successfully Published in Magazines*, St. Martin's Press, New York, 1990.

Kozak, Ellen M. *From Pen to Print: The Secrets of Getting Published Successfully*, Henry Holt, 1990.

Legat, Michael. *An Author's Guide to Publishing*, Robert Hale, London, 1987.

————. *The Nuts and Bolts of Writing*, Robert Hale, London, 1989.

————. *Writing for Pleasure and Profit*, Robert Hale, London, 1987.

McCormick, Mona. *The Fiction Writer's Research Handbook*, Plume, New York, 1988.

McKeown, Thomas W., and Cram, Carol M. *Better Business Writing*, Clear Communications Press, Vancouver, 1990.

Mencher, Melvin. *News Reporting and Writing* (3rd ed.), W.C. Brown, Dubuque, Iowa, 1984.

Messenger, William E., and de Bruyn, Jan. *The Canadian Writer's Handbook* (2nd ed.), Prentice-Hall Canada, Toronto, 1986.

Miller, Casey, and Swift, Kate. *The Handbook of Nonsexist Writing* (2nd ed.). Harper & Row, New York, 1988.

Neff, Glenda Tennant (ed.). *The Writer's Essential Desk Reference*, Writer's Digest Books, Cincinnati, 1991.

Peterson, Franklynn, and Kesselman-Turkel, Judi. *The Magazine Writer's Handbook*, Prentice-Hall, Englewood Cliffs, New Jersey, 1982.

Potter, Clarkson N. *Writing for Publication*, Plume/Penguin, New York, 1991.

Seidman, Michael. *From Printout to Published*, Carroll & Graf, New York, 1988.

Smith, Nancy. *The Fiction Writers' Handbook*, Piatkus, London, 1991.

Strunk, William Jr., and White, E.B. *The Elements of Style* (3rd ed.), Macmillan, New York, 1979.

Taylor, Bob (ed.). *The Canadian Press Stylebook* (rev.), The Canadian Press, Toronto, 1989.

Waller, Adrian. *Writing! An Informal, Anecdotal Guide to the Secrets of Crafting and Selling Non-Fiction*, McClelland & Stewart, Toronto, 1987.

Williams, Joseph M. *Style: Toward Clarity and Grace*, University of Chicago, Chicago, 1990.

Wilson, John M. *The Complete Guide to Magazine Article Writing*, Writer's Digest, Cincinnati, 1993.

Zinsser, William. *On Writing Well: An Informal Guide to Writing Nonfiction* (4th ed.), HarperCollins, New York, 1991.

Dictionaries & Thesauruses

The Collins Dictionary & Thesaurus, Collins, London and Glasgow, 1990.

The Concise Oxford Dictionary, Clarendon Press, Oxford, 1990.

Fowler's Modern English Usage (2nd ed.), rev. Sir Ernest Gowers, Oxford University Press, Oxford, 1965.

Funk & Wagnalls Modern Guide to Synonyms, ed. S.I. Hayakawa, Funk & Wagnalls, New York, 1986.

Gage Canadian Dictionary, Gage Educational Publishers, Toronto, 1983.

New Webster's Dictionary & Thesaurus of the English Language, Lexicon, New York, 1991.

The Oxford Thesaurus, Clarendon Press, Oxford, 1991.

The Oxford Writers' Dictionary, R.E. Allen, Oxford University Press, Oxford, 1990.

The Penguin Canadian Dictionary, Penguin Canada/Copp Clark Pitman, Toronto, 1990.

The Penguin Dictionary for Writers & Editors, Bill Bryson, Penguin, London, 1991.

Roget's II, Houghton Mifflin, Boston, 1988.

Webster's Ninth New Collegiate Dictionary, Thomas Allen, Toronto, 1991.

Yearbooks & Other Regularly Published Reference Sources

The Book Trade in Canada, compiled and edited by Eunice Thorne and Ed Matheson, Ampersand, Ottawa. (annual)

CARD (Canadian Advertising Rates & Data), Maclean-Hunter, Toronto. (monthly)

Canadian Publishers Directory, published biannually as a supplement to *Quill & Quire* magazine.

Literary Agents of North America (4th ed.), Arthur Ormont and Léonie Rosenstiel (eds.), Author Aid/Research Associates International, New York. (annual)

Literary Market Place: The Directory of American Publishing, R.R. Bowker, New York. (annual)

Matthews Media Directory, published 3 times a year by Canadian Corporate News.

Novel & Short Story Writer's Market, Robin Gee (ed.), Writer's Digest Books, Cincinnati. (annual)

Poetry Markets for Canadians, 5th ed., League of Canadian Poets and Mercury Press, Toronto, 1992.

Sources: The Directory of Contacts for Editors, Reporters & Researchers, published biannually as a supplement to *Content* magazine.

Writers' & Artists' Yearbook, A. & C. Black, London. (annual)

Writer's Market, Mark Kissling (ed.), Writer's Digest Books, Cincinnati. (annual)

Canadian Magazines for Writers

Books in Canada (see Chapter 2, Literary & Scholarly, p. 122)

Canadian Author (see Chapter 2, Literary & Scholarly, p. 123)

Canadian Writer's Journal (see Chapter 1, Consumer Magazines, p. 43)

Quill & Quire (see Chapter 2, Literary & Scholarly, p. 138)

Writer's Lifeline (see Chapter 1, Consumer Magazines, p. 50)

Major Canadian Magazine Publishers

Bowes Publishers Ltd., P.O. Box 7400, Station E, London, Ont. N5Y 4X3. Phone (519) 473-0010. Fax (519) 473-2256. (farm)

Canada Wide Magazines Ltd., 4180 Lougheed Highway, Suite 401, Burnaby, B.C. V5C 6A7. Phone (604) 299-7311. Fax (604) 299-9188. (consumer and business magazines)

Farm Business Communications, 1760 Ellice Avenue, Winnipeg, Man. R3H 0B6. Phone (204) 774-1861. Fax (204) 775-9052. (farm)

Key Publishers Ltd., 59 Front Street E., 3rd Floor, Toronto, Ont. M5B 1B3. Phone (416) 364-3333. (consumer and business)

Maclean Hunter Ltd., 777 Bay Street, Toronto, Ont. M5W 1A7. Phone (416) 596-5000; 1001 de Maisonneuve ouest, Suite 1000, Montreal, Que. H3A 3E1. Phone (514) 845-5141. (consumer and business)

Moorshead Publications, 1300 Don Mills Road, North York,
M3B 3M8. Phone (416) 445-5600. Fax (416) 445-8149.

Naylor Communications Ltd., 124 West 8th Street, North
Vancouver, B.C. V7M 3H2. Phone (604) 985-8711; 100
Sutherland Avenue, Winnipeg, Man. R2W 3C7. Phone (204)
947-0222; 920 Yonge Street, 6th Floor, Toronto, Ont.
M4W 3C7. Phone (416) 961-1028. Fax (416) 924-4408; 210 –
10139 117th Street, Edmonton, Alta. T5K 2L3. Phone (403)
428-6164. (business)

Sanford Evans Publishing Ltd., 1077 St. James Street, P.O. Box
6900, Winnipeg, Man. R3C 3B1. Phone (204) 775-0201. Fax
(204) 783-7488. (business)

Southam Inc., 1450 Don Mills Road, Don Mills, Ont. M3B 2X7.
Phone (416) 445-6641; 3300 Cote Vertu, St.-Laurent, Que.
H4R 2B7. Phone (514) 339-1399. Fax (514) 339-1396. (business)

Telemedia Publishing, 50 Holly Street, Toronto, Ont. M4S 3B3.
Phone (416) 482-8600. (consumer)

OTHER BOOKS OF INTEREST
TO CANADIAN WRITERS

PUBLISHED BY McCLELLAND & STEWART INC.

A PASSION FOR NARRATIVE: A Guide for Writing Fiction
by Jack Hodgins
"One excellent path from original to marketable manuscript. . . . It would take a beginning writer years to work her way through all the goodies Hodgins offers," *Globe and Mail*

Called "a superb teaching tool," by the *Calgary Herald,* this clear, comprehensive guide for writers of novels and short stories makes use of countless examples of fine writing and provides writing exercises for home work. Jack Hodgins is such a legendary teacher that, as *Quill & Quire* says, "reading and using this book is like taking a master class from a musician."

Trade paperback, 5¼ × 8¼, 298 pages

WORDS FAIL US: Good English and Other Lost Causes
by Bob Blackburn
"If every journalist were required to read a chapter . . . every morning before starting to write, our newspapers, magazines, and news broadcasts would be immeasurably improved." *Books in Canada*

This "accessible, often hilarious guide," as described by the *Daily News* (Halifax), is for all those who love English. Recommended to "anyone who seeks to communicate clearly, in the English language," by the *Calgary Herald,* it will make you acutely aware of your own contribution to the failings of the language, and help improve your writing.

Trade paperback, 5¾ × 8⅜, 240 pages

FINDING ANSWERS: The Essential Guide to Gathering
Information in Canada *by* Dean Tudor
"This handy book is full of ways to navigate the oceans of available information." *Globe and Mail*

This easy-to-read reference book outlines the essentials of how to find and use information, whether from print or other formats, from libraries, databases, associations, institutions, governments, and even from experts. *Quill & Quire* hailed *Finding Answers* as "a godsend."

Trade paperback, 5¼ × 8¼, 308 pages